The Psychology of Dreams

The Psychology of Dreams

by

Paul R. Robbins

McFarland & Company, Inc., Publishers
Jefferson, North Carolina, and London

Grateful acknowledgment is made to the following for permission to reprint excerpts from their copyrighted materials: *American Anthropologist*, for Bourguignon, E.E., Dreams and dream interpretation in Haiti, *American Anthropologist*, 1954, **56**, 262–268. *American Imago*, for Wilson, G.S., A prophetic dream reported by Abraham Lincoln, *American Imago*, 1940, **1**, 42–48. *Archives of General Psychiatry*, for Trosman, H.; Rechtschaffen, A.; Offenkrantz, W.; and Wolpert, E., Studies in psychophysiology of dreams: IV. Relations among dreams in sequence, *Archives of General Psychiatry*, 1960, **3**, 602–607, © American Medical Association; for Ryan, J. H., Dreams of paraplegics, *Archives of General Psychiatry*, 1961, **5**, 286–291, © American Medical Association; for Chang, S.C., Dream-recall and themes of hospitalized schizophrenics, *Archives of General Psychiatry*, 1964, **10**, 119–122, © American Medical Association; and for Carrington, P., Dreams and schizophrenia. *Archives of General Psychiatry*, 1972, **26**, 343–350, © American Medical Association. *British Journal of Medical Psychology*, for Ehrenwald, H., Telepathy in dreams, *British Journal of Medical Psychology*, 1942, **19**, 313–323. *Bulletin of the Menninger Clinic*, for Robbins, P.R., and Tanck, R.H., Sexual gratification and sexual symbolism in dreams: Some support for Freud's theory, *Bulletin of the Menninger Clinic*, 1980, **44**, No. 1, 49–58, © 1980, The Menninger Foundation. *Canadian Journal of Behavioral Science*, for Ogilvie, R.; Busby, K.; Costello, L.; and Broughton, R., The effects of pre-sleep suggestion upon REM sleep, *Canadian Journal of Behavioral Science*, 1975, **7**, 139–150, © (1975) Canadian Psychological Association, Reprinted by permission; W. Dement for Dement, W., The physiology of dreaming, doctoral dissertation, University of Chicago, Department of Physiology, 1958. *Ethos*, for Foster, G.M. Dreams, character, and cognitive orientation in Tzintzuntzan, *Ethos*, 1973, **1**, 106–121; and for Shweder, R.A., and LeVine, R.A., Dream concepts of Hausa children: A critique of the "doctrine of invariant sequence" in cognitive development, *Ethos*, 1975, **3**, 209–230. *International Journal of Psycho-Analysis*, for Mack, J.E., Nightmares, conflict, and ego development in childhood, *International Journal of Psycho-Analysis*, 1965, **46**, 403–428. *Journal of Altered States of Consciousness*, for Bakan, P., Dreaming, REM sleep and the right hemisphere: A theoretical integration, *Journal of Altered States of Consciousness*, 1977–78, **3:4**, 285–307, © 1978, Baywood Publishing Co., Inc. *Journal of Nervous and Mental Disease*, for Dement, W., and Wolpert, E.A., Relationships in the manifest content of dreams occurring on the same night, *Journal of Nervous and Mental Disease*, 1958, **126**, No. 6, 568–578, © Williams & Wilkins, 1958. *Journal of Parapsychology*, for Rhine, L.E., Psychological processes in ESP experiences (Part II. Dreams), *Journal of Parapsychology*, 1962, 172–199. *Perceptual and Motor Skills*, for Meier, C.A.; Ruef, H.; Ziegler, A.; and Hall, C.S., Forgetting of dreams in the laboratory, *Perception and Motor Skills*, 1968, **26**, 551–557; and for Griffin, M.L., and Foulkes, D., Deliberate presleep control of dream content: An experimental study, *Perceptual and Motor Skills*, 1977, **45**, 660–662. Princeton University Press, for *The collected works of C.G. Jung*, trans. R.F.C. Hull, Bollingen Series XX, Vol. 17: *The Development of Personality*, copyright 1954, © 1982 renewed by Princeton University Press. *Psychiatric Quarterly*, for Roheim, G., The song of the sirens, *Psychiatric Quarterly*, 1948, **22**, 18–44; and for Fleiss, A.N., Psychotic symptoms: A disturbance in the sleep mechanism, *Psychiatric Quarterly*, 1962, **36**, 727–733. *Psychiatry*, for Crapanzano, V., Saints, Jnun, and dreams: An essay in Moroccan ethnopsychology, *Psychiatry*, 1975, **38**, 145–159. *Psychoanalytic Quarterly*, for Greenson, R.R., The exceptional position of the dream in psychoanalytic practice, *Psychoanalytic Quarterly*, 1970, **39**, 519–549; and for Tokar, J.T.; Brunse, A.J.; Castelnuovo-Tedesco, P.; and Stefflre, V.J., An objective method of dream analysis, *Psychoanalytic Quarterly*, 1973, **42**, 563–578. *Psychoanalytic Review*, for Strean, H.S., A paranormal dream, *Psychoanalytic Review*, 1969, **56**, 142–144 (Reprinted from the *Psychoanlytic Review* through the courtesy of the Editors and Publisher, the National Psychological Association for Psychoanalysis, New York, N.Y.). *Psychological Reports*, for Robbins, P.R., An approach to measuring psychological tensions by means of dream associations, *Psychological Reports*, 1966, **18**, 959–971. *Science*, for Broughton, R.J., Sleep disorders: Disorders of arousal? *Science*, 1968 (March 8), **159**, 1070–1078, © 1968 by The American Association for the Advancement of Science.

Library of Congress Cataloguing-in-Publication Data

Robbins, Paul R. (Paul Richard)
The psychology of dreams.

Bibliography: p. 161.
Includes index.
1. Dreams. I. Title.
BF1078.R58   1988   154.6'3   87-29889

ISBN 0-89950-270-9 (acid-free natural paper) ∞

Printed in the United States of America.

McFarland   Box 611   Jefferson NC 28640

To Sharon

Contents

Introduction

This is a book about dreams and what they mean. The subject has fascinated and at times bewildered people from early times. The dream has found its way into our literature—in Shakespeare, Dostoevski, Joyce, to name a few authors—our religions, our beliefs and superstitions, and into our theories of personality. The capacity to dream is part of our phylogenetic heritage, something we seem to share only with the other mammals. Have you noticed when your pet dog or cat is sleeping, that at times he appears unsettled and his breathing becomes irregular? We believe that this is a period of dreaming.

There are many topics one could consider about dreams. These range from the "hard science" investigations of REM-related dreams in sleep laboratories to the parapsychological reports of predictive and telepathic dreams. In this book we will cover a wide range of topics relating to the dream, recognizing that both the amount and credibility of the evidence vary widely from topic to topic. We will not include daydreams in our researches, nor will we venture in any detail into the problems of pharmacology and dreams.

The book is divided into two major parts. The first part presents information about what we know about dreams. Beginning with a historical review of dream interpretation, there are chapters on theories of dreams, sleep laboratory studies of dreams, the content of dreams, the recall of dreams, the dreams of mental patients, symbols in dreams, dreams and creativity, anxiety dreams and nightmares, and telepathic and predictive dreams.

The second part of the book deals with methods of dream analysis. Here we shall consider such techniques as sketching and painting dreams, the Gestalt therapy approach of acting out elements of the dream, and techniques of free and directed associations to dreams.

The author is a psychologist who is a researcher and therapist. He has attempted to present the material in a non-technical fashion.

I. The Nature of Dreams

Chapter 1

A Look at Dreams in the Ancient World and Primitive Cultures

In writing a book about dreams, one must ponder where to start. Perhaps with the latest findings from our sleep laboratories, where subjects sleep with electrodes attached near their eyes to monitor the sudden bursts of activity that summon the technician to the bedside, to inquire, "Have you been dreaming?" Perhaps one could begin with Freud. His contributions to our view of dreaming were revolutionary. But even Freud wrote that there were others before him who thought deeply about the problem. Where then should we begin? My answer will be, in the beginning, or as near to it as we can, for this will put our entire inquiry into perspective. We will begin with what our forebears believed about dreams in the cradles of western civilization: Greece and the Near East.

In examining the conception of the dream among the early Greeks, we have to rely mainly on the literature that has survived. Reliance on literature, whether epic poetry such as the *Odyssey* or plays such as *Prometheus Bound*, present difficulties. Drama and literature are mirrors to society, but not exact ones. Can one say that television presents an accurate picture of American society? The rate of adultery on the afternoon soap opera and that of murder on the evening shows would be far higher than even our most severe moralists would claim is true in reality. A second difficulty is that the dream in literature is used as a dramatic device to move the plot. The dream is contrived to present information to the character, to clarify his feelings, to change his understanding, and to bestir him to action. Third, the characters of ancient literature are warriors, kings and gods. We learn little about the dreams of ordinary people. In spite of these difficulties, the dream in literature does suggest important ideas about the way the dream was conceived by these ancient peoples.

The *Iliad* and the *Odyssey* are epic poems attributed to the blind poet Homer. While the date at which Homer composed these poems is uncertain, he described events in the Bronze Age of Greece—a period in the shadows of history that we can only glimpse through the eyes of Homer and the excavation of archeologists. The poems describe the war of the Greeks against the city of Troy, and the subsequent wanderings of the hero, Odysseus, through a series of fantastic adventures to be finally reunited with his wife, Penelope.

3

Both the *Iliad* and the *Odyssey* contain dreams of the characters. Looking at these dreams, we are led to several conclusions: (1) Dreams were perceived as having meaning; they were not considered to be nonsensical, trivial, or just random ideas. (2) These meanings were interpretable. (3) The meaning could be prophetic, giving information about the future. (4) The dreams could be sent from external sources – serving as the bearer of messages. (5) The external source was generally a god.

As an example, let us look at the dreams of Penelope in the *Odyssey*. Penelope had been long suffering, waiting for the return of her husband while reluctantly playing host to a mélange of suitors who had literally taken over her estates. The suitors had placed her under extreme pressure to give up on her missing husband and to choose one of them in his place. Near the end of her trial, she had a dream. In the dream, she was at home watching the geese she kept – there were twenty in all – and they were eating wheat out of a water-trough. Suddenly a great eagle with a crooked beak came swooping down from the mountain. The eagle attacked the geese, ferociously breaking their necks, killing them all. Then the eagle soared into the sky, leaving the geese strewn in a pile. Penelope wept bitterly for her geese. In a while, the eagle returned, this time alighting on the roof. It spoke to Penelope in the voice of a man. "Take heart," it said, "this is no dream but a true vision that shall be accomplished for thee. The geese are the wooers, and I that before was the eagle am now thy husband come again, who will let slip unsightly death upon all the wooers."[1] Penelope then awoke from her dream and looked around. There were the geese in the court eating the wheat in the trough.

The meaning of Penelope's dream was couched in symbols. Human beings were represented by different animals. In this dream, the symbols were readily "decoded" and the message was assumed to be a valid predictor of future events.

In the Homeric epics, not all dreams were perceived as valid predictors; some were manifestly false. The dreamer had to distinguish between the true vision and the false one. Penelope describes this difference using an exquisite metaphor of two gates through which dreams enter the mind. "Twain are the gates of shadowy dreams, the one is fashioned of horn and one of ivory. Such dreams as pass through the portals of sawn ivory are deceitful, and bear tidings that are unfulfilled. But the dreams that come forth through the gates of polished horn bring a true issue, whosoever of mortals beholds them...."[2]

While Penelope judged her dream about the geese to be a true prophecy, sometimes the messages sent from the gods were false and misleading. In the *Iliad*, the chief of the gods, Zeus, was angry at the Greek leader Agamemnon and sent him a misleading dream. Zeus speaks to the dream as if it were a being. "Go quickly, baneful Dream, to the swift Achaean [Greek] ships, and when you reach the lodge of Atreus' son Agamemnon, tell him exactly what I told you. Tell him to hurry and arm the long-haired Achaeans, since now he may take the city of Troy and fill the wide streets with his soldiers...."[3]

The dream then appeared to Agamemnon in the form of a respected Greek elder who related the message from Zeus. Convinced by the dream that victory was his, Agamemnon marshalled his troops, and led them into a bloody, inconclusive battle.

In going over the dreams in Homer, one must note in passing another dream of Penelope's. In addition to its message quality, the dream contains erotic elements. It is as if Penelope is dreaming about something desired, and experiencing it in fantasy when reality seems to offer little hope. As such it suggests some of our modern theories about dreams. Referring to her dreams, Penelope said, "This very night one seemed to lie by my side, in the likeness of my lord ... and then was my heart glad, since methought it was no vain dream but a clear vision...."[4]

Moving ahead centuries in time, one comes to a new age in Greece, the beginning of that period which saw the flowering of drama, sculpture, and philosophy. The playwright Aeschylus, who had fought the Persians at the battle of Marathon, wrote many plays, though only a few have come down to us. His use of the dream seems similar to that of Homer in that dreams are used as messages to the dreamer—messages that can be deciphered. One of the most graphic illustrations of meaning and interpretation of a dream occurred in Aeschylus' play *The Libation Bearers*. This was the second play of a bloody trilogy involving adultery, murder and revenge. It was a bizarre dream of the mother, Clytemnestra, that set the stage for further bloodletting. The dream of Clytemnestra was related by a third party to her son, Orestes. The third party was the chorus that often plays a commentary role in Greek plays.

> CHORUS: I know, child, I was there. It was the dreams she had. The godless woman had been shaken in the night by floating terrors, when she sent these offerings.
> ORESTES: Do you know the dream, too? Can you tell it to me right?
> CHORUS: She told me herself. She dreamed she gave birth to a snake.
> ORESTES: What is the end of the story then? What is the point?
> CHORUS: She laid it swathed for sleep as if it were a child.
> ORESTES: A little monster. Did it want some kind of food?
> CHORUS: She herself, in the dream, gave it her breast to suck.
> ORESTES: How was her nipple not torn by such a beastly thing?
> CHORUS: It was. The creature drew in blood along with the milk.
> ORESTES: No void dream this. It is the vision of a man.
> CHORUS: She woke screaming out of her sleep, shaky with fear....[5]

And then Orestes interpreted it:

> See, I divine it, and coheres all in one piece. If this snake came out of the same place whence I came, if she wrapped it in robes, as she wrapped me, and if its jaws gaped wide around the breast that suckled me, and if it stained the intimate milk with an outburst of blood, so that for fright and pain she cried aloud, it follows then, that as she nursed this hideous thing of prophecy, she

must be cruelly murdered. I turn snake to kill her. This is what the dream portends.[6]

The philosophers Plato and Aristotle discuss dreams in their writings, and there were a number of Greeks who achieved some notoriety as interpreters of dreams. There is a trail of now dimly remembered names—Antiphon, Panyassis, Aristander—who performed this function for Alexander the Great. Most important of the dream interpreters was a man named Artemidorus. Artemidorus lived in the second century A.D. and was the author of a multi-volume set of books on the interpretation of dreams. A translation of Artemidorus' dream interpretations into English has been published. The ideas of Artemidorus about dreams represent a significant advance over the concepts of dreams we have seen in Greek literature. While some of his ideas reflect the superstitions of his time, there are some inspired guesses that make one think of Freud, 2000 years later. Glancing through his dream interpretations is a source of endless fascination.

The Greeks seemed to believe that information communicated by the gods through dreaming could be beneficial. This was particularly true when it came to treating sickness. If one were ill, one could visit temples where one could await help from the gods while one slept. Dr. M.G. Papageorgiou describes the procedure used at the sanctuary of Amphiaraus: The ill person would first fast for a day, then would sleep on the skin of a previously sacrificed ram. Amphiaraos would appear in the patient's dream providing therapy directly on the spot or would give advice on how to deal with the illness. Papageorgiou believes that the dream experience may have been psychotherapeutic. It seems like a kind of faith healing with the dream being part of the procedure.[7]

Dr. Sidney Cohen provides us with an illustration of this dream-visitation therapy, writing about a Greek author, Aristedes, who lived in the second century. Aristedes had terrible medical problems. He suffered from toothaches, earaches, asthmatic attacks, fever, bloated stomach, and muscle cramps. He apparently felt he was at death's door. Then he had a dream in which the god Asclepius gave him some advice. He was told to walk barefoot, ride horseback and take cold baths. As this medical advice seemed at least as good as what he had been receiving, Aristedes traveled to Asclepius' temple at Pergamum to continue the treatments. The god's advice, coming in dreams, seemed to be consistent, for one day Aristedes tore off his clothes and jumped into a freezing river. He swam and splashed and experienced a nearly euphoric state of well being.[8] Cohen does not indicate how many years Aristedes survived this kind of medical advice, but one cannot fault his enthusiasm.

The early Hebraic tradition as manifested in the Bible viewed dreams in much the same light as the early Greek tradition. Dreams in the Old Testament were viewed as meaningful, interpretable, as messages, and sometimes as prophetic. For the most part, the messages were from God. In fact, the Bible was quite explicit in stating that God used dreams to communicate with his prophets: "And the Lord came down in a pillar of cloud, and stood at the door of the tent, and called Aaron and Miriam; and they both came forward. And he said, 'Hear my words: If there is a prophet among you, I the Lord make myself known to him in a vision, I speak with him in a dream.'"[9] The exception was Moses, whom the Lord spoke to "mouth to mouth, clearly, and not in dark speech..."[10]

Dreams in the Bible occur to a number of persons. They include relatively obscure characters such as Abimelech, a contemporary of the patriarch Abraham, and central figures such as Jacob, Joseph, Solomon, and Daniel. The dreams of two important non-Hebrew figures are also related in the course of the Bible: the pharaoh of Egypt at the time of Joseph, and Nebuchadnezzar, ruler of Babylon.

Some of these dreams are in the form of a dialogue between God and the dreamer (e.g., the dreams of Abimelech and Solomon[11]). Sometimes the dream is a matter of instruction of what the dreamer is supposed to do or not to do (e.g., the dreams of Laban and Jacob[12]). The dreams that have fascinated readers, however, are not the simple message dreams; rather, they are the dreams laid out in symbols, requiring interpretation. The dreams of Joseph, for example, are rich in symbolism. Joseph related the following dreams to his brothers: "...behold, we were binding sheaves in the field, and lo, my sheaf arose and stood upright; and behold, your sheaves gathered around it, and bowed down to my sheaf." And later, "...behold, the sun, the moon, and eleven stars were bowing down to me."[13]

His brothers considered the dreams in terms of prophecy, saying, "Are you indeed to reign over us?" As the story unfolds, they reacted by selling Joseph into slavery, only to have the prophecy fulfilled years later.[14]

The reaction of Pharaoh in Joseph's time and of Nebuchadnezzar centuries later suggests the widespread, enduring interest in the meaning of dreams in the ancient Near East. When Pharaoh had dreams that troubled him, he sent for all the magicians of Egypt and its wise men to interpret them. Interestingly, none could, or apparently even tried. When Nebuchadnezzar was disturbed by troubling dreams, the Bible paints him as so skeptical of the powers of magicians and sorcerers he summoned that he insisted they prove their credibility by not only interpreting the dream, but first relating the content of the dream without being told what it was. The king was very severe with them, saying, "I know with certainty that you are trying to gain time, because you see that the word from me is sure that if you do not make the dream known to me, there is but one sentence for you." When the magicians replied that they could not do such a thing, the king was quite angry. The summary execution of the magicians was only prevented by the prophet Daniel, who was able to tell the king both the substance of the dream and what it meant.[15]

The dreams of Nebuchadnezzar, parenthetically, are some of the richest in use of imagery in the Bible. In one dream, he beheld a mighty image of exceeding brightness, with a head of gold, breast and arms of silver, thighs of bronze, legs of iron, with the proverbial feet of iron and clay. In another dream, he described a tree that grew so tall that its top reached to heaven and was visible to the end of the earth. Daniel decoded the first dream in terms of the emergence and destruction of successive kingdoms, culminating in a kingdom established by God. Daniel decoded the second dream in terms of the person of Nebuchadnezzar himself. The interpretation of this dream included a prophecy of the king's misfortune, which in time came to pass.[16]

The Biblical stories suggest that interest in dream interpretation in the Near East is very old. There is archeological evidence to substantiate this. Dr. A. Leo Oppenheim, a Mesopotamian scholar, has provided a translation of an Assyrian dream book and also mentions other cuneiform tablets dealing with dreams. Oppenehim believes that it is possible to distinguish several types of dream reports from ancient Mesopotamia. Like the Homeric epics, there were message dreams sent from the gods to kings and other high personages, calling to their attention some matter of importance. Sometimes the message dreams were clear and unmistakable; sometimes they were couched in symbols.[17]

In addition to the message dreams, there appeared to be considerable interest in disturbing dreams—what we would think of as nightmares. Such dreams were considered to be the result of evil, demonic powers that resided in the underworld and sought out men to do them harm. To prevent evil dreams from happening or to put an end to them once they started, one went through exorcism rites. Oppenheim writes that there were many cuneiform tablets providing exorcism rituals. He cites one such practice where the person first related the dream to a lump of clay. While certain prayers were uttered, the lump of clay was dissolved, purging the individual of his difficulties.[18]

We may think such rituals to be utterly naive, but the odds against a nightmare recurring in the near future are pretty high, and how was the troubled Babylonian to know it wasn't the lump of clay that did the trick?

The Mesopotamians had some theories about the process of dreaming. One of these theories was that the soul of the dreamer leaves the body (or is transported by a god) to the place viewed in the dream. In that sense the dream is external to the body and conceived of as a real or quasi-real experience.[19]

The seriousness with which dreams could be taken in the ancient Near East is suggested by a story related by the Greek traveler and historian Herodotus. Croesus, the King of Lydia, whom we think of mainly in terms of his wealth, had a dream that his favorite son would die as a result of a blow from an iron weapon. Croesus was so alarmed by the dream that he removed his son as commander of the Lydian army, forcing him to marry and settle down. Croesus also got rid of every weapon in sight in order to prevent an accident. His actions came to no avail, however, for his son was killed in a boar hunt, struck by an errant spear meant for the boar.[20]

A similar story was recorded by Herodotus about Astyages, King of the Medes. Astyages had some incredible dreams about his daughter. In one dream his daughter voided a stream that flooded not only his capital, but flooded the whole of Asia. In another dream a vine grew from his daughter's womb that overshadowed these same Asiatic lands. Like Croesus, Astyages was concerned and sought the meaning of these dreams from the magi, who were said to have the skill to interpret them. The magi said the dreams portended that his grandson-to-be would rule over Asia in place of him. To prevent this from happening, the king gave the infant to a trusted kinsman with instructions to bury him. Unwilling to do this, the kinsman passed him on to a herdsman, who elected to raise him instead of burying him. The child, named Cyrus, grew to manhood, and as surely as these things seem to happen in ancient tales, led a successful revolt against Astyages, succeeding him as king.[21]

In his historical review of dream interpretation, Dr. Morton Kurland indicates that belief in the prophetic and divine origin of many dreams continued into Roman times and was also evident in the Islamic civilizations that arose later in North Africa and the Near East. There is considerable dream material available from the Islamic culture. Samples of such dream material can be found in von Grunebaum and Caillois' book *The Dream and Human Societies.* Kurland points out that in Islamic dream interpretation, there were specific omens in dreams which forecasted favorable events for the dreamer, while other omens forecasted unfavorable events. Nonetheless, some of the ideas advanced about dream interpretation seem sophisticated. For example, it was recognized that dreams could be forgotten because of feelings that might arise that the dreamer would not wish to know.[22] This idea is not very far from Freud's theories hundreds of years later.

In summarizing this brief look at views of dreaming in the ancient world, we can see an apparently widespread belief that dreams were meaningful, used symbols to indicate this meaning, were interpretable, were prophetic, and at times served as messages from the gods. These conclusions reflect the fact that the peoples of these earlier times lived in prescientific cultures. They knew nothing of controlled experiments, sleep laboratories or psychoanalysis. They knew only what their cultures provided them with the tools to know.

One may agree with the substance of our analysis but still ask whether it is possible to cross-check our conclusions. There are people living today who know little or nothing of science. One thinks of the studies of anthropologists in villages and hovels in little-traveled places scattered about the globe. Would the people in these folk cultures, too, view dreams as external, as bearing messages from the gods, as prophetic?

In their journeys, some anthropologists have obtained the kind of information we seek about dreams. In trying to answer our question, we will look briefly at four very different groups of people who could have had little contact with each other: Mexican villagers, Zulu tribesmen, Moroccans, and Haitian peasants. Some of the ideas about dreams we find here seem remarkably similar to those we found in our look at the ancient world.

In some folk societies, dreams are believed to be external in origin, rather than something in one's mind. For example, among the villagers of Tzintzunt-zan, Mexico, Dr. George Foster found that nightmares (though not normal dreams) are not always distinguished from waking events. The most common form of nightmare is "a something; a three-dimensional *bulto*, or perhaps just an *aire*; an air, identified as death" that "enters through the door, circles the room, then sits beside or lies beside the human." This dream is often described by the villagers as if it were a real experience. Foster reports that during the experience, the person breathes with difficulty and "a great cold" is felt.[23]

Like the ancients, some individuals in the village believed that dreams could be transmitted by God or by the devil.[24]

Foster stated that there was a general reluctance to talk about dreams. Possibly this was due to the belief among the villagers that dreams are prophetic and there might be fear of what the dream foretold. Foster's informants were able to relate instances of dreams seemingly coming true. The most common interpretation given to dreams was death. Interestingly, a symbol in the dreams believed to indicate death was "much meat, much music, lots of fiesta"—a situation of seemingly good times. While Foster was collecting his data, one villager reported having repeated dreams of much meat. Shades of the prophecies of the ancients: The villager died in a matter of months.[25]

Dr. S.G. Lee made an extensive investigation of dreams of the African Zulus, talking to over 600 persons. Among the Zulus, dreams were viewed as containing messages. In this instance, the message came from ancestral spirits who are venerated in the Zulu religion. In dreams, the ancestors evaluate the behavior of the dreamer, letting him know whether they approve or disapprove of what he is doing. The ancestral spirits may also prophesy about the future, possibly pointing out a course of action for the dreamer to follow. Most of the Zulus questioned said they did not know the meanings of their dreams. The task of interpreting dreams fell to a few individuals who were recognized as diviners. These diviners were highly respected and also functioned as "medical consultants." The process of becoming a diviner involved first showing signs of the right aptitude (unusual mental symptoms), then undergoing formal training. These mental symptoms—fugue states, disturbed dreams and emaciation—might cause a person to be hospitalized for mental illness in this country. However, in Zululand, the symptoms are said to indicate possession by ancestral spirits. When this happens, the Zulu may become a trainee for two years, during which time the trainee's own dreams are analyzed (not unlike a prospective psychoanalyst), and is then eventually recognized as a diviner. Lee points out that about 90 percent of the diviners are women, and that the few male diviners are often transvestites.[26]

With this view of the function of dreams, it is not surprising that the most frequent dream reported by the Zulus was about people who had died. There was also a strong tendency for Zulu women to dream about water—ponds, lakes, still waters, and flooded rivers. This could reflect the daily work of the women. (As we shall see in our discussion of symbolism, however, some psychoanalytically oriented writers [e.g. Roheim] might have radically different interpretations of the water dreams.) Finally, like the Mexican villagers studied by Foster, the Zulus sometimes reported strong reactions to nightmares. Among Zulu men particularly, nightmares were regarded with horror. Lee reported that men were often hospitalized because of anxiety following nightmares.[27]

Dr. Vincent Crapanzano has studied the dreams of a group of Moroccans in the shanty towns of Meknes. Crapanzano reported that the Moroccans believed that when a person sleeps, his soul leaves the body and wanders about. It is the wandering soul which observes the dream, a presumably ongoing, external event.[28]

The Moroccans believed that dreams predicted the future. Sometimes, the meaning of these predictions was well known and generally accepted. For example, "if you dream you are riding on a female mule, then you will marry and divorce." However, "if you dream you are riding on a camel, then you will never have any problems."[29]

Bad dreams were thought to be caused by demons. These creatures were depicted as made up of vapor and fire and were said to be capricious and quick-tempered. Crapanzano's subjects believed particularly in a she-demon called 'A'isha Qandisha. In one of her guises, she was described as beautiful; in another as a hag, with "long straggly hair, pendulous breasts, and elongated nipples." She was said to be ready to "strangle, scratch, or whip anyone who insults her or does not obey her commands."[30] 'A'isha Qandisha obviously was no one to fool around with.

The Moroccans believed they could influence the character of their dreams—ward off the bad ones and bring on the good ones. To some extent, whether a person had bad dreams depended on the character of the person. A pious person had fewer bad dreams. Reading prayers might ward off bad dreams. According to Crapanzano, his subjects would actively try to influence their dreams by refraining from sexual relations, sleeping on their right sides rather than their left, and saying prayers before going to bed.[31]

If a person became the object of the demon's anger and was disturbed by bad dreams, he might turn to one of the wise men (traditional teachers) in the community for assistance. The wise man might give him an amulet to fend off the dream. Failing this, the dreamer might tell the dream to a rock. This action was supposed to dissipate the bad effects of the dream on the person.[32]

Dr. Erika Bourguignon (1954) reported some observations she had made about the concept of dreams among peasants in Haiti. Many dreams are considered supernatural visitations, coming from the dead or from the gods. Once again, the dream is believed to be a message to the dreamer. When the message comes from a god, the dreamer is thought to be possessed by the god. As the dreamer may also talk to the god in the dream, it is a two-way communication rather than simple instruction.[33]

The gods appearing in the dreams reflect a mixed Catholic, African and

Haitian origin. Some of the gods are identical to saints. Nonetheless, they are conceived as *Vodun* (voodoo) deities. Many dreams are believed to be a form of harassment by these gods. If the dreamer wants an interpretation of his dream, he may go to a Vodun priest or priestess for help. Disturbing dreams are generally believed to indicate a desire of the gods for feasts, sacrifices, or initiation. If the dreamer makes an attempt to appease the god by some religious ritual, the disturbing dreams are expected to subside. Bourguignon reports the belief that saying prayers before going to sleep will prevent dreams, as this act will satisfy the god. Also, she reports the belief that placing one's hand under one's head can cause the dream to be forgotten.[34]

In closing this chapter, we would like to note an interesting parallel between the conceptions of prescientific cultures about dreams and the beliefs of young children. Distinguished Swiss psychologist Piaget noticed that young children had magical ideas about dreams which gradually gave way to more adult concepts, usually by the age of nine or ten.[35] A study was carried out in Montreal by Drs. Laurendeau and Pinard which confirmed Piaget's observations. They questioned children of various ages about their concept of dreams, asking whether a dream was real or make-believe, where it came from, how it got to them, whether it was inside or outside of them, etc. Young children, aged four to five, often believed that dreams originated outside the head, had a material existence, and could be visible to others. As the child matured, these ideas gradually shifted to adult conceptions.[36]

The transitional patterns between the child's view of dreams as an external event and the adult view as a private internal experience are sometimes fascinating. Drs. Richard Shweder and Robert LeVine studied children at the Ahmadu Bello University in Nigeria. They were looking at developmental sequences in children's thinking, interviewing children in a market town in the northwest part of the country. Like Piaget and Laurendeau and Pinard, they found a remarkable difference in children's concepts of dreaming between ages six and ten.

In the transition period between these ages, sometimes dreams were conceived as mirages or hallucinations. For example, "I dreamt my younger sister fell into a well and died. (Did that really happen?) No, because I still see her. (Was the dream in your room or inside you?) The dream was inside the room. (If I had been there, could I have seen your sister dying?) Yes."[37]

The most typical kind of transitional thinking was a view of dreams as real events, but located within one's body. If somehow one could come inside your body, one would be able to see your dreams.[38] The idea is not too different from something I was told as a small child: that if I was able to get inside the large old radio we had, I would be able to see the events being dramatized.

In our review of the way dreams were understood in early history and in primitive cultures, we have underscored some common themes: the beliefs that dreams are meaningful, their reliance on symbols, their external origin, their prophetic nature, and their interpretability. It is interesting that all of these conceptions are very much alive today. There is a basic difference, however. We are now able to translate these ideas into more researchable questions and thus obtain more scientific information in regard to their validity. There is a whole spectrum of questions now under investigation by dream researchers. Even the seemingly far-out notion that dreams can serve as bearers of messages has received a new dress in laboratory studies of telepathy, where the question has been phrased, "Does the dream state increase the possibility (or probability, if you are a believer) of telepathic communcation?" We shall now examine some of these questions. Our focus will be first on the nature of dreams and then on what they can tell us about ourselves.

Chapter 2

Some Modern Theories of Dreaming

The most influential explanation of the nature and meaning of dreams was developed by Freud. It is at once original, ingenious, and far-reaching. Is it valid? In some respects, probably yes. In others, research evidence fails to support it. For example, one of Freud's ideas was that dreams served the function of maintaining sleep. When one is sleeping and is exposed to a disturbing stimulus, psychological processes would work to incorporate the stimulus into a dream rather than allow the person to awaken. A loud noise, for example, might be turned into thunder in the dream. As we shall see in our review of laboratory studies, this view of dreams as "the guardians of sleep" is not supported by the evidence.

Freud's theories are intricate and complicated and utilize a special technical language. We will make no attempt here to deal with the many details of his theory; rather, we will provide a sketch of it as it applies to dreaming.

At the risk of oversimplification, let us draw on a homey analogy. Imagine you put a pot of water on the stove, lighting the burner under it. Then you put a flat lid on top of the pot, not fastened securely, just lying there. As the water began to boil, the steam would exert pressure on the lid, and eventually knock it right off. If you wanted to keep the lid on, you might apply counter-pressure from above with your hand—enough to match the pressure from below. (We assume the lid has a handle on it, and your hand is none the worse for the experiment.)

Freud's view of psychological functioning is something like that boiling pot. Instead of boiling water submerged under a lid, think of psychological needs pushing for recognition and gratification. Imagine further that these are ideas of the most unacceptable kind—wishes or thoughts you would not want to admit to in a thousand years. Now, let's journey to the top of the lid, where we have been exerting a counter-pressure. Instead of your hand holding down the knob on the lid, imagine something called a censor. The censor is flashing signals below—something like, "Thou shall not pass." Finally, consider the lid as a kind of barrier between awareness and unawareness, or as Freud calls it, the unconscious.

In Freud's own words: "We may therefore suppose that dreams are given

14

their shape in individual human beings by the operation of two psychical forces (or we may describe them as currents or systems); and that one of these forces constructs the wish which is expressed by the dream, while the other exercises a censorship upon this dream-wish and by the use of that censorship, forcibly brings about a distortion in the expression of the wish."[1]

Freud makes it very clear that the function of the censor is *defensive*, to protect the individual from being faced in consciousness with what is unacceptable. During sleep, there is a process that reconciles the conflicting demands of the suppressed wishes and the responsibilities of the censoring agency. Freud refers to this process as the dreamwork.[2]

A dynamic system like this demands energy to keep it going. Returning to our boiling pot of water, imagine that there is a seemingly endless fuel supply heating the water from below, and you have to stand there holding your hand on it indefinitely to keep the lid on. Freud believed that sleep was one period in which the psychic counter-pressure exerted by the censor let up. It is like a period of truce following a battle. The censor is still active, but weaker. During this time, it is now possible for these unacceptable wishes in the unconscious to sift through the barrier, provided they are sufficiently disguised and would not be recognized for what they really are. As the wish attains this limited access to consciousness, presumably some of the pressure it has been generating is dissipated.

What the dreamwork does is to combine various elements (memories). One of these elements is a recent experience, usually something that happened in the past twenty-four hours. This experience is selected by the dreamwork to provide a link with other materials that relate to and give expression to the unconscious thoughts. These materials could be ideas that are recent, or they could be from the past, extending all the way back to early childhood. The dreamwork combines these diverse ideas into a kind of theatrical production. To achieve this synthesis and to satisfy the demands of the censor for distortion, the dreamwork uses a number of techniques.

One technique is to change the intensity of the original dream thought. The suppressed thought may be powerful, but the dreamwork may change that so it appears in the dream content as a trivial idea. Freud calls this process *displacement*. Another process is *condensation*. This is where a large number of suppressed ideas pressing for release are compressed into a few fragments. A third technique of disguise is the use of *symbols*. A dream thought may be represented by a symbol, generally an object in the dream content.[3]

Thus, in Freud's system, one deals with two levels: the actual dream content, which he called the *manifest* content, and the thoughts that have forced their way (albeit disguised) into consciousness through the dream. These thoughts that have given rise to the dream are referred to as the *latent* content.[4]

Now if one accepts this view, it is clearly the latent content which is important. These are the thoughts that are too disturbing to allow into consciousness.

If one understands what these thoughts are, and if one is able to accept their reality, integrating them into one's self understanding, then presumably psychic pressure should be relieved and one ought to function better. This is a keystone of psychoanalysis.

How does one discover the latent meanings of dreams? How does one work back from the manifest content – through the distortions of the dreamwork to uncover the thoughts that have given rise to the dream? Freud's approach to solving this problem was to use free-associations. In this method, the subject considers the various elements in the dream one at a time, lets his mind wander freely, and the train of thought tends to go over previous experiences and ideas. In this method, it is important that the subject report everything that comes into his mind, not suppressing anything for any reason. Freud was convinced that this free association process would lead to a chain of connecting thoughts that would tie in with the latent dream materials. These connections were like pathways, and there might be a number of them between the dream and the latent thoughts.

Now, what are these latent thoughts that have worked their way into representation in the dream? As we have indicated, Freud believed that when the work of interpretation had been completed, the thoughts would eventually lead back to a wish, and that the dream is the fulfillment of a wish. Sometimes, as in the case of children, the wish appears to be simple and straightforward, seemingly requiring no complicated process of analysis. It is usually possible to go deeper, however, and Freud leaned to the view that dream wishes are invariably derived from the unconscious. In Freud's case illustrations, these wishes frequently turned out to be sexual. However, Freud made it clear that he did not believe that all dreams required a sexual interpretation. "In particular, I cannot dismiss the obvious fact that there are numerous dreams which satisfy needs other than those which are erotic in the widest sense of the word: dreams of hunger and thirst, dreams of convenience, etc.," and later "the assertion that all dreams require a sexual interpretation, against which critics rage so incessantly, occurs nowhere in my Interpretation of Dreams. . ."[5]

Notwithstanding this disclaimer, even a casual reading of the Interpretation of Dreams reveals the heavy emphasis Freud placed on sexuality as a force underlying dreams. This is particularly true when we look at his view of the meaning of symbols. All kinds of objects may stand for the male and female genitals.

Freud stated that frequently dreams could have more than one wish underlying them. He believed that in a dream analysis, one might uncover a whole succession of wishes superimposed on one another, the bottom line being the fulfillment of a wish from earliest childhood. Here one would find evidence of instinctual impulses. The job of the dream analyst in psychoanalytic terms is something like that of an archaeologist digging a trench in an ancient city, looking for older and older remains.

Freud's theory of dreams, like his other theories of psychoanalysis, was not universally acclaimed. In the brief extract we have quoted, we can sense some of the flak thrown up by his critics. Even among his followers in the psychoanalytic movement, there were doubts expressed and revisions proposed. Dr. Robert Clark has written a paper describing some of these revisions.[6]

One of the first of the revisionists was a Viennese analyst, Dr. Herbert Silberer. He proposed that dreams could be interpreted from more than one point of view. Acknowledging the usefulness of Freud's approach, which yielded information about the impulsive life, he also felt that dreams could be interpreted on an allegorical level. Freud rejected Silberer's opinion outright. Another critic, Dr. Alfonse Maeder, a Zurich analyst, wrote that wish fulfillment was a one-sided explanation for dreams. Maeder also felt that one should pay more heed to the manifest content of the dream than Freud did, suggesting that a coherent, purposeful dream was an indication of successful coping with the problem. Freud responded by saying Maeder was wrong and that his own concepts were fully adequate to deal with Maeder's concerns.[7]

Even more revisionist was Jung. Once a disciple and close friend of Freud, Jung developed a distinctly different point of view about psychoanalysis and about dreams. As we did with Freud, we shall only sketch some of his ideas. Jung was careful to give Freud credit for his method of dream analysis, saying he was "the first to make the bold attempt to throw open the secret doors of the dream."[8] Having said this, Jung took out his rapier and cut a swath through the fabric of Freud's psychoanalytic ideas. While many people were impressed by Jung's thinking, the good doctor from Vienna probably threw his hands up in despair. For Jung was once his best and brightest.

Both Freud and Jung believed in an unconscious, but they had different ideas about it. The different points of view can become almost a theological argument, for our certain knowledge about the unconscious is scanty. The behaviorist may take an agnostic position, questioning whether there is any such thing at all. At best the unconscious is a construct, something we have inferred from bits and pieces of data and observations. Like heaven or hell, it can be populated with one's own fantasies, or one may accept the doctrines of a teacher like Freud or Jung.

We have glimpsed the Freudian concept of an unconscious. One senses a place where infantile wishes and unacceptable impulses are churning about waiting for release—a kind of Pandora's box. The connotation of Freud's unconscious is forbidding and negative.

Jung's concept of the unconscious is no place of delights, either, but it seems far less forbidding than Freud's. To be sure, the Jungian unconscious includes repressed materials relating to instinctual impulses—those basic Freudian discoveries. However, there are also materials with constructive potential as well. These materials were not buried to protect the person against unacceptable wishes; rather they are a reservoir of unused and forgotten ideas, ideas that could serve as a source of creative inspiration if they could be brought into consciousness. In this Jungian scheme of things, one could imagine a writer dreaming or fantasizing, and when aroused, inspired with an idea for a story. We shall encounter reports of just this sort of thing when we consider dreams and creativity later in the book.

In addition to this personal unconscious, Jung advanced a highly speculative notion, that all of us have something called a "a collective unconscious." This is "an impersonal layer of the psyche"—not acquired by the individual, but a function of the inherited brain structure, a residual of our ancestral life.[9] This may be a hard concept to grasp. I like to think of words such as ancestral, archaic and primitive when I use the term. Jung believed that both the personal unconscious, which reflects the individual's experience, and the inherited collective unconscious can influence our dreams, though the action of the collective unconscious is infrequent. It is the collective unconscious, however, which is responsible for the strange, vivid, fantastic dream—the kind that makes us wake up and wonder.

Jung offers us a definition of dreams. They "are products of unconscious psychic activity occurring during sleep.... The dream is a spontaneous process resulting from the independent activity of the unconscious, and is as far removed from our conscious control as, shall we say, the physiological activity of digestion."[10]

Jung further stated that dreams are "undisguised manifestations of unconscious creative activity."[11] This position represents two significant departures from Freud, for while both writers believed that dreams stemmed from the unconscious, Freud believed dreams were *defensive* in nature, *not creative*, and Freud believed dreams were *heavily distorted*.

Jung is very explicit about these differences. In regard to Freud's theory that dreams were disguised, Jung stated, "So, guided by long experience, I now proceed on the principle that a dream expresses exactly what it means, and that any interpretation which yields a meaning not expressed in the manifest dream-image is therefore wrong. Dreams are neither deliberate nor arbitrary fabrications; they are natural phenomena which are nothing other than what they pretend to be. They do not deceive, they do not lie, they do not distort or disguise, but naively announce what they are and what they mean."[12]

According to Jung, one of the important functions of dreams is to bring up ideas that the person is not aware of or has not been attending to. Jung believed that dreams provide information that can help the person restore balance in his life. Jung calls this tendency for dreams to bring up these unattended matters *compensation* . . . "for in my experience the vast majority of dreams are compensatory. They always stress the other side in order to maintain the psychic equilibrium."[13] A simple illustration of this would be a person who works long hours, thinking only about his job, and dreams of playing tennis or going to a party.

So Jung believed dreams were trying to tell the dreamer something important—something he ought to deal with in order to improve the quality of his life. The question then becomes, how can one understand the meaning of the dream?

Jung believed that in interpreting dreams, it is crucial to know as much as possible about the dreamer. One should know about the character of the dreamer, what activities the dreamer has been recently involved in, what his moods have been, etc. In a sense, this real life information represents one side of the clinical picture. To obtain information about the other side—the unconscious material from the dreamer—Jung follows Freud in using an association technique to the various parts of the dream. For Jung, the association technique was a more circumscribed task than Freud prescribed. Jung wanted the associations to be directly connected to the dream images, not an unlimited chain of ideas. The associations collected to the various parts of the dream may then be compared and contrasted with the conscious situation of the dreamer.

The ability to integrate dream associations with the waking life of the subject—to show what the dreams are suggesting in a compensatory manner—depends on the skill and knowledge of the analyst, and in Jung's view, is an art like diagnosis or surgery. And still, there is no guarantee of success. As Jung put it, "Moreover, there are dreams that defy every effort at interpretation. Often the only possible thing is to hazard a guess. At any rate, up to the present no open sesame for dreams has been discovered, no infallible method, and no absolutely satisfactory theory."[14]

Having discussed some of these ideas of Freud and Jung, one feels almost a compulsion at least to mention the views of Alfred Adler concerning dreams.

While Freud and Jung wrote extensively about the meaning of dreams, Adler's interest seems relatively peripheral. Adler viewed dreams as attempts to cope with problems, to work toward the solution of difficulties that lay ahead. He thought it followed from this premise that if you faced up to your problems in waking life, you would have little need to dream and therefore would have few dreams.[15] As we shall see in our review of laboratory dream studies, this conclusion is incorrect.

While Adler saw the chief function of dreams as overcoming problems, he did not see the solutions presented by dreams as necessarily good ones. In dreams, he says, we may only fool ourselves. The solutions offered in the dream may be temporarily satisfying, but may not advance the person realistically toward his goals. Furthermore, if the dream is recurrent, it is a repeated answer to the same type of problem. So, if the solution is misleading, one may fool oneself time and again. [16]

Adler agreed with Freud that the real meaning of the dream is different from its manifest content and in the value of associating to the dream to uncover its meaning. Like Jung, Adler did not agree with Freud's emphasis on sexuality and wish fulfillment. Adler was opposed to fixed rules for dream interpretation, pointing to the truism that everybody is different, and that interpretation of dreams must be undertaken in the context of the dreamer's problems, behavior and retrospections of earlier life.[17]

Adler expressed some interesting ideas. One of these was that you could *make up* a dream which would be every bit as good as a real dream in expressing your life style. This idea of "fantasizing" has found its way into psychological tests called projective techniques.

Another provocative idea of Adler's was that the emotions expressed in a dream could spill over into waking life. He cited a case of an unhappily married man who was prone to criticize his wife. One night he had a dream that a child was lost because of his wife's negligence. (In fact, there was no such child.) In the morning he woke up angry, proceeding to criticize his wife.

Finally, Adler believed that dreams, like poetry, utilize the language of metaphors. A student facing an examination might not dream of taking the test per se; rather he might dream of engaging in battle or an athletic contest, or facing some other type of challenge.[18]

Speculation about the nature of dreams has continued to the present time, both among psychoanalytically oriented writers and among psychologists and psychiatrists who have engaged in research on dreams. Dr. Jane Dallett has written a paper summarizing some of these views. One of the themes Dallett has identified among contemporary writers is a belief that the dream state is essentially continuous with waking thought, rather than being a radically different condition. Another view shared by these theorists is that dreams have adaptive value and may help the individual in coping with his problems.[19]

It would take us too far afield to compare the ideas of the many authors listed in Dallett's paper, but it seems worthwhile to close our brief discussion of dream theories by considering one of these writers, Dr. Louis Breger. He presents a concept of dreaming in terms of "information processing" which is a different kind of model from the psychoanalytic theorists we have considered.

Breger is one of several psychologists who has written about an "informational processing" concept of dreaming. Breger seems sympathetic to many of the observations Freud made about the nature of dreams, but feels the model Freud developed to explain dreams is incorrect. Breger rejects the notion of an organism which is passive and reacts only to build-ups of stimulus energy.

Breger conceives of the mind as "interrelated memory systems."[20] One must imagine something like an intricate computer system whose memory banks are stored with what one has experienced and learned from the past and whose programs can call up this information and use it. This mechanism controls and processes incoming information, then transforms this information into thought, fantasy, dreaming, and motor activity.

Dreams, like other mental processes, are constructed from these stored memories. The difference between dreams and other mental processes is that dreams are a transformation of information that occurs during a period (sleep) when little new stimulation is coming into the system and little action is possible. As such, dreaming is a pure psychological transformation.

Breger assumes that some memory systems are more likely than others to be involved in dream transformation. These are memories involving emotional issues. Breger also assumes that there are special programs guiding the transformation of the memory systems during sleep. These programs permit "a much freer combination of memory elements including association by shape, color, common sound or function...."[21] Breger also believes that such programs include those used in earlier years of intellectual development. This would introduce the logic of the young child into dreams.

Dreaming for Breger, then, is a psychological transformation of old memories taking place under the aegis of special programs—programs that permit more creativity than in the usual waking state. Breger believes that under these conditions, the emotional materials introduced into the dream content may be integrated with other memory structures. Some of these memory structures may have "previously proved satisfactory in dealing with similar material," and may contribute to a solution of the problem.[22] In addition, the diverse memories brought up by special programs may throw new perspective on the problem, and new solutions may be conceived. Viewed this way, dreams are adaptive, useful processes in coping with life's problems.

Chapter 3

The Scientific Study of Dreaming

Observation, speculation and theorizing are early phases in the scientific study of natural phenomena. This was true in the natural sciences, where alchemy preceded chemistry and astrology, astronomy. We have already seen how man's speculations about dreaming date well back into recorded history, culminating in the searching observations of Freud. The full application of the scientific method to the study of dreams has been quite recent. The scientific approach requires a method to obtain data that are accurate, sensitive and reliable. Moreover, one must be able to examine these data objectively; independent observers should be able to look at the same information and describe it in essentially the same way. The scientific method also places a premium on the possibility of replicating studies to see if similar results are found. Finally, whenever feasible, controls are utilized to prevent extraneous factors and biases from influencing the results.

The first requirement—that of acquiring accurate data—has been a bugaboo for the study of dreams from time immemorial. The fleeting nature of dreams was recognized by the ancients. In Aeschylus' *Agamemnon*, there is a poetic description: "It is vain, to dream and to see splendors, and the image slipping from the arms' embrace escapes, not to return again, on wings drifting down the ways of sleep."[1]

The problem was to study a phenomenon that was gone almost before you knew it—a now-you-see-it-now-you-don't kind of thing. One could put a notebook beside one's bed, or a tape recorder, but still it would be a catch-as-catch-can procedure. To compound the problem, one may dream several times in the same night, adding confusion to one's recollection the following morning.

The solution to the problem of obtaining more accurate dream reports was advanced markedly by a discovery in the sleep laboratory of the University of Chicago in 1952. The story is recounted in William Dement's very readable book, *Some Must Watch While Some Must Sleep* (San Francisco: Freeman, 1974). The laboratory was under the direction of Dr. Nathaniel Kleitman, a pioneer in sleep research. One of Kleitman's students, Eugene Aserinsky, was assigned the task of monitoring the eye movements of a student during the night to see whether these movements changed with the depth of sleep. Aserinsky did not

22

look at the subject's eyes, but looked at a continuous recording of wavy lines on chart paper. One may obtain such recordings by taping electrodes to the scalp and face of the subject, and attaching the electrodes in turn to a polygraph. The systems used in the sleep laboratory provided a continuous recording of brain waves, eye movements, and other data during the course of the night. What Aserinsky noticed on the chart recordings was that while the subject was sleeping, his eyes were sometimes acting like he was wide awake. Instead of resting during sleep, at times the eyes moved about as though the sleeper were looking at something.

These rather startling observations were confirmed and followed up by a great deal of systematic study. It was discovered that there are periods of rapid eye movement during sleep (REM periods) and periods in which these movements do not occur (NREM, the N standing for non). The REM and NREM states differ physiologically and very importantly in the report of dreams.

Brain wave studies indicate that REM periods occur during times of relatively light sleep. These REM periods are characterized by irregular breathing and increased blood flow in the brain. Sleep during NREM periods is relatively quiescent, characterized by slow, steady breathing. If you awaken the subject a few minutes after the onset of an REM period, the odds are about four out of five that the subject will say he's been dreaming. If you awaken the subject during an NREM period, the report of dreaming is much less frequent.

The tie-in between REM sleep periods and report of dreams made it possible to obtain immediate recall of dreams. Instead of waiting till morning, an investigator would watch the unwinding chart paper for the indications of rapid eye movements, wait a few minutes, then awaken the subject, asking him to report his dream. Not only were the difficulties of recalling dreams noticeably reduced, this procedure also made it possible to obtain some basic information about the nature of dreaming. We will take a look at some of the directions in which this research has gone.

Studies have shown that REM periods occur in cycles during the night, alternating with NREM periods. During a period of eight hours of sleep, a person may experience five REM periods of somewhat different lengths. The average REM period lasts about 20 minutes. As sleep progresses, REM periods tend to grow longer. Approximately 25 percent of a night's sleep is comprised of REM periods. This is fairly consistent from night to night.

If you awaken subjects after the onset of rapid eye movements for each period during the night, you may find dreaming occurring in each instance. The subject may report five dream experiences during the night.

Before we proceed further with our discussion of the REM phenomenon, it seems a good point to examine the implications of this discovery for one of Freud's ideas about dreaming. It will be remembered that Freud believed that dreams served as "the guardians of sleep." Freud believed that if an ongoing stimulus were disturbing to the sleeper, this stimulus would be incorporated into a dream, permitting the person to remain sleeping. We now know, however, that dreaming is a regular activity. As far as we know, REM and accompanying dreaming occurs whether one feels hungry or has an empty stomach, whether it is quiet as a tomb or whether the night is filled with thunder. It seems clear that a disturbing stimulus does not instigate a dream; the dream seems to occur when it is *biologically* time to dream. As we shall see later, an outside stimulus may influence the content of an ongoing dream. In such instances, it may be possible that the dream could help prolong sleep.

Returning to our subjects in the sleep laboratory, if we have awakened them during each REM period, we may have elicited dream reports from each period. We might then ask, are these several dreams identical? Or if not, are they parts of the same dream? Our answer to date for both questions seems to be no.

In a study carried out by Drs. William Dement and Edward Wolpert, not only did the dreams appear to be different during the night, there was only occasional evidence of continuity between dreams. In describing their results, the authors concluded:

> In the 38 nights' sequences, no single dream was ever exactly duplicated by another dream, nor were the dreams of a sequence ever perfectly continuous, one taking up just where the preceding had left off. For the most part, each dream seemed to be a self-contained drama relatively independent of the preceding or following dream.[2]

In a subsequent study, Dr. Harry Trosman and his associates studied two subjects for seventeen nights each in the sleep laboratory. From the thirty-four nights of dreams, the researchers could identify only one instance of a clearly continuous series of dreams. This atypical sequence went as follows:

> Dream 1. I am in a garage cutting up wood to put on a truck to take away.
> Dream 2. I am in the same place cutting up a door, getting it ready to throw out.
> Dream 3. I am completing the work in the garage, carting off some things and breaking others that are too big to throw away; then I lock up the garage.
> Dream 4. The garage was all cleaned out.[3]

We must throw in a cautionary note here. While these two studies reported the virtual absence of dream continuity, they used a total of only ten subjects. It is of course possible that there are people who tend to report sequential dreams. It is also possible that even without clear continuity between dreams, there may be a common theme underlying several of the dreams, or that associations to these dreams might lead to the same underlying concern. Both teams of researchers noted instances of common themes underlying dreams of the same night.

If dreams seem to differ one from the other during the night, are there any trends at all in the content of dreams as the night unfolds? For example, do dreams become more bizarre or more sexual the longer one sleeps? An investigation by Drs. Bill Domhoff and Joe Kamiya provides us with information bearing on this question.

These researchers awakened subjects during the first three REM periods of a night's sleep, obtaining dream reports. They found that the content of dreams for these three REM periods was fairly similar. There was about the same number of bizarre elements; there was a general lack of explicit sex in the dreams of all three periods; and the tendency to bring in events from one's past was approximately the same. One major difference was a tendency for hostile and violent elements to find their way into dreams somewhat more frequently as the night went on.[4] Does this point to a decrease in censorship activity in the latter stages of the night? Possibly, but one might also expect a similar increase of sexual content, and this was not the case. While the findings of this study do not extend into the later REM periods, these data point to the essential similarity of dream content during the night.

Let us return to the rapid eye movements themselves. If you inspect them closely, you will find that they are not all alike. They differ in the direction of the movement (some are up and down, some are back and forth), in the size of the movements (some look like large peaks, others like small hills), and in number (sometimes there are a lot of markings, sometimes only a few). Researchers wondered whether these differences had any significance. Did they relate in any way to what was being experienced in the dream?

Consider the direction of the eye movements. Suppose the direction of the eye movements monitored on the chart were upward. Would the subjective experience in the dream also be that of looking upward?

In his doctoral research, Dement reported some fascinating observations. He monitored subjects' eye movements, waiting for clear-cut examples of either pure vertical or pure horizontal eye movement to occur. He had to be patient because much of the record of eye movements is a mixture of directions, not sustained one way or the other. When a pure vertical or horizontal eye movement lasted for a full minute, he awakened the subject and asked what he was dreaming.

Five of his subjects had pure vertical eye movements. Their five dream reports all involved acts of looking upward and downward. Dement summarized these dreams as follows:

One subject dreamed of standing at the bottom of a tall cliff operating some sort of hoist and looking up at climbers at various levels and down at the hoist machinery. Another subject dreamed of climbing up a series of ladders looking up and down as he climbed. Another dreamed of throwing basketballs at a net, first shooting and looking up at the net, and then looking down to pick another ball off the floor. The fourth subject dreamed he was standing before a staircase leading up into a building. He was anxiously peering at the address which was carved in the sidewalk at his feet, and then looking up toward the top of the stairs. In the fifth, the subject was watching a blimp that hovered above him. The occupants of the blimp began dropping leaflets and the subject recalled alternately looking up at the blimp and down at the dropping leaflets.

The one subject observed who experienced pure horizontal eye movements dreamed of watching two people throwing tomatoes at each other.[5]

In the same report, Dement also looked at the difference in dream content between periods of frequent, large eye movements and periods of infrequent, small eye movements. He thought the large eye movements might be reflected in more active dreams. To study this possibility, he had a number of dreams rated for the level of activity taking place, and found a clear tendency for the larger, more frequent eye movements to be associated with more active dream content.[6]

In thinking about Dement's findings, one gets the feeling that the person is somehow actively involved in the dream. The dreamer's eyes seem to dart back and forth in at least a rough relationship to the event being experienced. But then one looks at the dreamer, his body resting quietly, almost motionless as he sleeps. The eyes may be hard at work, but the body appears to be anything but active. Perhaps the dreamer is more of an observer than an actor, watching rather than doing. However, if you continue to look at the dreamer carefully and are *very* patient, you may eventually notice movements in the arms or legs. Is it possible that these movements, too, are reflected in dream content?

The answer to this question seems to be yes. We are indebted to Wolpert and to Dr. Russell Gardner and his associates for studies of the problem. The researchers used the electromyogram (EMG) to sense muscle movements. This is the same type of machine that has become so popular in biofeedback therapy, allowing one to become aware of one's own muscle tensions. Gardner and his co-workers attached electrodes to their subjects' legs, forearms, and the flexors of their wrists and fingers. While the EMG recorded muscular movements, they observed the sleeping subject to make doubly sure that a muscular movement actually occurred.

I think one can summarize their findings by saying that activity in the muscles appears to relate to activity in the dream. More specifically, they found: (1) When both upper and lower body muscles were observed as active, there was greatest activity occurring in the dream. (2) When both groups of muscles were quiet, there was least dream activity. (3) The location of muscle activity observed was related to the type of activity depicted in the dream. Generally speaking, when movements of the upper part of the body were observed, similar movements were also reported in the dream. The same held true for movements observed for the lower part of the body.[7]

A graphic illustration of how limbic activity in a dream may mirror actual leg movement was related to me by a student. In the student's dream, he was having an argument with his sister about summer vacation plans. He became very angry at her. Storming out of the house, he tried to start his car. The car wouldn't start. This upset him further and he kicked the car. In reality, he reported, he had kicked the wall beside the bed, and when he got up he felt pain in his left foot.

The suggestion is that the dreamer is more than a mere observer of the dream, that his muscles respond at times as if he were participating in the drama. In these instances, is it possible that the person is actually living the dream? This is, of course, speculation. If it were true, it would cast dreaming into a model that was at once elegant, simple and understandable. I doubt that the nature of dreaming is as straightforward as that. However, let me present one other bit of evidence that suggests there could be truth in the idea.

We used the word drama as a descriptive term for the dream. After all, a dream is something like theater, complete with action and sometimes words. There is often conversation in dreams. I remember giving a lecture (about dreams!) in a dream. We might wonder, do the muscles of our lips and chin become active when we talk in our dreams?

Once again, the answer seems to be yes. By way of background, we know that the muscles involved in speech work "covertly" when one is reading silently or thinking. A neat demonstration by Drs. F.J. McGuigan and Robert Tanner showed that these speech muscles appear to be active during conversational dreams as well. Using the electromyogram, they recorded muscle action from the lip, chin, and neck. When dreams occurred which included conversation, there were increases in the amplitude of these EMG measures. What is equally important is that these changes did not occur during dreams which were purely visual.[8] So we have more grist for the mill.

While we were discussing the involvement of the external muscles in dreaming, the reader may have been wondering about what was happening inside. We know that exciting situations can affect one's breathing and pulse. When you are feeling anxious, you can feel these effects sometimes to the point of becoming uncomfortable. Some dreams can be quite stimulating. Shouldn't we expect an increase in breathing and heart rates during dreams?

In the original paper by Aserinsky and Kleitman describing the REM phenomenon, it was noted that both respiratory and cardiac rates were slightly higher during the REM periods than in preceding and subsequent periods. In a later paper, Dr. Aserinsky took a closer look at breathing patterns during the REM periods themselves. Looking at the detailed eye movements in a way somewhat analogous to examining a specimen under a microscope, Aserinsky delineated "bursts" of REMs adjacent to relatively quiet periods within the overall REM stage. Aserinsky compared breathing during the relatively quiet REMs and the REM bursts. When a REM burst came, breathing became more rapid. When the eye movements quieted, breathing returned to normal, although it was still somewhat more rapid than during other sleep stages.[9]

The increase in heart rate during REM states is probably not a problem for the person with normal heart functioning, but may be a possible hazard for persons with heart trouble. Persons with cardiac abnormalities have shown increased cardiac problems during REM periods. This was documented by a greater incidence of premature ventricular beats in one study and reports of angina pectoris in another. Dr. Gerald Rosenblatt and his co-workers feel that the REM state may be an especially vulnerable period for the heart patient. They theorize that this could be a time in which heart patients are more likely to experience fatal attacks. They suggest that drugs modifying REM action might be useful for such patients in preventing potentially fatal arrhythmias.[10]

Some of the other physiological changes that have been reported for REM periods include a decrease in the number of galvanic skin responses and an increase in grinding of the teeth! Among males there is also an increase in erections. In one study, Dr. Charles Fisher and his colleagues reported that erections occurred in 95 percent of all REM periods studied, while in another study carried out under the leadership of Dr. I. Karacan, erections were reported in 80 percent of the REM periods. In both studies, erections were infrequent in NREM periods. Usually erection coincides with the onset of the REM period. These erections usually occurred in the *absence* of any manifest sexual content in the dream.[11]

The regularity of the erection cycle during sleep suggests that it is biologically determined rather than being a specific response to sexual stimulation. Interestingly, though, the experience of anxiety in the dream may inhibit erections. Karacan and his associates found that when erections did not occur during REM periods, the subjects tended to report more anxious dreams.

These, then, are some of the physiological changes that take place during REM periods. An increase in heart rate, the sudden spurts in breathing, the cycle of erections—all of these are nightly features of our sleep, sensed dimly if at all. These processes accompany the endless theater of the dream, regularly occurring throughout one's sleep; a matter seemingly of our biology, a mechanism developed in the evolution of the species. But if dreaming is an evolutionary development, should it not have some meaning, some purpose in helping us cope with our problems? We believe that this is so, and we will offer some ideas about the usefulness of dreams later in this book. For now, we shall turn to an intriguing attempt to explore the question of the function of dreams in the research laboratory.

If one is interested in studying the function of a biological or psychological process, a direct (though possibly disastrous) approach is to interrupt the process—stop it from occurring and observe the consequences. Where the effects are likely to be harmful, animals, of course, are used as subjects. Still, there are circumstances in which human volunteers may be safely studied. The effects of sensory deprivation are an example of research that comes readily to mind. There was an occasion when an experimenter had himself lowered into a dark tank of water and remained isolated, out of sensory contact with his normal world, to see what the experience would be like.

Nothing quite so dramatic is required for dreaming. The research objective is simple enough. Markedly reduce dreaming for a period of time and see what happens. If dreaming is really important, we should expect some consequences to follow from dream deprivation. How does one accomplish this? The answer is, if REM periods are indeed good indications of dreaming, then preventing these periods from occurring should effectively reduce the amount of dream time.

The basic procedure was reported by Dement in 1960. His subjects went to sleep in the laboratory. At every sign of REM activity, they were awakened and required to sit up in bed for several minutes. The subjects were allowed to sleep fully only during NREM periods. These REM deprivation procedures were carried out for five consecutive evenings. Following these deprivation nights, the subjects were allowed to sleep without interruption for several nights in the laboratory while their sleep was monitored. Those post deprivation nights were called "recovery nights."

Two major observations were made. The first was that during the recovery nights, the amount of REM time recorded on the charts was unusually high. On the first recovery night, there was a substantial increase in REM time over a pre-experimental baseline period of normal sleep. It was as if there were some kind of compensation for previous loss of dream time. This phenomenon was called REM rebound.

The second observation was behavioral. The experimenter reported that the subjects showed signs of anxiety, irritability, and difficulties in concentration during the period of REM deprivation.[12]

Taken together, the two observations suggested that dreams have an important psychological and perhaps biological function. The data seemed consistent with Freud's theory that dreams served as a means of discharging psychological pressures.

The discovery was provocative and led to further research. These follow-up studies have led to some revision in our conclusions about dream deprivation.

The REM rebound effect has been confirmed in a number of studies, though not in all. The psychological effects of REM deprivation (anxiety, irritability, difficulties in concentration) have not been confirmed. Subjects who are awakened periodically during REM periods do report more fatigue, confusion, less ability to think clearly, and discontent than before starting the experiment. But as Dr. D.A. Chernik points out, many of these feelings are also reported by subjects who are awakened periodically during NREM periods. Lack of sleep in general rather than specific REM deprivation seems to be the principal source of psychological discomfort.[13]

Chernik's conclusions were based on asking his subjects to fill out mood scales while in the sleep laboratory. Dr. David Foulkes and his co-workers wanted to find out what their subjects were doing when they were outside of the laboratory. They recruited some assistants (watchers) to follow the

REM-deprived subjects around and observe their behavior. The watchers reported nothing unusual in the subjects' behavior, though one of the subjects complained vociferously about being watched![14]

In revising his thinking, Dement later reported that subjects had been deprived of REM sleep for as much as sixteen days without serious adverse effects.[15] So the psychological effects of REM deprivation observed in the first experiment have not proved to be reliable.

We are still left with the very significant finding that REM deprivation with accompanying loss of dreaming may result in increased dreaming during subsequent nights. There seems to be something in our biological makeup which requires us to maintain a certain amount of dream time. So the dream does appear to be important. But why? Perhaps this cannot be fully answered by experiments. Perhaps this may only become clearer when we begin to analyze the meaning of dreams themselves.

In the rush of excitement to exploit the possibilities of studying dreams using the REM-identification technique, there was a tendency to ignore the NREM periods. The assumption was made that these periods were relatively barren of mental activity. An important study by Foulkes, however, forced some modification in this view. He found that NREM periods were not barren at all; there were considerable thought processes at work – not necessarily vivid dreams, but mental activities, nonetheless. In investigating the nature of NREM reports, Foulkes found that they tended to be less vivid and elaborate than REM reports. NREM reports seemed to be more thoughtlike in character, frequently being recapitulation of everyday activities.[16]

Foulkes presented some illustrations of the differences between NREM and REM dream reports. In the following examples taken from an adult male subject, one can see a difference in the dramatic quality of the reports taken from NREM and REM periods.

> 1. He asked an acquaintance at work for a hammer, so that he could fix something in his apartment. (NREM)
> 2. He was thinking of a point made in his tax class, that you have to provide over half of a person's support to claim him as a dependent. (NREM)
> 3. He received a phone call in the middle of the night from a girl identifying herself as from the University of Chicago. She said that it was time for his "35-day evaluation." He chided her for calling so late at night. She replied that it was the only time they could get him in. (REM, 3 minutes after onset of eye movements).[17]

The discovery of the different qualities of reports from the REM and NREM sleep has led to speculation as to how and why this takes place. One of the more intriguing theories, described by Dr. Paul Bakan, is that REM sleep is associated with a transitory dominance of the right brain hemisphere. Compared to the left hemisphere, which Bakan described as "typically involved with language, logic, propositional thought and analytic functions," the "right, 'non-dominant' hemisphere is associated with perceptual-spatial and non-verbal functions, visual and body imagery, music, and non-analytic functions." In Bakan's analysis, during REM sleep, the two hemispheres become more functionally independent, and in cyclical periods, the right, less logical hemisphere, dominates.[18] When this happens, it would not be surprising to find more dreamlike, less logical quality in the reports of the subjects.

In considering theories like this, one has to keep in mind that the difference between REM and NREM sleep reports is far from absolute. Researchers have noted considerable dreamlike materials in reports from NREM periods.

The resurgence of interest in NREM periods has had important implications for one important type of dream: the traumatic type of nightmare known as the night terror. This is a dream that is terrifying. The dreamer's heart rate accelerates rapidly, and he may scream in his sleep. Unlike most dreams, these rare experiences tend to occur during NREM, not REM periods. We will consider these night terrors in detail later in the book.

The study of dreams in the sleep laboratory has been a major breakthrough in our understanding of dreams. It has enabled us to make a much more precise study of the nature of the dreaming process and of its physiological correlates. The limitations of the laboratory procedure are, however, clear. It is an expensive procedure, involving a great deal of time and effort on the part of experimenters as well as inconvenience for the subjects. Consequently only a small number of subjects are used in any given experiment. This limitation makes it difficult to generalize results. It also makes it difficult to study certain types of problems. For example, if we are interested in learning what types of persons remember dreams best, this requires a large number of subjects and would be a major undertaking for a sleep laboratory. Research on this question, therefore, has relied mainly on dream reports recorded in the home.

There is yet another limit imposed by the inconvenience of the laboratory: the use of dreams in the clinical work of psychotherapy. If we are interested in a patient's dreams in order to learn something about him, we cannot refer him to a sleep laboratory, as a physician might do for X rays. It is hardly practical. The same is true for the person who wants to analyze his own dreams. In both instances, we must rely on dreams recorded at home. And yet as Dr. David Cohen points out, recalled dreams constitute only a small fraction of actual dreams and could be an unrepresentative sample.[19]

The question then becomes, are there differences in the content of laboratory and home dreams? And if so, are the differences substantial? The answer to the first question seems to be yes. A study by Domhoff and Kamiya suggests that the home dream may include somewhat more sex and aggression or misfortune, while the laboratory dream may contain more characters and "bizarre elements." This latter finding probably reflects the apparatus used in the laboratory, which often finds its way into the dreams of the subjects.

Still, for the most part, the differences reported between home and laboratory dreams are small in terms of percentage. So, with certain differences that
should be kept in mind, one could consider the home dream a reasonable approximation of the laboratory dream. This is reassuring to those who continue
to study and utilize dreams without the facilities of a sleep laboratory.

Chapter 4
The Manifest Content of Dreams

The discovery of REM periods made it possible to pinpoint when a dream is occurring, but once you have the dream transcribed, how do you analyze it? How can you describe a dream in such a way that you have (1) adequately covered its content, and (2) used a sufficiently clear procedure that someone else using it would come out with essentially the same description? In other words, how can you describe dream content meaningfully and objectively?

Let us look at dreams reported by two students. As you will see, they are very different.

> I was sitting in the car outside the house (our old one). The young man and I were talking when the sky lit up. As we watched there was a circular path of light which was high up off to our right. As we watched, a ball of light followed the path and as it reached the bottom, it collided with a bright red ball in the path. A Chagall like figure outlined in light appeared. Outside the car we noticed my father watching the sky with binoculars and a man dressed in a gown and pointed sorcerer's hat. It was dark green and patterned but not with stars or crescents. He seemed to be directing the ball of light. He decreed all people be married, and married the Chagall figures which were soon over-populating the earth. The ball of light kept going around and around producing more figures and then I woke up.

> I used to go to camp. I was both a camper and in later years a counselor. I haven't gone for two summers now and last night I dreamed of camp. We were there the first day of camp. The children all lined up and us counselors [were] comparing the children—the good ones and bad ones.

These two dreams differ in several ways. For example, the first dream is considerably longer, and along with the added length, there are many more details. The actions of the first dream are bizarre, involving strange illuminations and a mysterious sorcerer-like person, while the actions of the second dream deal with what was usual and familiar in the dreamer's experience. Also, the first dream reports elements of color, while the second does not.

Let us now look at another dream.

> Throughout my dream (which seemed to last all night), I was an American spy in Russia. I believe it was Czarist Russia. The first part of my dream concerned how I got into Russia unnoticed. I encountered many different people

33

including a plantation owner freeing his Negro slaves, and some other American spies camping out by a roadside.

The next major portion of my dream, I worked in some sort of kennel for the important people's pets. I spent a lot of time taking care of the animals and learning what I could about these important Russian people.

At last, I became an important spy and worked out of a library in Moscow. My name became Sabie Lawrence, and my job was hiding Americans who were being sought after by the Ukrana. Toward the end of my dream, I was trying to hide this American girl. We were being sought after by the Cossacks. I felt the only safe place to hide her was in the library. We were racing down the steps of this library, hiding in and out of rooms. The Cossacks wore bright red and black uniforms, carried swords, and rode gray horses. At last, we were caught. The girl was immediately taken to a prison cell. I was questioned and beaten until I finally was sent to my cell. The cell was a dirt block with no windows. I curled up into a corner and thought about my past experiences.

In the third dream, we find that the dreamer plays an active role in the dream, in contrast to the relatively passive roles played by the dreamers in the first two dreams. The dream has definite scenes, offering more of a story line. We find a wider range of characters, including animals. There are also acts of aggression, which are not evident in the first two dreams.

If we added a fourth dream, we would find some similarities with the preceding dreams and probably some new elements as well. If we added a fifth, sixth, etc., dream, we would eventually cover most of the situations occurring in dreams. From such notes, we should be able to lay out a rough scheme for classifying dreams.

This procedure of developing a classification system and then applying it to new dream reports is called *content analysis*. It is a procedure social scientists like to use and has been applied to literature, movies, television, and all kinds of interview data. In essence, content analysis is a matter of looking at what's there, working out a scheme to make sense out of it and then using it. It is akin to what archaeologists did to samples of ancient pottery, the ancient astronomers did in making configurations out of the stars, and the grammarians did to language.

Some of the ways one might look at dreams are obvious and straightforward. For example, is it a long dream or a short dream? Who are the characters? Is there just one character—the dreamer? If there are several characters, do they interact with each other? If they do interact, what is the emotional tone? Is it friendliness, anger, sympathy? What is the setting like? Is it a usual or unusual place? Are there words spoken in the dream? Is the dream in color?

These are fairly obvious characteristics one might look at. One might also work out schemes to assess more subtle or esoteric psychological characteristics. For example, if one is researching Freud's theories, one could draw up a list of sexual symbols. Dr. Emil Gutheil has provided us with such a list.[1] If one is interested in researching Jung's ideas, one might try to work out a system for identifying the influence of the collective unconscious in dreams. This is not an easy task, for the researcher must define the meaning of the term very carefully and provide explicit examples in terms of dream materials. Despite these difficulties, studies of this sort have been carried out.

Over the years, there have been a number of schemes proposed for the analysis of the manifest content of dreams. Content analysis schemes have been developed to extract from dreams indications of a wide variety of psychological concepts including anxiety, hostility, homosexuality, dependency, masochism, ego strength, and orality. We are going to take a brief look at some of these schemes and then highlight some of the major findings uncovered. This will include facts about the settings, characters and emotions of dreams, the use of color in dreams, differences between the dreams of men and women, the dreams of children and the frequency of "typical dreams."

One of the most interesting studies of the manifest content of dreams was carried out by Dr. Peter Hauri and his colleagues at the University of Chicago. They first collected 127 dreams from subjects studied in a sleep laboratory. Then they rated these dreams on a variety of characteristics, such as the length of the dream, how imaginative it was, how pleasant it was, whether there was hostility, sexuality, etc. They fed these data into a computer, using a factor analysis program. This program extracts what is common or shared by the many separate measures. For example, if you asked people a series of questions like "Do you like to go to parties?" "Do you like to go to the movies alone?" "Do you spend a lot of time by yourself?" and "When you have problems, do you usually talk things over with friends?" a factor analysis of the answers would probably point to the presence of a general factor such as extroversion-introversion.

Probably the most important factor Hauri and his co-workers identified in regard to dreams was a measure called "vivid fantasy." The researchers described the factor as follows:

> This factor reflects feelings of *unreality* (imagination, distortion) coupled with *intensity* of experience (dramatization, clarity, emotion). Productivity (length of dream report) is also highly loaded. These three elements—the extent of a dream, its unreality, and intensity—are central to what is commonly referred to as a "good dream" (a lot of strange and wonderful things seem really to be happening).[2]

Another important factor identified was called "active control." This is the extent to which the dreamer is "active and exerts control."[3] Remembering our dream examples, we can see how the first dream would have been high on vivid fantasy while low on active control, while the third dream would have been high on both scores (at least till our dreamer was captured).

In summarizing their findings, Hauri and his co-workers feel one can learn a good deal about dream content by asking the following questions:

1. How intense and unreal is the dream?
2. How much is the dreamer, as a participant, actively trying to influence what is going on?
3. How pleasant is the dream?
4. How much verbal aggression is there?
5. How much physical aggression does the dreamer display?
6. How much heterosexual activity is there?
7. Is the dream more perceptual or more conceptual?
8. With what time in the dreamer's life is the manifest content of the dream associated?[4]

The most widespread studies of the manifest content of dreams were carried out by Dr. Calvin Hall and reported in two books, *The Meaning of Dreams* (New York: Harper and Brothers, 1953) and *The Content Analysis of Dreams* (New York: Appleton-Century-Crofts, 1966), the latter co-authored by Dr. Robert Van de Castle. Hall's studies provide us with our basic facts and statistics about the nature of dream content. When he wrote the first book, Hall had a collection of some 10,000 dreams to draw on, certainly one of the largest collections extant. Hall's approach to dream analysis tended toward the straightforward rather than the esoteric, although he has included measures of such psychoanalytic concepts as orality and regression.

In his earlier book, Hall analyzed dreams in terms of four categories: settings, characters, actions, and emotions.

The most frequent settings for dreams were houses or rooms in houses. About one-third of the dreams he analyzed occurred in this commonplace setting. Most often, the dream occurred in somebody's living room. Other commonplace settings were automobiles and recreational settings such as parties or beaches. In about one out of ten dreams, the dreamer was just out walking somewhere.

What about the characters? Hall found that in most dreams (about 85 percent) there was more than one character. The solo dream seems to be relatively rare. Typically there were three people in a dream. Very frequently these people were members of one's immediate family. Hall reported that younger people tended to dream about their parents, while the older people dreamt about their spouses or children.

While there was a good deal of dreaming about friends, there was also considerable dreaming about strangers. In fact, four out of every ten characters were strangers!

Not all characters in dreams are humans. As we saw in one of our dream examples, dreams sometimes include animals. What does this mean? Van de Castle has made some interesting analyses about dreams of animals. Comparing 150 dreams in which animals were present with a large sample of dreams in which no animals were mentioned, he found that the more animal characters were mentioned in the dream, the more anxiety, aggression and misfortunes also occurred. One might speculate that the presence of animals in dreams provides a vehicle for the expression of more primitive or deep-seated emotions.

When Hall analyzed dreams in terms of actions, one thing he did not find was an abundance of routine, daily activities. There was little sewing, typing, cooking or bathing. Dreams do seem to take one away from his usual routine of living.

The analysis of dreams in terms of emotional tone revealed that dreams are more likely to be unpleasant than pleasant. In fact, Hall reported that unpleasant dreams (characterized by fear, anger or sadness) were twice as likely as pleasant dreams (characterized by joy and happiness). Of these unpleasant emotions, fear was most frequent, anger next, and sadness least.

It is interesting that very similar findings were reported by Foster in his study of the Mexican village of Tzintzuntzan. Unpleasant emotions predominated and fear was the emotion most often noted.[5] So, these patterns reported by Hall apparently transcend American culture.

In the subsequent book Hall wrote with Van de Castle, most of these findings were confirmed, refined, and put into precise statistical form. The statistics were based on a sample of 1000 dreams collected from 200 subjects, half of them male, half female. The tables provided are useful in providing "norms" one can use to judge the typicality of dreams one may collect. This information is presented in great detail. For those who are curious about such things, elephants appear twice in a sample of 1000 dreams. Flower pots appear only once despite their potential as a Freudian female sexual symbol. There are four references to pajamas, thirteen elevators, twenty-four airplanes, one hundred and three doors, and one hundred and forty-nine automobiles in this sample of 1000 dreams.

More interesting, from a psychological standpoint, are the data provided on sex and aggression in dreams. Manifest sexuality in dreams (sexual intercourse, petting, kissing, etc.) was reported in only fifty-eight of 500 male dreams and eighteen of the 500 female dreams. The overall percentage would be rather small, about 8 percent. The authors suggest that this small figure might be due in part to their subjects' withholding information because of its sensitive nature. Other statistics I have seen are close to this figure. My own experience has been that the report of manifest sexuality in dreams is infrequent.

The tables indicate that there is frequent aggression in the manifest content of dreams. Nearly half of the sample of 1000 dreams contained at least one instance of aggression. There was little difference between males and females in this respect. Most often the dreamer was the "victim" of the aggressive act, not the perpetrator. Some of the aggressive acts were merely witnessed by the dreamer. Most typically these were instances of males being aggressive toward other males.

One interesting feature of these dreams was that the aggressive act frequently occurred without any clear expression of anger in the dream. The authors report only ninety-seven instances of anger in the 1000 dreams. It would seem that the emotion of anger and the act of aggression have been split off from one another in many dreams.

One of the intriguing visual features of dreams is that some appear in black-and-white while some appear in color. It was once thought that only a small fraction of dreams were in color. Hall's estimate was 29 percent. This figure was in line with the findings of other investigators who relied on questionnaire techniques. Using the REM method of obtaining more immediate recall, Dr. Edwin Kahn and his associates came up with a much higher figure of 70 percent. These findings were confirmed in a subsequent study by Dr. Herman and his co-workers at Yeshiva University, who reported the presence of color in 68 percent of REM-obtained dreams.[6] It would seem from those results that dreaming in color is very common, but recall for color is very poor.

One question that is frequently asked is whether the dreams of men and women tend to be alike, or if they differ in any respects. One difference was noted by Hall and Domhoff: Men most often dream about male characters in their dreams (about 64 percent of the characters are male), while women seem to dream equally about males and females. Not only was this difference observed for dreams of college men and women, but the same tendency was noted for dream reports from other cultures, the Hopi Indians and the Yir Yoront of Cape York, Australia. Drs. Alan Grey and Don Kalsched found the same general pattern holding among students at the University of Allahabad in Uttar Pradesh, India.[7] Hall believes the tendency for males to more often dream about males is nearly universal.

It is a little difficult to account for the difference. This author's own guess is that it reflects a historical pattern throughout much of the world of placing more importance on the male of the species. Since it was the male that was thought to matter most, it seems reasonable that the male would be most frequently the subject of dreams. If this interpretation is correct, we might expect this difference in dreams to diminish with the advent of the movement for women's equality.

In looking through the tables provided by Hall and Van de Castle, one notices some additional differences between the dream reports of males and females. In general, these differences seem to reflect the different roles that men and women play in their everyday lives.

As we indicated, dreams containing sexual behavior were reported more frequently by males than females. This may reflect a more guarded attitude on the part of women about relating sexual dreams. Women tended to report more emotion in their dreams than men. This seems to reflect the real differences one finds in waking behavior where society permits women to express fear and grief, but frowns upon such behavior by males. On the average, the dreams of women tended to have more characters in them. This was particularly true for dream characters of infants and children. There were nearly three times as many children in the dreams of the female subjects. Once again, this finding seems to reflect difference in the social roles men and women play, where child care is usually the responsibility of the women.

Dreams of male subjects showed a modest preference for occurring in an outdoor setting, while dreams for females were somewhat more likely to occur indoors.

Both sexes were about equally likely to report aggression in their dreams. Men were about equally likely to express this aggression in actions or in words. In the dreams of women, aggression was expressed mainly in words, not deeds.

What about the dreams of children? How do they differ from the dreams of adults?

The study of children's dreams poses some problems. Adult subjects can place a note pad and pencil by their bedside, and if they are sufficiently energetic at that time in the morning can write down what they remember of their dreams. It is possible to enlist the aid of a parent to interview the child, but this depends on finding very cooperative parents. Some alternatives are asking the child in a general way whether he has ever dreamt about such-and-such, or using the sleep laboratory REM-awakening technique.

Some of the earlier studies seem to emphasize the fearful elements of children's dreams. We shall have more to say about these dreams when we discuss nightmares. Recent studies conducted by Foulkes and his colleagues, however, suggest that pleasant dreams are much more frequent than anxiety dreams in normal children.

Foulkes and his collaborators carried out sleep laboratory studies of the dreams of children. They discovered that it was just as easy to identify periods of REM sleep in children as it was in adult subjects. They used an informal interviewing technique with the children to elicit their dream reports. Over a period of years, they have collected more than 700 dream reports. What they found was that the dreams of children tended to be free of unpleasant emotions and seemed to mirror the realities of the child's daily experience. Dreams were about riding tricycles, flying kites, going to school, playing in the back yard, being left at a baby sitter's house, etc. There were also dreams of animals, including one of a "teddy bear eating cereal."[8]

The dreams of these children usually occurred in an outdoor setting and were concerned with play.[9] As the child matures, the focus of dreams shifts to indoors. The emphasis on play eventually gives way to the more "serious business" of work, study, and social relationships of the adult.

Considering adult dreams, one might wonder whether there tend to be changes in dream content as a function of advancing years. Dr. Harold Zepelin investigated this problem using male subjects ranging from 27 to 64 years in age. He took samples of dream reports from both the sleep laboratory and home diaries. Zepelin found few, if any, differences in dream content that are related to age within the age range sampled.

We cannot leave the subject of the manifest content of dreams without discussing "typical dreams." People frequently ask, what does it mean if you are flying, or naked, or late for an appointment? There are a number of such dreams that many people experience at one time or another. As to what they mean, I think one is safest in looking at the individual case, making an assessment based on the dream, associations, and the life circumstances of the dreamer. Granting this, one might still ask, are there typical meanings for such dreams? The answer to this is there *could* be. The problem is the lack of hard scientific evidence one way or the other that one can draw on to back up one's speculations. There is no shortage of ideas, just a shortage of facts. With this disclaimer, let us look at some examples of ideas that have been advanced.

Dr. Emil Guthiel discussed a number of typical dreams and their interpretations in his book, *The Handbook of Dream Analysis* (New York: Liveright, 1951). While Guthiel's approach to these dreams is essentially psychoanalytic, he is far from dogmatic. Frequently, he presents several alternative interpretations.

Let us consider the dream of flying. We know something about how many people experience such dreams from an interesting survey carried out by Dr. Richard Griffith in an American University and his colleagues, Drs. Otoya Miyagi and Akiro Tago, in Japan, using college students in Tokyo. About one-third of the American students and 45 percent of the Japanese students said they had dreamt of flying or soaring through the air. The survey did not indicate how often such dreams took place.[10]

As interpretations for this common dream, Guthiel mentions Freud's view that there is a connection between flying and sexuality (erection in men and erotic fantasy in women), Stekel's view that there are death symbols in some dreams of flying, and Jung's idea that such dreams represent overcoming the difficulties of life.

Another common dream is falling. In the survey, such dreams had occurred in about 80 percent of the respondents, with little difference between the Japanese and Americans.[11] Guthiel feels that dreams of falling sometimes indicate loss of emotional equilibrium, such as loss of temper or self-control.

Dreams of appearing naked were experienced by 42 percent of the Americans surveyed and by 17 percent of the Japanese.[12] This appears to be a fairly large cultural difference. Guthiel mentions two interpretations for such dreams of appearing naked. The first is an exhibitionistic wish based on infantile needs. The second is an expression of feelings of inferiority.

Dreams of arriving too late were reported by 63 percent of the Americans surveyed and by 48 percent of the Japanese.[13] In my studies of the dreams of college students, I sometimes come across such dreams. Being late for an examination is one form of the dream. One student I knew had these dreams repeatedly before examinations. Invariably, he was late, couldn't find the room, went to the wrong building, forgot his paper and pen . . . all this in his dreams. When the day of the examination came, he was invariably early and usually got "A" grades.

Guthiel believes such dreams relate to frustrations and conflict. The conflict Guthiel sees is a wish to go and a wish not to go. Psychologists sometimes call this an approach-avoidance conflict. In this interpretation, the dream solves the problem by the person getting there too late.

Guthiel also feels such dreams could reflect a state of fatigue; the dream is sending a warning sign that the dreamer is overtaxing his resources. So much for speculation!

Chapter 5

The Stimulus and the Dream

Dreams are constructed out of one's past experience. Freud believed that a recent event—something that happened in the past twenty-four hours—usually acted as a trigger for the dream. This trigger set off more distant memories, which became combined in various ways in the dream content. Is there evidence for this trigger stimulus? Are very recent events, those of the past day, typically found in dreams? In exploring this question, Dr. Ernest Hartmann analyzed a sample of some 800 dreams. When the dreams were recorded, the procedure was to note any "day residue" items. These would be events that happened during the day which were included in the dreams. Over half of the dreams contained such day residues, providing some confirmation for Freud's observations.[1]

Then Hartmann went a step further. He tried to pin down the time of day the events incorporated into the dream actually occurred. He found that most of these events happened during the evening hours, reaching a maximum two hours before bed time. Things that happened just before going to bed were seldom incorporated into the dream.[2]

Hartmann's evidence substantiates the importance of the recent stimulus in the production of dream content. Investigators have long wondered whether the use of an artificial stimulus could influence dream content. Suppose you made a loud noise while a person was sleeping. Would that be incorporated into his dream? Or suppose you showed him a film before he went to sleep. Would this influence the dream? Or what would happen if you gave him instructions to dream about something specific, perhaps under hypnosis?

We are going to try to answer these questions as well as explore the effects of stimulus deprivation on dreams. In doing this, we are getting into the question of artificially shaping dreams. Once during a lecture, a student asked me whether it was possible to do anything before going to sleep to insure that she had good dreams that night. I am not sure of the answer, but some of the studies we will consider suggest that this may be within the bounds of possibility. So when someone says "Pleasant dreams," perhaps there will come a time when we may nod and reply, "Yes, I am planning on that."

The attempt to influence dream content by stimulating the dreamer while he is sleeping is not a new idea. In his *Interpretation of Dreams* (New York:

42

Basic Books, 1955; first edition published 1900) Freud mentions a number of such attempts in the nineteenth century, including some personal experiments conducted by Maury. Maury had himself stimulated in various ways while sleeping. These stimuli included light from a candle, a drop of water on his forehead, being pinched on the neck, and given eau-de-cologne to smell. Sometimes, Maury's dreams reflected these stimuli. For example, the drop of water on his forehead was followed by a dream report of sweating and drinking wine.

Maury's experiments were ingenious, but lacked the rigor of scientific controls. Essentially, the same problem was studied years later by Wolpert and Dement, who now had the advantage of the sleep laboratory and the REM-monitoring technique. These investigators were able to stimulate the dreamer during the actual time of dreaming. They waited for REM periods, then experimented with three types of stimuli: a tone sounding for five seconds, a lamp shining in the subject's face, and a fine spray of cold water. After using the stimulus, the experimenter waited a few minutes before waking the subject (if he had not already awakened) to inquire about dreams. Of these stimuli, the water spray was most frequently incorporated into the dream content (42 percent of the time). Less evidence was found for incorporation of the other two experimental stimuli, the tone and the light.[3]

In his doctoral thesis, Dement presents some illustrations of the effects of water stimulation. For example:

> The subject was sleeping on his back. . . . An eye movement period started, and after five minutes, cold water was sprayed on his feet and legs. One minute later he was awakened. The first part of the dream involved being in a room talking to some friends. Then, "two children came into the room and came over to me asking for water. I had a glass of ice water and I tipped the glass to give it to them. I was sitting, and I spilled the water on myself. The children wanted the ice and tried to grab it, but it slipped away. I got mad, because they were so greedy and tried to shove them away from the chair. . . ."[4]

Some investigators have tried to influence dream content by exposing subjects to an experimental stimulus before sending them to sleep. One procedure has been to show a motion picture film that is unusual and has a strong intensity. For example, Dr. Rosalind Cartwright and her associates studied the effects of erotic movies on dream content. Her subjects were male students at the University of Chicago. One of the films was blatantly pornographic – a ten-minute stag flick, showing a couple engaged in foreplay, oral sex and intercourse. The study took place in 1968 – a time before hardcore pornographic films were shown routinely in commercial movie theaters – so the effect of the film could be expected to be both novel and strong.

The investigators were interested in learning how frequently parts of the film might be incorporated into dreams. Six hours after viewing the film, the subjects went to bed in a sleep laboratory. They were awakened during REM periods and their dreams were transcribed. The content of the dreams was compared with that taken during the previous night in the laboratory, which was used as a "baseline" measure.

The major finding of the study was that the film had little immediate impact on dream content. Actions reflecting the film's sexual content occurred in only 8 percent of the dreams. In contrast, activities connected with the sleep laboratory occurred in 29 percent of the dreams.

The investigators monitored the subjects' dreams for three additional nights. They found that sexual incorporation increased on the second night to 20 percent, then fell off.[5]

In looking at the study, one wonders why the impact of the film on the dream was not stronger. One possibility is that the subjects were involved in a large amount of laboratory activity during the day (having blood samples taken, being interviewed, and taking an electrocardiogram), and these activities may have been a competing stimulus with the film.

The finding that sexual incorporation in the dreams rose after the first night seems at first blush inconsistent with Freud's observation that stimuli in the preceding twenty-four hours are the most frequent trigger mechanisms in the formation of dreams. It is possible that the clearly taboo nature of the film set up a defensive process, resisting immediate incorporation of the film. This seems possible in view of the fact there was an unusually large number of "I don't remember my dream" responses the night the film was shown, compared to the preceding and succeeding nights.

Some investigators have used films which are known to elicit stress reactions. One such film shows initiation rites in a primitive tribe. The camera follows a number of subincision operations carried out on the penis of young tribesmen. Goodenough and his co-workers used this film along with a second film showing the birth of a baby with the aid of a vacuum extractor. As control films, they used travelogues. One of these films about the English countryside was so dull that several of the subjects fell asleep just watching it.

The researchers predicted they would find more emotionality in the dream content following showing of the two stress films than the control films. This turned out to be the case. The dreams following the stress films were rated as having more anxious content than those following the neutral films.[6]

The "tricky nature" of this phenomenon, however, is illustrated by another study, carried out at about the same time by Drs. Joseph M. DeKoninck and David Koulack. They used a film called It Didn't Have to Happen, which shows workshop accidents. Among other things it portrays a worker's finger being cut off, with a close-up of the bleeding finger. The researchers report no increase in the anxiety level of the dream over and above a baseline measure.[7] So in one study you find the effect, and in the other you don't.

DeKoninck and Koulack looked for evidence of incorporation of film elements into the dream. They found very little. They tried another procedure, however, which did appear to pick up more elements from the film into the dream. What they did was to play a portion of the film soundtrack during REM sleep periods. The sound track included the sound of the finger-cutting circular buzz saw. This "reminder" played during sleep tended to increase the number of film elements in the dream.

We have looked at the effects of films as pre-sleep influences on dreams and have found them to be only marginally effective in shaping dreams. How about the effect of pre-sleep suggestion? Suppose you told a person to dream about such-and-such. Would this affect his dreams?

Dr. Priscilla Walker and Dr. R.F. Johnson have reviewed many of the studies seeking to demonstrate this possibility. In some of the experiments, the suggestions were made while the subject was under hypnosis. One of the early studies cited by Walker was conducted by Schroetter. Schroetter first hypnotized his subject, then gave her a suggestion of what to dream about, released her from hypnosis, then inquired the following morning about the dream. In one instance, Schroetter suggested that the size of the objects in the first part of the dream would be very small, while in the second part of the dream, they would be very large. In the subsequent dream report, the subject said she was so small she could pass through the eye of a needle, but as the dream went on, she became very large.[8]

More recent research carried out by Dr. Johann Stoyva and by Drs. Charles Tart and Lois Dick confirmed Schroetter's observation that hypnotic suggestions can influence dream content. These studies suggest that frequently, but by no means invariably, hypnotic instructions can find their way into dreams.[9]

In their review paper, Walker and Johnson point out that instructions do not have to be given under hypnosis to influence dream content. Some researchers have demonstrated that merely giving a suggestion, such as "you will dream about such-and-such," may be effective in influencing dream content for some subjects.[10]

Pre-sleep suggestion seems to be able to influence the content of dreams. Is it possible that such suggestions can also influence the actual capability of dreaming as indicated by REM measures? If you instructed a person to dream "more" or to dream "less," would this actually happen?

Dr. Robert Ogilvie and his associates tried to influence capability of dreaming using the following pre-sleep suggestion: "We would like you to concentrate on or focus your attention on dreaming tonight. Try to bring your dreams more into your awareness, and try to extend [sometimes the instructions were shortened] your dream episodes when they occur throughout the night. We should emphasize again that the research in this area indicates that you must really concentrate on the task of increasing [decreasing] your dreaming time."

These instructions had no perceptible impact on the percent of sleep time classified as REM periods. Ogilvie and his colleagues then looked within the REM periods and counted up the many separate rapid eye movements. They calculated how many movements there were during each period. What they found was when subjects were told to increase their dreaming, there were many more eye movements during a given period of REM time. Pre-sleep suggestion, then, had a measurable effect on the process of dreaming.[11]

The results of these investigations lead us to the conclusion that it seems possible to modify one's dreams. How to do this on a practical level is quite another question. If one is troubled by dreams of missing examinations at school or being chased by thugs and would prefer to dream of chocolate sundaes or a romantic rendezvous, how can one bring this about? There have been attempts to work out procedures for doing so. For example, in her book *Creative Dreaming* (New York: Simon & Schuster, 1974), Patricia Garfield described some techniques for influencing the content of one's dreams. Do these techniques work? Not according to the studies carried out in Foulkes' laboratory. Researchers Griffin and Foulkes tried Garfield's procedures out twice in controlled studies with essentially negative results. They concluded that the ability to control the content of dreams "must be much more difficult to achieve than enthusiasts such as Garfield (1974) generally intimate." Subsequent studies which have attempted to influence the content of dreams by voluntary control have produced some negative results (Ogilvie and his coworkers) and some positive results (Belicki and Bowers).[12]

While there seems to be a real possibility that one could influence the content of one's dreams, there is no proven procedure readily available for one to do so. If you are curious and want to experiment yourself, try thinking about your wished-for dream several hours before going to bed. Give yourself the suggestion, "I am going to dream about this tonight." I have no idea whether this will work, but if it does, you may be on to something.

We have seen that sometimes pre-sleep stimuli will influence dream content in a predictable direction—such as increasing the level of anxiety in the dream. Sometimes, we have observed that pre-sleep stimuli have little or no effect. There have also been instances in which such stimuli did not act to enhance the dream; instead, the reverse seems to be true. For example, a strong, pre-sleep aggressive stimulus has at times led to somewhat less aggressive content in dreams. Dr. Foulkes and his collaborators found this tendency after showing a film with aggressive content (a western film) to children. Along the same lines, Hauri had subjects undertake physical exercise before sleeping and found less such activity in their dreams.[13] I should also mention some observations Dr. Roland Tanck and I made in a study some years ago.

The observations I shall report were in a real sense fortuitous—not the result of some carefully designed experiment. In the spring of 1968, at George Washington University, Dr. Tanck and I were involved in collecting data for one of our studies using the Dream Incident Technique. The materials for the

DIT, along with some other psychological tests, had been put together into a rather cumbersome workbook. As we had only a limited number of the workbooks available, we decided to divide our subjects into two groups. The first group would receive the workbooks immediately, the second group later in the semester. The first group went about completing the tasks in the workbook more or less cheerfully under normal external conditions. The workbooks were then collected and given to the second group. Shortly after the workbooks had been distributed to the second sample, massive civil disorder broke out in the city, looting for several days. Martin Luther King, Jr., had been assassinated, and many citizens in Washington's black neighborhoods were outraged and reacted furiously. There were widespread fires, looting, and arrests. The situation was so bad that twelve thousand troops had to be called into the city to keep order. Some of the scars in the city's riot corridors remained visible for years.

During this period of violence and disorder, our subjects had the task of reporting dreams. When we collected the data, we knew of course that we had in our hands something like a natural experiment: One group had been exposed to a stimulus of considerable violence, and the other had not, and could serve as a control. We analyzed the manifest content of the dreams for the presence or absence of aggression, using two raters working independently on the data. The raters showed a high degree of agreement. In looking at the results, we anticipated that the subjects exposed to the community violence would probably show more aggression in their dreams. We were surprised when the opposite proved to be true. There was less aggression, and the difference was significant, statistically.

We did some checking to try to rule out artifacts that might have caused this difference. Comparing the two groups on a personality measure of aggression, we found they were at about the same level. We also looked at other measures of dream content, such as the level of vivid fantasy, and found that they did not drop off from group one to group two as aggression had.

Having checked out alternative possibilities as far as we were able to, we were left with the observation that a very strong outside stimulus for aggression had apparently depressed aggressive tendencies in the manifest dream content. Based on a suggestion by Arnold Meyersburg, we speculated that the data indicated a kind of reciprocal hypothesis: that when there is a clear external expression of aggression, there may be less need for intrapsychic expression of these impulses. We also thought that it might be possible that the intensity of the external aggressive stimulus could have elicited a strong counter-process (stiffening up the dream censor, in Freud's terms) making it more difficult for aggressive impulses to appear undisguised in dream reports.[14]

A report from Israel concerning the dreams of high school students who lived in a border town with a history of terrorist activity seems to bear out our observation. Drs. Yacov Rofé and Isaac Lewin reported that continuous living in the war environment since early childhood was related to a reduction in unpleasant and aggressive dreams.[15]

In discussing phenomena similar to this, DeKoninck and Koulack use as an explanatory phrase "compensation."[16] It is like our reciprocal hypothesis and would appear to be Jungian, both in name and conception. One will recall Jung's belief that dreams call attention to what is out of balance in one's life — what needs to be brought to one's attention.

Let us now look at the other side of the stimulus problem. Instead of introducing a new or added stimulus and seeing how it affects dreaming, what happens if you deprive a person of stimulation? What is the effect of lack of stimulation on dreams?

There have been experiments in sensory deprivation in which persons were deprived of sight, sound, touch, etc., for varying periods, but I do not know of any systematic attempt to study the effect of this extreme condition on dreams. The closest approximation I have heard about is a study by Wood. In his doctoral dissertation at the University of North Carolina, Wood studied the effects of pre-sleep isolation on dreams, and found an increase in social content in the dreams.[17]

Another approach to studying the impact of lack of stimulation on dreams is to examine the dreams of persons who are blind, deaf, disabled or confined for one reason or another. Inasmuch as dreams are primarily a visual experience, one of the most far-reaching kinds of understimulation would be blindness. What does the absence of vision mean for dreams?

Judging from research to date, blindness has a detrimental impact on the quality of the dream. Drs. Jerome Singer and Bella Streiner studied the fantasy and dreams of eight- to twelve-year-old blind children. The dreams the children described were rated for creativity and imagination, using such criteria as originality, variety of characters, and changes in space or time. When these ratings were compared with those obtained on children with normal sight, the researchers found that dreams of the blind children were less imaginative. The blind children rarely introduced content into their dreams that differed from their recent daily experiences. Their dream characters were most frequently parents and brothers and sisters. In contrast, dreams of the sighted children were more varied in both characters and situations.[18]

These findings are supported by Drs. Donald Kirtley and Katherine Cannistraci's study of blind adults. They found that the dreams of the blind persons differed from those of sighted persons in a number of ways. For one thing, there was much more conversation in the dreams of the blind. The authors believe this reflects the reliance of the blind on the spoken word as a means of defining reality in place of vision. Secondly, the settings of the dream tended to be different from the sighted persons': Among the blind, there was less frequent mention of the outdoors and of travel. Instead, there were dreams of being in the house and dealing with common household articles. Along with this emphasis on the familiar and concrete, the blind subjects dreamed more about the human body, probably their most concrete reference point of all.[19]

All of these findings suggest that one of the effects of blindness is to focus the content of dreaming on what is most familiar, substituting tactile and verbal contact with the environment for visual.

An interesting experiment of the effects of *selective* loss of visual stimulation was carried out by Dr. Edward Tauber and his co-workers. Imagine that you have been given tightly fitted goggles containing lenses which decreased all colors except those in the red-orange-yellow range of the spectrum. You are asked to wear these goggles continuously for several days. If you were like Tauber's subjects, you would find that your dreams contained more red-orange-yellow background and object colors and less of the blue-green.[20]

If the dreams of the blind emphasize the verbal, we might correspondingly expect the dreams of the deaf to emphasize the visual. According to a study carried out at Gallaudet College by Dr. Jack Mendleson and his colleagues, this is exactly what happens.

The earlier deafness occurs, the more intense the visual experience of dreams seems to be, with the congenitally deaf person reporting the most visual dreams of all. Their dreams were typically described as occurring in bright colors and were quite vivid on recall. The congenitally deaf reported a very high frequency of dreaming. Eighty-four percent of those interviewed said they dreamt every night. There was practically no sound experienced in the dreams of the congenitally deaf. Conversation in the dreams was usually in the form of sign language and gestures.[21]

Some studies have been made of the dreams of paraplegic men and women. In the paraplegic patient, the lower half of the body is totally paralyzed and anesthetic, producing severe limitations on physical activity. Dr. James Ryan was interested in the emotional problems experienced by paraplegic patients and sought to explore these through their dreams. One of the clearest tendencies he noted in their dreams was reports of normal, often energetic physical activities. For example, the patients reported the following dreams:

> At swimming meet for paraplegics. Yet all paraplegics are walking around. Not in chairs.

> I am out walking. Then playing baseball in park with gang of boys. I play first base.

> Drive in sport car to home town. I walk in big healthy steps around town. I swim and go skiing.[22]

As Dr. Ryan put it, "The patient appears to be expressing and experiencing pleasurable fantasies of behavior which is frustrated by the reality situation."[23]

In addition to these dreams of physical activity, the patients also reported dreams of sexual activity. Dr. Ryan also made the observation that some of the dreams of paraplegics contained indications of inadequacy and humiliation. "The patients experience feelings of being alone, unwanted, or in some cases, not even being visible."[24]

While some paraplegic males are capable of sexual intercourse, most are not, and ejaculation is rare. Dr. A. Estin Comarr and his colleagues reported that following spinal injury, there was a decline in the number of persons who reported sexual dreams, but the majority of the patients continued to have them.[25]

Some revealing cases reported by Dr. John Money show that sexual dreams of paraplegics can be both vivid and frequent. For example, one subject reported that sometimes he had such dreams for "three or four nights, or a week, going straight...."[26] We know from other studies that explicit sexual dreams are not very common among persons who have no such bodily injuries. For example, in the sleep laboratory study conducted by Domhoff and Kamiya, only 2 of 219 dreams included sexual acts. In home dreams, Hall and Van de Castle's figures are in the 8 percent range.

Not only were there apparently frequent dreams of sexual acts among these paraplegics, their dreams sometimes contained vivid imagery of orgasm despite a total lack of body sensation from the genitals. In Money's subjects, the loss of function was followed by dreaming that seemed to normalize the loss.[27]

We have talked about various kinds of deprivation—sensory deprivation and deprivation caused by lack of function or mobility. There are other types of deprivation we could consider. However, I think we will conclude the discussion by bringing up a type of deprivation that may seem far afield, yet is quite instructive. This kind of deprivation takes place in addictions. Having consulted on a drug addiction ward, I can testify to the profound difficulty patients have in finally giving up use of an addictive substance. As the patient deprives himself of what was formerly a mainstay of his life, what happens to his fantasies? Would he tend to dream more about the substance than would the person who still uses it?

Dr. Sei Choi tried to answer this question for alcoholic patients, administering a questionnaire to persons under treatment in the outpatient clinic. The subjects were persons whose alcohol history included blackouts, benders, cirrhosis and tremors. On the questionnaire, Choi asked whether they had dreamed about drinking since they had ceased drinking. He found that the patients who had dreamed of drinking had been abstinent for longer periods of time than the other patients. Eighty-three percent of the alcoholics who had been abstinent for more than one year had dreamed about drinking compared with 37 percent of the patients who had been abstinent for less than a year. The same pattern held when he looked at a shorter span of abstinence, three months. Deprivation of alcohol seemed to be followed by increased need to dream about it. It was as if the need for drink were being satisfied in the dream—a safer way than in reality.

The patients who reported these drinking dreams, however, seldom reported feelings of happiness during the dream. If anything, they reported feelings reflecting conflict about drinking—feelings of guilt, panic and failure. Happiness was a feeling they experienced when waking up. Choi reports that there was a universal feeling of relief that it had only been a dream and they had not succumbed to the impulse to drink.[28]

In trying to summarize these findings, one is led to the conclusion that the impact of stimulation on the dream is complex. The evidence indicates that dreams may be influenced by ongoing stimulation during sleep, incorporating elements of the stimulus into the dream. The dream may also be influenced by a pre-sleep stimulus. Verbal suggestion seems to be effective in some subjects, with or without hypnosis. The effects of films on dream content seem to be variable, but on the whole, less than one might suppose. At times the effect of pre-sleep stimulation does not enhance dream content, but works in the opposite direction, possibly evidence of defensive processes or compensation. A gross lack of stimulation such as occurs in blindness seems to limit what one dreams about. Less restrictive limits on stimulation, however, appear to produce compensatory dreaming or wish fulfillment.

Chapter 6
Dream Recall

Like many psychotherapists, I ask patients about their dreams in my clinical work because dreams are often very revealing about the patients' problems. Some patients have great difficulty remembering dreams, particularly when they are depressed. I had been working with a man for some months who had been depressed and was now recovering. Routinely I had inquired about dreams and routinely there was a negative shrug. Then one day he came in smiling broadly. "I dreamt last night," he said, and proceeded to tell me a most interesting dream that was an encapsulation of his major problem. When we analyzed the dream, he was astonished at how closely it described what he had been going through. In contrast, I was seeing a patient at the same time who was also depressed, but never showed significant improvement. She never reported any dreams in therapy and had only one vague recollection of a dream in her entire life.

These patients were hardly unique in having poor dream recall. Many people who seem to be doing quite well in life will tell you, "I don't dream." Others will say, "I can't remember my dreams." I suspect the first statement is incorrect. Since we know that REM periods are part of our biological makeup and that REMs are good indications of dreaming, it seems unlikely that people who say they "don't dream" are right. In fact, when such people are put in sleep laboratories, many are able to recall dreams. Under normal conditions, they just have very poor recall of dreams. Why is it that some people readily report dreams while others cannot?

In this chapter, we will consider several possible explanations. The first of these theories or explanations of dream recall is very simple. It starts with a fact observed in countless studies in psychological laboratories and buttressed by everyday observation—and that is, people differ considerably in how good their memory is. Why shouldn't this difference in ability to remember daytime events also apply to memory for dreams?

Dr. David Cohen, who has written extensively on the subject of dream recall, has discussed another straightforward explanation, which he calls an *interference hypothesis*. What this hypothesis boils down to is that new thoughts or other distractions occur during the process of awakening and afterwards. These new stimuli interfere with the memory of the dream; presumably, the more interfering events, the less likely the dream will be recalled.[1] The interference hypothesis follows from laboratory studies of memory in which new materials are interpolated between learning of information and efforts to recall that information. Such interpolation usually results in diminished recall. The phenomenon is called *retroactive inhibition*.

A third theory of dream recall follows from the Freudian concept of censorship. Freud put it this way. "We have seen that waking life shows an unmistakable inclination to forget any dream that has been formed in the course of the night and we have recognized that the agent chiefly responsible for this forgetting is the mental resistance to the dream which has already done what it could against it during the night."[2] What Freud is suggesting is that the content of the dream, already disguised by the censoring psychic agency, is still "too loaded" for comfort. The unacceptable is still in the dream. The censoring agency would like to see it obliterated altogether—and strives to do so. In the Freudian scheme of things, inability to recall dreams is another solution to the problem of affording release to unconscious pressures. The pressure of the latent dream thoughts is vented via the dream, and no damage results from the act, for the material is forgotten. This theory of dream forgetting which posits that there are internal forces actively seeking erasure of dream memory is usually called the *repression hypothesis*.

In this use of the term "repression" we are referring to the obliteration (or, as some have referred to it, the "after expulsion") of the dream from consciousness after awakening. Shapiro and his co-workers suggested that one particularly sensitive indicator of this effect might be the *contentless dream*.[3] This is the realization that one has dreamed but the inability to recall what the dream was about. It is as if the dream content had been expunged.

The contentless dream is frequently observed in studies using home dream reports, but seldom appears in the laboratory, where on-the-spot reports are taken. Shapiro and his team found only 3 such dream reports in a total of 169 awakenings. A subject who had the contentless dream experience in the sleep laboratory "reported the dream was 'on the tip of his tongue' as he was awakening but suddenly it was 'sucked away.'"[4]

A fourth possible line of explanation for dream recall (or lack thereof) relates to the rapid eye movements correlated with dreaming. Perhaps dreams which occur with greater numbers of accompanying eye movements are easier to remember, or perhaps dreams with bigger, more pronounced eye movements are easier to recall. One might speculate that more intensive eye movement activity might be reflected in more vivid dreams, and vivid dreams might be easier to remember. It sounds logical, but is either of these assumptions correct? Indeed, is there any relationship at all between what happens in a dream and our ability to recall it?

The more one speculates, the more questions occur. So, it seems time to turn to the available research to see what the evidence looks like. Let us begin with the first of the four theories, the one dealing with memory.

The hypothesis that people who recall dreams better have better memories for waking experiences has not received the attention it merits. Simple-minded possibilities sometimes elude the researcher fascinated by more intriguing theories.

In looking at the research, we will begin with some indirect evidence that seems to support the memory theory of dream recall at a gross level. We know that the memory of old people, particularly the "short-term memory" involved in fixating new information, is frequently poorer than in younger people. It was found that dream recall for older people, even with the aid of awakenings during REM periods, is not very good. Drs. Edwin Kahn and Charles Fisher found the rate of dream recall in their sleep laboratory for subjects in the 70- to 90-year range was only half what one finds for college students.[5]

Brain damage which obviously impairs memory also reduces dream recall. Drs. Milton Kramer and Thomas Roth found in a sleep laboratory study that patients with mild organic damage had only fair dream recall upon REM awakening. Patients with severe organic brain syndromes had still poorer recall, less than half of what one obtains from normal subjects. The authors reported that they tested four subjects who were *both* aged and brain damaged. These subjects recalled only 8 percent of their dreams during REM awakenings.[6]

In looking at the relationship of waking memory and recall of nocturnal dreams, one has to ask, memory for what? Memory for new incoming information, for events of the distant past, for pictorial stimuli like paintings, for patterns of sounds like symphonies, for historical dates, facts and figures? Not all memory is the same. What does one test?

Traditionally, psychologists have been interested in memory for verbal materials: for words, fragments of words, even fragments of words which make little or no sense and are appropriately called nonsense syllables. One might be asked to memorize a list of such syllables and be tested at a later time to see how much is recalled. When a researcher begins a study in psychology, he or she often prefers to use available techniques, for we know more about them. Thus it is not surprising that researchers have started with tests of verbal memories in looking at dream recall.

Two studies have examined the relationship between memory for verbal materials and dream recall. Both studies were part of doctoral dissertations, one conducted by Bernice Barber and the other by Stuart Anish. I think it is sufficient to report that the results were negative.[7] This aspect of waking memory seems to have little to do with memory for dreams.

Dr. Thomas Cory and his colleagues felt that memory for *visual materials* rather than memory for verbal materials might be more relevant in dream recall. They reasoned that dreams were primarily visual images in nature—and the ability to recall visual materials should be important in memory for dreams. To test this idea, they devised a number of visual memory tests.

Let us imagine that you were a subject in the study. For twelve days you filled out a dream diary, every morning upon awakening. When you completed this task, you went to a laboratory, where you were told you would be taking a test for color perception. You were instructed to write down the color of some slides that would be projected briefly on a screen. Fifty slides were then shown for 1/15 of a second. They included drawings of a policeman, ambulance, arrow, an alligator, and a flower. When you viewed all the slides, you might have been ready to leave for lunch, but the experimenter asked you to perform a new task — to write down the names of as many of the objects as you could remember. These were the data the experimenters were really interested in.

In analyzing their data, Dr. Cory's research group found that high recallers of dreams had better memory for these visual stimuli than low recallers of dreams. The researchers also used another series of slides with the same subjects, this time telling the subjects that they were taking a memory test. The results were the same. In both cases, visual memory related to dream recall.[8]

Cory's study then supports our first theory: Some elements of the waking memory system seem related to the ability to recall dreams. Some additional support for this theory was recently reported by Dr. Raymond Martinetti. Martinetti used a test for short-term memory that is routinely used in intelligence testing: reading a series of numbers (single digits) to the subject and asking the subject to repeat the series. Martinetti found that subjects who had better dream recall tended to do better on the digit recall task.[9]

With some evidence suggesting the usefulness of the first theory, let us take a look at the second line of explanation, the interference hypothesis. Cohen believes that the interference hypothesis has a very significant role in explaining morning dream recall. It is a theory involving normal distractions and competing stimuli that demand attention. Interposed between the fact of the dream and later attempts to recall it, these stimuli serve to weaken the memory of the dream. This theory seems particularly plausible in the case of the dream, for the dream is not fixated in memory under normal conditions of waking attention.

Cohen and his associate, Gary Wolfe, ran an experiment which demonstrates how even a modest distraction upon awakening can diminish dream recall. They divided their subjects into two groups. Upon awakening, one group was instructed to dial the weather report and write down the predicted temperature range for the day before reporting their dreams. The other group was asked simply to lie quietly for an equivalent period of time (about 1½ minutes) before reporting their dreams. While about 80 percent of the subjects in both groups reported dreaming during the night, subjects in the "dial-the-weather group" were not as able to recall what they had dreamed about. They were much more likely to report that they had dreamt but could not recall the content of the dream.[10] Thus, a simple distraction appeared to weaken the ability to report dreams. We might imagine what the more compelling events of normal life would do.

Much attention has been given to the Freudian hypothesis that forgetting of dreams is related to the activity of censorship, or put more broadly, to repression. Repression is a process of keeping psychologically threatening materials out of awareness. It is not conceived as a conscious effort such as "I just won't think about this any more"; rather, it is an automatic process that we are unaware of.

Psychotherapists have long noted that some people are more aware than others of their conflicts and problems. We have been tempted to assume that people who bring up and talk about these conflicts are more open or in touch with themselves and might therefore be considered *less* repressed individuals. If there is any validity in this idea, it should be possible to measure, at least crudely, the extent to which people tend to be repressed or at least to use repression as a defense mechanism.

In the 1960s Dr. Donn Byrne developed a scale using items of the MMPI which he believed measured a psychological dimension called *repression-sensitization*. After the scale had been used in a number of studies with some success, attempts were made to use it in the study of dream recall. The hypothesis was simple enough. If people score high on the repressor end of the scale, shouldn't they be less likely to remember their dreams?

Dr. Tanck and I were among the researchers who tested this hypothesis. We administered the Repression-Sensitization Scale to undergraduate students. Then we asked the students to write down two dreams over a period of several weeks. Not all the students were able to do this; some reported only one dream, some none at all. We considered the students who were not able to report the two dreams our "low dream recall" group. When we compared these students with the others on their Byrne scores, we found no difference. Repression as measured by this scale had nothing to do with recall of dreams. Similar negative results were reported by Cory and his associates and by Dr. Gwendolyn Gerber. Gerber found a positive relationship between the Byrne scale and a questionnaire asking subjects about the frequency with which they dreamed, but when the subjects were put to the test of recording dreams in a diary, the relationship vanished.[11]

Findings like the above cast some doubt on the repression or dream censor hypothesis, but are hardly reason to discard it. A paper and pencil test such as the R-S Scale is probably only a rough indicator of the tendency to repress. Perhaps the best way to study the repression theory is with experiments. The study by Cartwright and her colleagues showing erotic movies is an experiment in this direction. It will be remembered that there was a tendency for students not to remember their dreams the night they viewed the movie, which could be evidence for repression. Along the same lines, Goodenough's team found that after viewing subincision and birth films, their subjects gave somewhat more contentless dream reports than after viewing neutral films. While both of these studies provide some evidence for the influence of repression, the evidence is inferential and not very strong.[12]

There have been some other experiments designed to study the repression hypothesis and dream recall. However, to date, I have seen nothing which provides a crucial test of the hypothesis and am inclined to consider the hypothesis neither demonstrated nor disproved. In this respect, I find myself in agreement with the position expressed by Goodenough and his colleagues:

> The absence of convincing laboratory evidence for the repression hypothesis at this moment hardly warrants its rejection. . . . The dearth of research on repression is a consequence of the very real difficulties involved in creating and manipulating in a laboratory setting the circumstances under which repression is likely to occur.[13]

The fourth theory of dream recall suggests (1) that the amount of rapid eye movement activity influences the quality of the dream – the more REM activity, the more vivid the dream – and (2) that more vivid dreams are more likely to be recalled. This line of reasoning has been called the *salience hypothesis*.

In looking at the first assumption – that greater REM activity is associated with more vivid dreams – we might recall the original work of Dement. When there were larger eye movements recorded, there was more activity in the dream.[14] One may find additional support for this position in Cohen's review of research relating to dream recall.[15] While not all the findings are consistent, there does seem to be a tie-in between the underlying eye movement activity and the vividness of the dream.

There is also positive evidence for the second part of the salience hypothesis – that more vivid dreams are better recalled. Cohen cites a study from his own laboratory which indicates that the dreams of frequent recallers are more interesting and more vivid than the dreams of infrequent recallers.[16] Even more direct evidence is found in research by Meier and his associates. These investigators followed a single subject for *fifty* nights in a sleep laboratory. The subject must have been unusually cooperative and probably deserves a place in the Guinness Book of Records. At any rate, he was awakened during REM periods, recording between three and four dreams per night. In the morning, he was asked once again to recall the dreams of the previous night. He remembered about two-thirds of these dreams. All of the REM-awakening dream reports were then rated for intensity (whether "impulse, conflict, strong emotion, misfortune and dramatic events occurred"). The relationship was clear; dreams rated as most intense at the time of REM awakenings were better recalled in the morning.[17]

The study by Meier and his co-workers, ingenious as it was, used only a single subject, and would not be convincing by itself. A study carried out by Goodenough's research team, however, supports Meier's conclusions. Dreams reported during REM awakenings that included strong emotions such as depression or hostility were better recalled in the morning. In discussing their findings, the authors state, "Dreams not recalled in the postsleep period were pallid in content when compared with recalled dreams."[18]

The evidence to date, then, points to a role for the vividness of dreams (and the eye movement activity underlying this vividness) in the recall of dreams.

In trying to understand the process of forgetting dreams, it may be well to start with the observation of Goodenough and his colleagues that reports of contentless dreams in the laboratory are exceedingly rare.[19] If you awaken a sleeper during REM periods and he is aware of dreaming, he will recall the details of the dream whether it is vivid or mundane. Therefore, it seems reasonable to assume that at the starting gate, dreams are more or less equal in terms of immediate recallability. It seems likely that vivid dreams have more "staying power" in memory—they are less likely to get wiped out during the night. It is as though you etched two lines in beach sand, one deep, one shallow. When you etched them, they would both be visible, but after some time of exposure to the elements, only the deep line might remain visible.

While our analogy of the beach sand is at best a rough one, it does suggest the erosion or frittering away of the dream memory as time elapses during sleep. There is little doubt that something like this takes place. Suppose you wake up a sleeper right after the cessation of REM activity. There is an excellent chance of a dream report. However, if you waited a while after the REM activity stopped and then awakened the subject, the likelihood of a coherent dream report would go down. Wolpert and Trosman found that the longer they waited to awaken the subject, the more fragmentary the dream reports became. Indeed the dreams seemed to wither away.[20] So it is that when morning comes, the dreams that occurred in the latter part of the night seem best recalled.

If we ask what causes this withering away, we might point to several possible factors: poor consolidation of the dream in short-term memory, the influence of repression, and the interference of subsequent competing ideas. We remember that even during NREM sleep, some thought processes are operative. Although the effects of such nocturnal interference are difficult to study, the effects of interference upon awakening are very clear.

In summary, we have looked at four types of explanations to account for observed differences in ability to recall dreams. For three of the theories—differences in waking memory, the effects of interference, and vividness of the dream content—there is research evidence to support the theory. For the fourth, the repression theory, there is insufficient evidence either for or against. One could conclude from this that the conditions which tend to maximize the efficacy of memory play an important part in dream recall, in a manner more or less similar to waking life. If you have a good capability of recalling visual materials, if the dream is vivid, and if you are not distracted upon awakening, your chances of dream recall are improved.

This is a straightforward view, and is not essentially different from what might influence your recall of a TV show. If the show were vivid and you were not distracted afterwards by other events, you would likely have better recall for the show. While the explanation is straightforward, I doubt that it is complete. Dreams often deal with uncomfortable materials. It is hard to believe that such discomfort is entirely unrelated to the forgetting of these materials. Consequently, I am far from ready to discard the repression hypothesis — or something like it. We must wait for more crucial experiments before we can make that decision.

Chapter 7
Dreams and Mental Illness

From time to time writers have speculated that there may be a link between dreaming and symptoms of mental illness, particularly the bizarre symptoms of schizophrenia. Schizophrenia is an illness of unknown etiology with
symptoms that at times seem strange and unusual. There may be loss of reality
contact and social withdrawal. In some patients, there may be delusions of
persecution—the communists or the FBI may "be after" the patient. Sometimes
the delusions may be bizarre—a snake may be in the patient's stomach, or he
may be married to the Virgin Mary. Some patients may experience hallucinations, seeing what simply isn't there. Other patients may present a rigid
posture.

There are some obvious correspondences between these symptoms and
dreams. When one dreams, one sees visual pictures that seem real enough, but
are not really happening. One might wonder, are these pictures not similar to
hallucinations? Then, too, dreams sometimes contain bizarre happenings. Are
not these, too, like the bizarre ideas of some schizophrenics that we call delusions? Dr. Arthur Fleiss argues that "such phenomena as symbolization, condensation, displacement, projection, use of neologisms, and depersonalization
with feelings of strangeness and unreality" are common to both dreaming and
schizophrenia.[1] Is it possible that there is an underlying identity shared by the
dream state and schizophrenia? This is an intriguing idea, for if it were true,
we might obtain some basic insight into the schizophrenic process, a mental
illness that afflicts millions of people.

The question has generated much research. Judging from a review article
by Dr. Gerald Vogel, the facts and implications of this research are still in some
dispute.[2]

Schizophrenic patients have been studied in the sleep laboratory. One
question investigated was concerned with hallucinations. Does the awake
schizophrenic patient who is actively hallucinating show the same brain wave
patterns and rapid eye movements that we find during periods of dreaming?
If the same processes are involved in hallucinations and dreams, we might expect this to be true. Research findings, however, are negative. The
physiological correlates of dreaming and hallucinations apppear to be
different.[3]

A second area of investigation concerned the effects of REM deprivation. Interest in this question followed Dement's initial observations that normal subjects become psychologically disturbed during REM deprivation. It was theorized that schizophrenics might not have normal amounts of REM time while sleeping. Vogel cites a number of studies indicating that REM time for schizophrenics is not appreciably different from normal controls.[4] Once again, it looks like a negative finding.

A third question investigated was whether schizophrenics show the usual rebound in REM time after REM deprivation. While this matter is in some dispute, there is some evidence suggesting that there may be some differences here. Vogel reports evidence from his own research, however, which indicates that REM deprivation does not appear to exacerbate the symptoms of schizophrenia.[5]

Judging from Vogel's review, laboratory studies have thus far found only limited evidence of distinctive features in the REM patterns of schizophrenics. Their dreaming patterns may not be very different from those of normal persons. How about the content of their dreams? Are the dreams of schizophrenics different from those of normals? The answer seems to be yes. They are very different.

We will introduce this subject by looking at the dreams of a catatonic schizophrenic patient. The dreams were reported in a study by Dr. S.C. Chang. What is interesting about these particular dreams is that when the interview was conducted, the schizophrenic symptoms had remitted, and the patient in his more normal condition was able to look back over his dreams. The threatening world of the schizophrenic's dreams that will emerge in our inquiries can be clearly glimpsed here, but there is a muted quality in these retrospections compared to the more savage overtones we sometimes encounter during the symptomatic stages of the illness.

> Many of my dreams are in color; others a very dark black. I remember seeing myself in a white convertible driving around during some national calamity. It seemed to be a violent windstorm or earthquake. Everyone seemed panicky except me. Other times I've seen myself going through deserted mansions and homes; and once driving at night or at dusk with my mother in a convertible. Usually the roads are deserted and there is no sun shining, and everyone had their headlights on. I have also seen myself standing on an open plain in my hometown; and seen the ocean come right up to our house. I see myself with former friends and people I once knew in strange places such as an exclusive pool or gymnasium. Once I was with my sister and one of her close friends, at this beautiful ultramodern home. In front of the home was a large pond or lake. It was very dark and a huge tornado-like cloud came out of the sky and destroyed our glass house, but none of us were injured. Many of my dreams always seem to be in some fantasy world or in some other world. Once I was with someone on the edge of a huge forest, and we both were running through the woods scaring all the animals, especially the deer! Then again some of my dreams are centered around sex, and I've seen myself dancing with women but never having relations with them.

For one dream I was going through those underground tunnels or passageways; it was like a dungeon and there were caged animals underground. Some of the animals reminded me of pre-historic times.

Once I was in this strange town, or in some part of N. Town which I wasn't familiar with. Part of the town was being destroyed by fire, and meanwhile there was this flock of blackbirds flying around. I distinctly remember being frightened by these birds. Usually I'm trying to help others while the town is being destroyed, but they pay no attention to me and just continue sitting or going about their daily chores while the town is being consumed in flames.

Many of my dreams seem to be in some other time zone or another era, in which no one is working. None of my dreams seem too symbolic but just parts or glimpses of unfinished stories and fantasies.

In all these calamities, earthquakes, windstorms, etc., I usually am rather calm and not disturbed while others are in a panic. Usually the people I am with are very calm and relaxed and don't seem upset at all.[6]

Let us now turn to studies of the dreams of schizophrenic patients in more acute stages of the illness.

An illuminating study was carried out by Dr. Patricia Carrington. Carrington obtained the dreams of hospitalized female schizophrenics. Most of the patients were in acute conditions, taking tranquilizing medications. When the dreams were collected, they were compared with those of college women of the same age.

There were sharp differences between the normal women and the schizophrenic women. The dreams of the normal women "tended to be practical, realistic, and detailed."[7] Dream content for normal women included shopping, cooking, parties, dates, etc., the events of everyday life. The dreams of the schizophrenic women were much more dramatic, stark and grim. The dreams of the schizophrenic women were described as "overwhelmingly threatening."[8]

There was much more aggression committed against the dreamer in the schizophrenic dreams. Moreover, much of this aggression was life-threatening; in some instances the dreamer was actually killed in the dream. Other instances of aggression included rape and sexual assaults.

The dreams of the schizophrenic group were often bizarre, sometimes depicting total disasters. Instances cited by Carrington included "a volleyball hits a girl and pulverizes her into a million pieces; an alligator eats the dreamer alive; a dreamer's head is pressed into quicksand."[9] Many of the dreams contained episodes of explicit mutilation. Carrington reports that these scenes were often savage and brutal. Examples are given: A "dreamer burns her arm which then falls off exposing raw veins and bloody flesh," and "a woman kills her husband and stuffs part of his body into camels' heads," and "cut-up pieces of people are hung on rocks with blood oozing and mingling with the sawdust on the floor." No one in Carrington's control group reported dreams of such grizzly mutilation.[10]

Carrington considered the following schizophrenic dream as typical:

I was decapitated. My ribs were picked clean, no skin, no muscle. My body was cut in half. I was just a pile of bones. They didn't know who it was but I still knew who I was. I wanted to pull myself together, but I couldn't.[11]

Not only did the dreams of the schizophrenics depict a threatening and at times gruesome world, the dreams also portrayed the dreamer as being unable to cope with the threat posed. In contrast to the dream actions of the normal subjects, who were constantly trying to deal with the problems posed, the schizophrenic subjects frequently appeared hapless and helpless in their dreams. The one coping mechanism mentioned was a violent outbreak.

Carrington believes that her data point to the conclusion that a strong (healthy) ego in waking life will produce dreams which are integrated and resourceful, while the disturbed ego will produce the opposite.[12]

Carrington's study used female students as controls. Drs. Milton Kramer and Thomas Roth compared the dreams of schizophrenics with the dreams of normals and of depressed patients. While they approached the problem differently from Carrington, using REM awakenings and the Hall–Van de Castle system of content analysis, some of the results seem consistent. The characters in the schizophrenic dreams tended to be strangers rather than anyone known. There was a great deal of aggression in the dreams, and the predominate emotion expressed was apprehension. The ingredients of a threatening environment are certainly here.[13]

In comparing a group of paranoid schizophrenics with groups of psychotic depressives and hysterical character disorders, Dr. Robert Langs arrived at similar conclusions. Speaking about the paranoid schizophrenics, he stated that their dreams "reflect a proneness to conflict with others, and a view of the environment and others as predominantly traumatizing and overwhelming."[14]

As we have indicated, schizophrenia has acute phases. Here the patient may experience breaks with reality, his life patterns are thrown out of kilter, and he often is hospitalized. Schizophrenia can also become a chronic illness where the patient may remain hospitalized for years. Chang was interested in possible differences in the kinds of dreams reported by patients in relatively acute and chronic stages of the illness. He found that the dreams of the acute patient tended to be longer than those of the chronic patient. The dreams of the acute patient also encompassed a wider range of content. The dreams of the chronic patient were simpler and briefer. Chang observed that in many instances, the dreams of the chronic patient dealt with family members.[15] This is noteworthy in view of the long physical separation from the family. It was as if in dreams, the patient were hanging onto something long absent in reality.

What have these studies told us about the relationships of dreams and schizophrenia? I think it fair to say that there is little evidence that a common process underlies the two phenomena. They are both curious mental states with superficial similarities, but we have no reason to believe that schizophrenia is a dream state or vice versa. What we have learned is that the dreams of the schizophrenic patient are fraught with anxiety-provoking situations. We all have these experiences occasionally in dreams, but in the schizophrenic they seem to be running rampant. It is as if the control mechanisms that protect us from being overwhelmed by anxiety have gone out of kilter. One has a sense of flood gates that do not work. We do not understand why this happens, because we have as yet no clear understanding of the cause of the disease. The dreams portray the situation in a dramatic way, but do not answer the essential questions of why and what to do about it. These must await other lines of inquiry.

There are of course, other types of mental illness besides schizophrenia. One form of psychological disturbance follows from brain damage. We have already seen in our discussion of dream recall how organic brain damage can severely limit one's basic capability of remembering dreams. Excluding various kinds of neurotic behavior, the other major category that we think of as mental illness is depression. We are not talking about the limited, transitory episodes of the blues most of us experience at one time or another, but rather the more serious episodes requiring intensive therapy or hospitalization.

There are a variety of "subtypes" of depression. In some patients, depression alternates with periods of manic states; in others, it occurs alone, and we call it *unipolar depression*. Sometimes depression occurs after an upsetting event such as the loss of a loved one, and we call it a *reactive depression*. In any case, depression is usually characterized by such feelings as sadness and hopelessness.

Do the dreams of depressed patients reflect these sad feelings? Most of the research to date suggests that when the depressed patient is experiencing the worst of his depression, his dreams are not unhappy. The dreams are often short and commonplace. As such, the dreams seem to be split off somehow from the main thrust of conscious experience. Dr. John Miller, working with hospitalized patients, found that most of the patients who were in a deep state of depression reported pleasant as well as bland dreams. For example, one patient related a dream of being in a coffeehouse in Venice where there were beautiful girls and entertainment. To cap off the pleasant imagery, a man came in announcing they would sail around the city in a gondola.[16] Such dreams sound like Freud's wish fulfillment dreams.

When Miller looked at the dreams of depressed patients who were *improving*, paradoxically he noticed more conflict and evidence of disturbance. There was interpersonal stress in the dreams; sometimes the dreamer was being coerced by others. For example:

My husband was in a boat fishing and had the outboard motor running. I wanted to get in the boat also but he insisted I stay on the shore and wait while he fished. I decided my fishing license had expired so I wouldn't be able to fish anyway so it was safer I stay on the shore.[17]

There have been other reports taken at the time of deep depression, emphasizing the impoverished, banal nature of the dreams. This was reported in a paper presented at a French psychiatric meeting in 1967 by Baer and his colleagues. The investigators drew on a very large number of dreams from depressed cases. Dream activity appeared to be reduced when the depression was severe. The dreams of those patients with severe depression were banal, and the conscious problems of the depressed person seldom appeared in the dream. These researchers, as Dr. Miller had earlier, noted the possibility for the depressed patient to experience happy dreams, even though he is depressed when awake.[18]

Another example is Langs' study, which included the dreams of patients with psychotic depressive reactions. Langs' patients were selected using such criteria as psychomotor retardation, hopelessness, loss of self-esteem, and impairment of reality contact. The patients' dreams were described as brief, vague and empty. There was little evidence of either happiness or unhappiness. Examples of typical dreams included, "Sometimes I dream I'm by my sister, and then I wake and I'm not," and, "Dreamed I was with the whole family as it was in former times."[19]

One other feature has been noted in the dreams of some depressed patients. Dr. Aaron Beck and Clyde Ward noted that among depressed patients in psychoanalytic treatment, dreams were often characterized by painful experiences such as disappointment, rejection or injury.[20] These dreams, interpreted as masochistic, sound something like the conflicted dreams experienced by Miller's improving patients.

Rejection and masochistic themes continue to be characteristic of the dreams of formerly depressed patients who have recovered and are functioning in the community. Using a sleep laboratory to obtain his data, Hauri found this while comparing the dreams of patients who had recovered from depressions with those of normal controls. He also found that the dreams of the recovered depressed patients tended to be short; about 40 percent of the dreams were described in fewer than seventy words. When there was emotion reported, it was more likely to be unhappy than happy. Compared to the control subjects, the dreams were focused more on events of the past and were more likely to include depictions of inanimate external forces, such as storms blowing.[21]

While there are some apparent inconsistencies in the data collected to date on depressed patients, the general picture seems to be that during the depth of the depression, dream life tends to be shut off from the emotional debacle of waking life. Generally, dreams seem to lack emotion; they seem short and bland. At times there are pleasant dreams. These have possible psychological value in coping with the depression, offering hope in fantasy where none seems to exist in reality.

As the symptoms of the depressed patient begin to clear up, there is more of a tendency for dream life to reflect unresolved problems in the depressed person. These problems frequently concern feelings of rejection. Such dreams continue into the period when the patient recovers from the symptoms. The shortened nature of the depressed dreams persists even in recovery and may be characteristic of the depressed syndrome.

Chapter 8
Symbolism

The belief that ideas in dreams may be represented in the form of symbols is an old one. One will recall Penelope's dream in the Odyssey,[1] where geese were interpreted as wooers and an eagle as Odysseus. Or the dream interpreted by Daniel in the Bible, where an immense tree was interpreted as King Nebuchadnezzar.[2]

When Freud wrote *The Interpretation of Dreams*, he discussed symbolic interpretation of dreams made by his predecessors and contemporaries. Freud was not happy with what he saw. For example, he called Wilhelm Stekel's use of symbols "reckless."[3] Freud argued against starting dream interpretation with a this-means-that approach; rather, the way to begin was with free association. It was only when the free association technique ran into difficulty that he recommended turning to symbols to fill in the gaps.

Symbols for Freud were one of the means by which latent dream thoughts were disguised in the process of being represented in the manifest content of the dream. Freud stated that there were some symbols that typically had the same meaning in dreams from person to person. Still, one had to be cautious in making an interpretation, for at times symbols could have several meanings, and the analyst could make the correct judgment only from considering the context.

When Freud begins to discuss typical symbols, it becomes obvious that there is a very strong emphasis on sexuality in their interpretation. He stated, "All elongated objects, such as sticks, tree-trunks and umbrellas—may stand for the male organ."[4] He added some weapons to this list such as knives, daggers, pikes, revolvers, rifles and sabers, and machinery and tools like ploughs and hammers. Among animal figures in dreams, a clear-cut symbol of the male organ was the snake.

Symbols of female sexuality were said to be "boxes, cases, chests, cupboards and ovens" as well as "hollow objects, ships, and vessels of all kinds."[5] He added that "rooms in dreams are usually women,"[6] tables laid for a meal may be a symbol for a woman, and wood in general had a female connotation.

The act of sexual intercourse was represented by "steps, ladders or staircases," or by "walking up or down them."[7]

This is only a partial list of symbols mentioned by Freud. Animals, land-scapes, clothing—all may have symbolic meaning referring to the genitals.

Gutheil has expanded on Freud's list of sexual symbols. For symbols of the male genitals, he included such items as rats, squirrels, mice, horses, bulls, cow's udders, birds, bananas, pears, the stalks of flowers, trees, roots, trunks, fingers, noses, hair, arms, teeth, sails, flagpoles, keys, fishing poles, pencils, brushes, baseball bats, syringes, golf clubs, rope and common names such as John, Dick and Henry. He also includes janitors, burglars, and dwarfs. For female symbols, Gutheil included ears, eyes, cabbage, leaves, roses, shells, oysters, kittens, pockets, rings, front doors, figs and peaches. This, by the way, is not a complete listing; there are more![8]

Freud made it clear that sometimes one interprets objects such as these literally and not symbolically. The object is what it is, and does not stand for something else. Still, even before Gutheil's addendum, Freud had developed quite a list, and one wonders why he complained that his critics viewed his dream theories as being so sexual in orientation.

The reader may have the feeling that some of this is rather dubious, to say the least. He is certainly entitled to ask the question, how do you know this is so? An answer that might be offered is that these ideas are derived from a theory which is based on considerable clinical experience. From a scientific standpoint, however, this is not enough. Science requires a firmer footing for acceptance of ideas than the opinions of men, no matter how authoritative they appear. In the last analysis, a scientific theory must be tested objectively.

The question, then, remains: How valid is the idea of symbolism in dreams? I must admit that at this point, because there is relatively little research that is useful, I haven't reached any firm conclusion.

Tanck and I carried out a study to try to test the theory. Our rationale was as follows. If, as Freud believed, dreams make use of symbolism for disguis-ing latent thoughts which are largely sexual in nature, then individuals who are gratifying their sexual desires in behavior presumably would be subjected to less pressure by these unconscious forces. That is to say, there would be less need for sexual symbolism in their dreams. Translated into the language of for-mal hypothesis, we predicted that individuals with satisfying sexual relation-ships in their daily lives would use less sexual symbolism in their dreams than individuals who did not have such relationships.

In our study we used a questionnaire to separate two groups of college students. The first group dated frequently and had satisfying heterosexual rela-tionships. The second group hardly dated at all. Then we looked at the dream reports of our subjects, scoring them for symbolism. We used the following list, taken from Freud as our guide.

For male symbols: Any clearly elongated object, sticks or poles, tree trunks, umbrellas, knives, complicated machinery, ploughs, tools, weapons, snakes, airships, overcoats, hats, neckties.

A dream example:

...driving down the road. It was very snowy and icy.... A cement pole had ice and snow on it.[9]

For female symbols: boxes, cases, chests, cupboards, ovens, ships, containers, hollow objects, tables.
A dream example:

I was back at my old high school. I was just visiting.... When I came out of class, for some reason I started looking for a locker. All of the lockers in hall except one had a lock on it. I went to the open one and started to clean the things in it out. The locker number was my old girl friend's locker. All of the things in the locker belonged to her. I took them all out and put my things in.[10]

For representation of the sexual act: steps, staircases, elevators, escalators, ladders; walking up and down, climbing, being run over.
A dream example:

...four people and I are in a department store. Put a nightgown that is very expensive but on sale, on hold. Then I and another woman are waiting for an elevator. Man and woman and another man get out—I get in the elevator and go to the top of the building....[11]

The dreams were coded without knowledge of which group the subject belonged to. As a further check, two analysts coded a random sample of dreams independently with a high degree of agreement. Then we compared the two groups in terms of the total number of dream symbols reported.

Our results? We found as predicted that the group of subjects with ongoing sexual gratification in their daily lives had less sexual symbolism in their dreams.[12] Thus we found some support for Freud's theory.

Our findings are but a drop in the bucket when it comes to proving or disproving such a provocative theory. I would like to point to other studies of dreams which test Freud's symbolism theory, but I can hardly find any. Must we then rely on faith in accepting the theory? Not entirely. There is research on symbolism outside the context of dreams which bears on Freud's theory.

As we know, symbolism can be found in paintings, stories and poems. In terms of research, it is possible to stimulate subjects by exposing them to sexual materials and then asking them to make up stories. A study of this sort was carried out by Drs. Russell Clark and Minda Rae Sensibar. They found that male subjects stimulated by pictures of nude females tended to use more symbolic content in their stories than subjects not stimulated.[13] A little more support for Freud.

A more subtle form of stimulation is music. Dr. Michael Wallach asked a group of Radcliffe undergraduates to rate certain classical music selections in terms of how much they felt "sexually aroused" while the music was playing.

All the selections were impressionist pieces and, for those interested in creating a romantic mood, the winner was a section from Debussy's *Petite Suite*. Wallach then played the three musical selections to undergraduate students, instructing them to write brief stories after each segment of the music. Wallach also administered a scale measuring the anxiety level of the subjects, figuring that the more anxious subjects would be likely to express their desires symbolically. He used a complex method of scoring the stories for symbolic content that included the presence of Freudian symbols, acts of penetration, indications of rhythm, and body movements. Wallach found what he predicted: The students with higher levels of anxiety used more symbolic content in their stories.[14]

Tanck, Houshi and I have extended Wallach's work, carrying out research in which we have found a relationship between self-report of anxiety and the use of Freudian symbols in the subject's dreams.[15] Nonetheless, it is still a long jump from Wallach's undergraduates responding to soft music with literary symbols to interpretations such as Roheim made about Odysseus.[16] If the reader is not convinced that Freud's ideas of sexual symbols are correct, I would not blame him. I am not convinced, myself. The problem has to do with the nature of the beast. Freud's theory of symbolism, like his theory of dreams in general, is a theory of unconscious processes at work. The dreamer does not choose to dream about boxes or spears; that is the action of the dreamwork. A valid test of Freud's ideas must take place in the context of unconscious processes. That is why it is so difficult to study and our knowledge is so limited.

There has been some research of what symbols mean to people on a *conscious* level. As such, these studies could neither validate nor invalidate the Freudian theory. However, some of the findings are important and revealing.

One basic question that has been explored is whether shape has sexual meaning. Do people tend to identify pointed or elongated shapes as male and rounded shapes as female? The answer seems to be yes. A representative study was carried out by Dr. Ken Lessler using students in the public schools of East Lansing, Michigan.

Lessler told his subjects, "I have some cards with figures or pictures on them. I would like you to place each card in the pile to which you think it belongs. If it reminds you more of a father, brother, boy, or man, place it in this (pointing) pile. If it reminds you more of a mother, woman, girl, or sister, place it in this pile. They will not look like anything, so you will have to guess. Please turn the cards over when you put them down."[17]

Students tested in both the fourth and ninth grades tended to sort the elongated figures as male and the rounded figures as female. The same held true for a sample of college students.[18]

We must add a proviso to the rule that shape connotes sex. This proviso is that cultural usage may override shape in determining sexual designation. Let us try to clarify this abstraction by putting a case to you. A needle is an elongated object, which makes it a likely candidate for selection as a male sexual symbol, yet it is something women are much more likely to make use of than men. If you drew a picture of a needle and asked people to designate it as male or female, what would they do? The answer was provided in a study by Dr. Rosalea Schonbar and Dr. Joel Davitz. They found that the great majority of their subjects responded "female." Likewise for lipstick and broom, elongated in shape, but nonetheless designated female. Objects such as a tobacco jar, basketball net, and drum—shaped like female symbols, but associated with male use—were overwhelmingly designated male.[19] These findings seem to indicate quite clearly that in conscious experience the cultural meaning of an object can take precedence over sexual meaning based on shape.

The importance of cultural experience in giving meaning to potentially symbolic objects is also clearly demonstrated in a more recent study by Dr. Roger Richardson. Richardson wondered what would happen if you presented slides of elongated and rounded shape to people from different countries. Would they agree that the elongated figures were male and the rounded figures female? Richardson obtained his data in Baton Rouge, Louisiana. The experimenter boarded foreign flagships visiting the port, and, using their captains as interpreters, showed his slides to the passengers. The slides were exposed briefly, using a device called a tachistoscope. What Richardson found was that his various groups of subjects—Chinese, Swedes, and Americans among them—disagreed substantially in identifying the slides as male or female. In his discussion, Richardson makes the point that a tube of lipstick (an elongated object), which may be viewed as female by most Americans, may resemble a bullet to a plains Indian, and be judged as male.[20] These studies do not indicate that shapes of objects are devoid of sexual connotation. We have already seen that shape does play a role. They do point out that one cannot ignore the culturally defined meaning of objects.

The Freudian approach emphasizes the sexual meaning of symbols. It seems clear, however, that symbols may have meanings other than sex. A flag is a common symbol of patriotism, a dove of peace, a cross of Christianity, and there are many symbols of death. These are nonsexual symbols based on shared cultural experiences. One finds such symbols replete in the art, literature and religions of the world. The followers of Jung would also add, to these cultural symbols, various symbols which they believe have their origins in the collective unconscious. According to the Jungians, modern man has lost his understanding of these archaic symbols. The Jungians have looked to the beliefs of primitive societies and to mythology in order to shed light on their meaning. Jung's views of symbols can be explored in a beautifully illustrated book, *Man and His Symbols*, written by Jung and some of his associates shortly before Jung's death.

It would take us too far afield from our study of dreams to venture into the manifold use of culturally defined symbols. However, it would be appropriate to close our discussion with an experiment suggesting that people may react "unconsciously" to such symbols.

A study conducted by Dr. W.W. Meissner looked at the emotional impact of possible death symbols. The experimenter presented a list of words to a group of Catholic seminarians, asking them to give the first association that came to mind. This is Jung's time-honored procedure, wherein, the stimulus word "dog" might be followed by "cat," or "boy" by "girl." Meissner's list of words contained a number of possible death symbols such as "black," "stranger," "bird," "water," and "statue." The list also contained some neutral words. While the subject was giving his associations, his galvanic skin response, a subtle physiological measure of emotional reactions, was being monitored. What happened in the experiment was that the seminarians reacted more strongly to the postulated death symbols than to the neutral words, demonstrating the impact of these symbols.[21]

Symbolism is an intriguing subject that has given rise to much speculation. Freud's theory of dream symbols is a fascinating idea, but like most of Freud's ideas, it does not lend itself to easy testing. The evidence for or against the theory is scanty. The idea that sexual symbolism based on shape is a universality would seem to need some modification, for we know that cultural experiences may determine the meaning of objects beyond the suggestion of shape. Freud himself was not unaware of this possibility, for some of his symbolic references depended on language. The larger question of whether in fact objects in dreams can stand for something other than what they seem to be, and if so, what these symbols actually mean, is a matter requiring much more investigation. We would be remiss to treat Freud's views of dream symbolism as much more than an intriguing theory until more convincing evidence has been developed to support them.

Chapter 9
Dreams and Creativity

We live in a time of fads and fashions. Anything that can be attuned to self-help is merchandized. You can improve your chance of success in life by subscribing to a magazine which gives you tips on how to get ahead. You may expand the horizons of your personality and experience inner growth by joining groups of like-minded persons striving for personal development. And you can unleash the dormant forces of your creative self by harnessing the energies of your dreams. Or at least, so they say. Is it true? I can only think of an old-timer standing on the edge of his front porch, biting on his pipe, grunting, "Well, maybe."

The notion that dreams may foster creativity is hardly a new one. The idea probably goes back to Artemidorus, if not before. We encountered it in Jung's theory of dreaming and saw it developed into a sophisticated theory in Breger's information processing model of dreaming.

As a way of approaching the problem, let us recall Breger. Breger assumed that the special conditions under which dreaming takes place permit freer combinations of memories than are possible during waking thought and that dreams are less subject to the constraints of social acceptability. Both of these conditions should produce solutions to problems that differ from those attained under the rigors of critical thinking in the waking state.

The logic of the argument would have to say that these dream solutions are somehow more unusual, atypical, or odd than waking solutions. This assumption is not difficult to grant, because the material of dreams is often put together in unusual ways. The next assumption which seems to follow is that dream solutions are actually viable in practice. This is much more dubious. If one does as one dreams, one may end up in all sorts of difficulty. Nonetheless, one could argue that if only a small percentage of atypical dream solutions proves to be workable, there could be a basis for the belief that dreams can be creative. Moreover, if even unworkable solutions lead to a reexamination of the problem in waking thought, the idea that dreams can be sources of inspiration may have merit.

Let us look at some anecdotal evidence and then follow with some research.

Over the years there have been a number of persons—some of enormous reputation—who have said (or have been alleged to say) that some of their creative ideas came in dreams. How much of this is truth and how much is hearsay is difficult to assess, for some of these perons died centuries ago.

Dr. Roy Dreistadt has collected many reports of creative dreaming of famous people, summarizing these in an interesting paper. Some of the cases involved composers. For example, Dreistadt reported that Richard Wagner wrote a letter stating that he dreamt his opera *Tristan and Isolde* and could not have invented it purposely. Other cases involved poets and novelists. Coleridge said that his poem *Kubla Khan* occurred to him in a dream. Robert Louis Stevenson stated that the basic plot for *The Strange Case of Dr. Jekyll and Mr. Hyde* came to him in a dream in which the actual splitting of the character's personalities took place.[1]

Dreistadt also provides illustrations of dream-solutions reported by scientists. One case was that of Otto Loewi, who won a Nobel prize for his studies of the chemical action of the nerve. As the story is related, Loewi was trying to find a way to test his hypothesis concerning the role of chemicals in transmitting nervous impulses. One night he had a dream in which two ideas—his hypothesis, and a technique he had used for another problem— occurred in association. Loewi woke up, wrote down some notes about the dream, only to find in the morning he couldn't make out what he had written. The following evening the dream was repeated. Unwilling to tempt fate again, Loewi hastened to try the experiment suggested in his dream, and as a good story should end, the procedure worked![2]

Other examples of scientific discoveries said to result from creative dreams are given in a paper written by Drs. Stanley Krippner and William Hughes. They describe a dream of Niels Bohr which helped him formulate a model of the atom, and dreams of Louis Agassiz which guided him in his studies of fossils. They also relate a story about Elias Howe, the inventor of the sewing machine. Howe had a dream that he had been captured by savages. In the dream the king of the savages told Howe that if he didn't have a sewing machine ready within twenty-four hours, they would kill him with spears. Unable to perform this task, Howe awaited his own execution. As he looked at the approaching spears, he observed that they had eye-shaped holes near the point. Howe awoke from the dream with the idea that he should try relocating the hole in his machine needle near the point of the needle. The idea worked very well, and we are now blessed with sewing machines.[3]

Dreistadt's list of creative works said to follow from dreams is impressive: Mozart, Voltaire, Descartes, Dante, Shelley, Tolstoy, and Poe are just a few of the persons mentioned. The latter was said to base some of his stories on nightmares.[4]

In addition to reports of ideas coming in dreams, some famous people reported that ideas emerged in the twilight period of awakening from sleep. This is a stage of incomplete arousal, not the same thing as dreaming, and could be a period of relatively uncluttered mental activity. Charlotte Brontë was said to have experienced a clearer view of her story of *Jane Eyre* as she awakened from sleep.[5]

So much for the dreams of history's creative geniuses. What do we find for more ordinary mortals? Looking through a sample of the dreams of college students, I came across relatively few clear-cut dreams of problem solving. They do turn up on occasion. For example, I have read dream reports of students in which they were solving problems in genetics, mathematics, and chemistry. I cannot vouch for the quality of the solutions. Sometimes the problems solved in dreams are more mundane. For example, one student reported that she dreamt of figuring out a monthly budget in a dream. Another student struggled in her dream with the problem of polishing her boots. The dream contributed the unusual solution of using a washcloth.

I might also mention a problem-solving dream of a middle-aged divorcee. She was quite concerned about finding a job. One night she had a dream that she retired early because of a disability. In the dream she added up a disability pension she might receive from social security with the interest from her savings account, finding that it was enough to get by on. The interesting thing is she did have a disability, but had never considered using it to obtain early social security benefits before dreaming about it.

The infrequent occurrence of clear-cut cases of problem-solving dreams does not mean that many dreams are not oriented in this direction. Problems and solutions may be stated in a diffuse manner in dreams, requiring some unscrambling. We have come up with some evidence for this point of view in our studies with the Dream Incident Technique. We have found that the real life experiences underlying dreams are often viewed by the dreamer as incidents in which he was trying to solve problems.

Despite the attractiveness of the proposition that dreams may foster creative ideas, there has been relatively little useful research on the question. Some writers take it for granted that there is a relationship between dreams and creativity and go on from there, espousing ways of capitalizing on the process. But hypotheses are not the same thing as findings, and anecdotes such as we have reported are a long way from hard evidence.

Let us examine some of the systematic studies that have investigated possible relationships between dreams and creativity. The earliest of these studies was carried out by Dr. Joseph Adelson. Adelson enlisted the cooperation of college women taking a creative writing course. The college instructor chose the ten most creative students and the ten least creative students—a judgment based on "literary inventiveness, originality in the choice of theme and treatment."[6] Adelson looked at the dream reports from the two groups of students. He found that the dreams of the more creative women more frequently seemed fanciful in content. They portrayed more fantastic situations (e.g., walking on air) and utilized unusual dream characters (e.g., Roman soldier). Also the creative subjects showed a tendency to transform themselves in their dreams into new roles such as an actress, artist, or mother. Both Adelson and a more recent team of investigators (Sylvia, Clark and Monroe) found that the dreams of creative subjects seemed more likely to occur in unusual and diverse places than the dreams of noncreative subjects, whose dream settings were frequently their homes.[7]

Adelson's observation that the dreams of creative students seemed more fantastic than the dreams of noncreative students was supported in subsequent research carried out by Dr. Naomi Schechter and her colleagues. These researchers began with the idea that *artists* would be almost by definition a group of creative people. They also felt that scientists and engineers would be less creative than artists. I am not sure that scientists or engineers would agree with this, but it was their assumption.

The investigators collected dreams from art students (mostly from Cooper Union in New York) and from science and eingineering students at City College of New York. The dreams were then rated independently by two analysts on a rating scale. The low point of the scale indicated logical, realistic dreams; the high point, incoherent and bizarre dreams. The researchers found that the dreams of the artists tended to be less logical and realistic than the dreams of the engineers and scientists; stated another way, they appeared to be more imaginative. The art students also recalled dreams somewhat better than the scientists and engineers, and particularly had better recall of color in their dreams.[8]

In discussing their analysis of the dreams, the authors made the following observations:

> Analysis of the thematic content, development, and detail of the dream protocols indicates that the dreams of the artists were characterized by fantastic situations and events, by greater development of plot and setting, and by complex variation of themes within a single dream. By contrast, the non-artist groups tended to report dreams that were strongly rooted in reality. The plots of their dreams were concerned with situations that could easily have occurred and were centered about the dreamer or people related to him.[9]

They also report some typical dreams. For example, from the nonartists:

> I was among some of my friends. One boy that I know started a fight with some of my friends. I came to the aid of my friends and defeated him with numerous blows.

And from the artists:

> I am lying in bed staring at the ceiling. A young girl who I imagine to be my sister (I have no sister) crashes through a skylight. There is blood and glass all over the blue stone floor. I feel no particular emotion about this—I rise from bed and proceed to paint a painting—I paint this painting time after time but have no conscious recollection of what it looks like—then out-of-doors, I find myself bound and waiting for torture which never comes—I am

consciously disappointed. In the sky I perceive *it* changing from clouds and blue to it. Changing *it* is white and shaped like a whole—immense and fearsome.[10]

One might hesitate in drawing conclusions from the study. Cooper Union may have attracted a different kind of student from City College, and the results might reflect factors other than the differences between art and science majors. Dr. George Domino, however, has carried out a study which confirms the major thrust of the Adelson and Schechter studies—that creative people have less logical, more bizarre dreams. To find a group of creative people, Domino asked high school teachers to nominate students who had shown evidence of creativity in actual productions. These students were compared with controls—students not nominated as creative—in terms of their dream reports. As was true in the Schechter study, the dreams of the creative group were judged as more unusual and bizarre.[11]

Domino took a closer look at the elements that went into the more unusual dreams of the creative students. He found that there was more use of symbolism in these dreams, more condensations, and more unlikely combinations of ideas. Interestingly, Freud thought such dream processes were used to disguise latent dream thoughts, serving a defensive purpose. Domino's data, however, suggest that these processes occur in the creative, not constricted, individual.[12]

The Adelson, Schechter and Domino studies provide valuable data, but they do not tell us anything about the direct effect of dreaming upon creativity. Did dreams actually influence Adelson's creative writers or Schechter's artists? An interesting study that has attempted to tackle this difficult problem was conducted by Cartwright.

One of the measures of creativity Cartwright used in her investigations is a test called the RAT. It has nothing to do with the animal of that name, but simply stands for Remote Associates Test. The underlying idea of the test is that the creative person has the capability of pulling out of his mind or memories more *disparate* ideas in developing solutions to problems. Remote associations or ideas might lead to unusual or novel solutions, rather than a tendency to fixate on what is directly in front of a person.

Cartwright conducted her study on creativity in a sleep laboratory, putting her subjects on various schedules. First, her subjects were tested on the RAT. Then they were allowed to sleep for three and a half hours. To make sure her subjects actually dreamed during these hours, their sleep was monitored for rapid eye movements. After the subjects were awakened, they were retested on the RAT. Cartwright found that her subjects did no better on the test for Remote Associates after a period of sleep and dreaming than after an equal period of waking time.[13] So dreaming had no perceptible influence on this task.

One might ask, "Well, how about trying something involving more productive activity—like writing a story, or drawing a picture?" Perhaps one could induce some art majors to enter the sleep laboratory and sketch an assigned subject after a period of dreaming.

As part of her study, Cartwright looked at the possible effect of dreaming on completing a story. The subjects first wrote out a brief story in response to pictures depicting a conflict. One conflict was described as follows: "This is Walter and his mother. They are at home. They have been arguing because he wants to live on his own. That's the problem. Write how they feel and how they work this out...." The subjects wrote out their stories. Later, after awakening from REM sleep, they were asked to write out new solutions to the story. Cartwright expected the solutions to show more successful endings after dreaming. However, the opposite proved to be true. After dream sleep, the hero of the story was *less able* to solve the problem.[14]

Cartwright also looked at the possible effects of dreaming on more routine problem solving. She expected to find little impact, and she was right. In one procedure, she asked her subjects to work crossword puzzles after awakening in the sleep laboratory. The students were no more effective in solving the puzzles after dreaming than under waking conditions.[15]

When one thinks about these findings, one may argue, "Well, why should one's ability to solve various and sundry problems be better after dreaming— particularly if the tasks involved have no specific relationship to the dream?" The dream is dealing in a diffuse way with particular problems of relevance to the individual life. The dream may have little or no relevance to other problems. What one needs are problem-solving tests that are related to the dream itself.

How can one do this? One possible approach might be to use hypnosis, instructing subjects to dream about a specific problem situation. For those who do, we could ask them to write out a solution to the problem. Such solutions could be compared with solutions formulated to similar problems without an intervening dream.

Robert Davé reported an intriguing study which approximates this approach. Davé recruited subjects who were faced with problems that seemed for the moment intractable. For example, several of his subjects were trying to write prose or poetry and were getting nowhere. Another subject was trying without success to develop a thesis proposal. Unlike most studies in experimental psychology, Davé dealt with problems that were real. Davé hypnotized his subjects with the aid of highly repetitive background music. While under hypnosis, the subjects were asked to visualize the elements of the problem they were facing. Then they were told, "Even though you cannot see these elements any longer, they are still very alive in the back of your mind, out of sight. In fact, they have a life of their own where you can't see them and when I count to three they will cause a dream or dreamlike experience to come into your mind's eye...."

Some of the hypnotized subjects were able to report dreams or dreamlike experiences on the spot. For these people, Davé repeated the procedure twice. Finally, all the subjects were given the following posthypnotic suggestion: "Every night, including tonight, for the next seven nights, the elements of your project/problem will become very lively and will represent themselves in your dreams in one way or another. You will be able to remember everything about these dreams once they are over."[16]

How much success did this hypnotic dream manipulation have? Davé reported considerable success for six of his eight hypnotic dream subjects as against only one of sixteen subjects in control conditions. For example, one of the hypnotized subjects had been working unsuccessfully on a poem. On the third night after hypnosis she awoke after a dream and composed three stanzas. She reported that the images which had appeared to her during hypnosis reappeared at this point and she was able to add additional verses.[17]

Davé's results are obviously limited by the small number and highly selective nature of subjects used. Nonetheless, the study suggests that creativity may be unlocked by a procedure involving both hypnosis and dreamlike experience. We will have to wait and see if more studies along this line produce similar results.

At the present time, it is not possible to draw firm conclusions about the role of dreams in creativity. The claims for creative effects of dreaming seem far in excess of what has been scientifically established at this time. We know that a number of outstanding creative artists and scientists have reported receiving ideas in dreams. Such reports raise the hypothesis that dreams produce creative inspirations, but they do not prove it. Proof requires more systematic, verifiable data. Research demonstrating that nocturnal dreams will give rise to creative productions is scanty. At this point, it seems probable that the dreams of more creative and less creative individuals appear to differ—that those of the more creative persons appear to be more unusual. However, we know little about how such dreams are related to the creative act. Surely, this is a problem calling for vigorous research.

Chapter 10

Nightmares

In sketching the history of the word *nightmare*, Dr. Roger Broughton points out that the root word for nightmare (as well as the French equivalent *cauchmar* and the German *nachtmar*) is the early Teutonic *mar*, which means *devil*. The word nightmare alludes to a night devil, reflecting the views of more superstitious times, that demons encroached on the sleeper during the night, pressing against his chest, causing the nightmare. Broughton illustrates this belief with a reproduction of an eighteenth century painting by Johann Heinrich Fussli, titled *The Nightmare*. In the painting, the sleeper's head hangs down over the bed, arms extended toward the floor. A demon reposes on the sleeper's chest and there is the figure of a horse in the background. This superstition may have arisen from the content of many nightmares in which the dreamer felt that he was being crushed or smothered. Psychoanalyst Dr. Ernest Jones wrote a pioneering book on nightmares in which he delineated three characteristics of the nightmare. One of these characteristics is this feeling of oppression on the chest with accompanying difficulties in breathing. The other two characteristics are intense dread and a sense of paralysis.[1]

The feeling of intense dread is probably the hallmark of the nightmare. The reader will recall our discussion of the dreams of primitive tribes where such experiences resulted in acute psychological disturbances. Among the Zulus, Lee found that men regarded nightmares with horror; they often were hospitalized because of the anxiety aroused.[2] Foster described the nightmare among the people of Tzintzuntzan as "a terrifying experience, which robs ego of the power of movement and speech, and which leaves him in a cold sweat, awake."[3]

We must imagine that the normal degree of fear experienced in the nightmare is augmented among primitive peoples because of their beliefs about the causes of the dream. It is one thing for a person educated in a modern society to awaken from an anxiety dream, reacting with relief: "Thank God, it's only a dream." It must be quite another experience for the person living in a prescientific culture to awaken with the thought that a malevolent spirit has possessed him, portending future harm or misfortune.

While dreams involving intense dread are exceptional for most people, almost everyone has had dreams in which anxiety-laden events occurred. To document this, we can draw once again on the survey of college students conducted in America by Griffith, and in Japan by Miyagi and Tago. Considering only the American students, about four out of five college students reported that at one time or another, they had dreamed of being attacked or pursued. About an equal number reported they had experienced dreams of falling. More than half of those questioned reported dreaming at least once of being frozen with fright, while almost half said they had experienced dreams of being smothered, unable to breathe. Somewhat less frequent were dreams of wild, violent beasts, and seeing oneself dead.[4]

These survey data collected by Griffith and his colleagues asked about dreams "ever" experienced and not for what was typical. Still, dreams characterized by some anxiety are not unusual. Apprehension was the most frequent emotion found in Hall and Van de Castle's analysis of a thousand dreams.[5]

If there is any validity at all to Freud's theory, there is bound to be some anxiety inherent in the process of dreaming, for dreams are dealing with materials that make us uncomfortable. Even with Jung's less instinctual approach, we are dealing with problems that are unresolved and potential sources of tension.

One particular type of dream which many people experience, the *recurrent* dream, is frequently anxious in nature. Robbins and Houshi found that recurrent dreams (which frequently date back to childhood) typically depict the dreamer in a situation where he or she is being threatened or pursued. The threatening agents may be monsters, burglars, wild animals or natural forces like storms, fires and floods. Dr. Roy Lacoursiere and his colleagues have observed recurrent anxiety dreams in combat veterans suffering from post traumatic stress neuroses. Judging from the work of Drs. Gentil and Lader, there may be a tendency for persons experiencing high levels of anxiety in daily life to have dreams where they are the targets of aggressive behavior.[6]

There is experimental evidence that when one tries to revisualize a dream, anxiety is aroused. Drs. Howard Morishige and Joseph Reyher asked subjects to visualize a previous dream while they were being monitored for physiological reactions. The investigators reported both changes in the galvanic skin response and desynchronization of the alpha rhythm (a measure of brain wave believed to indicate a relaxed state).[7]

While we do not fully understand the function of anxiety in dreams, there is evidence that it can influence one's biological processes. We will recall that anxious dream content seems to inhibit the usual erection cycle for males in REM sleep periods. We also have learned from a study carried out by Carolyn Winget and Dr. Frederic Kapp that pregnant women who experience anxiety in their dreams tend to have shorter periods of labor during delivery.[8] In this instance the experienced anxiety in the dream may have had a useful purpose in the efforts to cope with an impending problem. Obviously this may not always be the case. For example, we will recall that in persons with heart conditions, dreams may cause exacerbations of coronary symptoms, and we might imagine anxiety dreams would be singular in this regard.

Anxiety, then, is commonly experienced in dreams and may underlie many more dreams. But some anxiety experienced in a dream is not necessarily a nightmare, and certainly not the traumatic dream known as the night terror. When does an anxious dream become a nightmare? What distinguishes the nightmare from the night terror?

The answer to the first question is not as easy as it may seem. If we could accept the criteria proposed by Jones, the answer would be simplified. The nightmare would be characterized by intense dread, a feeling of oppression on the chest, and motor paralysis. The problem with this is some people report nightmares without recalling a sense of oppression or paralysis. Therefore, I would be inclined to rely mainly on the first index — intense dread. Stated this way, the difference between nightmares and other anxiety dreams lies in the severity of discomfort experienced. The dreamer can best tell you when that line is crossed.

If we must hedge on the definition of a nightmare, we can still say something about the content of such dreams. In making an analysis of nightmares, Drs. Marvin Feldman and Edward Hyman found that these dreams contained many dangers, including death and physical injuries. In the dreams, the target of these attacks was usually the self. Moreover, the self was usually depicted as helpless in the face of the threat, unable to cope with the problem. When anxiety became too intense, the dreamer might awaken.[9]

In an early study, Dr. Hulsey Cason interviewed 125 adults bothered by nightmares. From his data, he selected some typical examples. These examples seem very consistent with the themes of threat against the self and accompanying helplessness noted by Feldman and Hyman. Some of these dream reports were as follows:

> I saw myself with my father in the apple orchard of an uncle for whom I had worked during the summer. It vaguely seemed as if my mother and two sisters were there also. While talking (the topics were not recalled), we were attacked by a wild pig or an animal much like one. We took refuge in a tree, and were forced down only when the creature attacked my mother and sisters. I reached the animal first and was attacked and knocked down by it. I was screaming and seemed to see father making towards me with a club in his hand.[10]

> A good friend stole a car in which we rode away, chased by the police. The car became smaller and smaller until it was the size of a toy, and then it would not run. I picked it up, put it under my arm, and tried to run with it. I found myself in a large empty room trying to find some place to hide. The walls began to close in, and I woke up.[11]

> I was standing on the bank of the lake watching three launches. The launches went a short distance, turned around, and then came back. The middle

launch was quite narrow and high, it was rocking back and forth, and it finally turned over. Everybody just stood on the shore helplessly watching my father and fiance drown. I saw every agonizing motion they went through, and could not offer any aid.[12]

I suddenly became conscious that something was taking place. I saw the sheets began to move in wave-like fashion, and the waves became increasingly violent. I looked at the end of the bed, and it slowly began to move. The walls began to go away, and everything moved further and further from me. I began to sink into space, and then made a desperate effort to wake up, and finally succeeded.[13]

I was being washed towards the top of a waterfall at an alarming rate. It was impossible to make any movements that would save me. My hands, legs, and voice seemed paralyzed. Water was rapidly running in my nose and mouth when I woke up.[14]

In looking through a recent collection of several hundred dreams of college students, I came across some cases where the students reported having nightmares. These contemporary dreams seemed somewhat less disturbing than the reports of Cason's subjects, who were frequently bothered by nightmares. However, the themes of these dreams involving personal threat and helplessness were still evident. While most of the threats dealt with violence and potential physical injury, there were instances in which the threat was psychological and the loss was interpersonal. An example of this would be the dream of a husband discovering evidence that his wife was unfaithful.

While the nightmare can be uncomfortable, it seems to be a relatively mild experience compared to the night terror. Actually, the night terror seems to be in a different category from the anxiety dream or nightmare.

An illuminating paper on this subject was written by Charles Fisher and his associates. They have been doing extensive work on nightmares and night terrors at the Mount Sinai Medical Center in New York. The basic distinction between the nightmare and night terror is that the nightmare is a dream occurring during REM sleep, while the night terror occurs during NREM sleep, a period of normally relatively little dreaming. Of these two types of anxiety dreams, the night terror is much more severe. The night terror frequently includes talking in one's sleep, sleepwalking, sudden increases in heart rate, and screams of fear. The researchers report that some of these screams are "blood-curdling" with "animal like intensity."[15]

In the night terror, the rise in heart rate is very sudden and quite pronounced. Fisher and his associates report that the heart rate in the period preceding the night terror appears normal. The change in pulse is abrupt and dramatic. In one of their illustrations, the pulse rose from a restful sleep rate of 56 to a rapid 164 within the space of a minute. In contrast, the more common REM nightmare shows a more gradual acceleration in heart rate with a much less substantial rise.[16]

The night terror seems to be just that—sudden and terrifying. The person is seen to talk, ambulate, and utter screams. His memory for all this, however, is poor. Recall for these events tends to be fragmentary, and there are instances of pronounced amnesia.

Fisher's group lists the most common types of night terrors observed in its research. Some of these dream reports were fear of aggression against oneself, being trapped in a small space, being left alone or deserted, and falling. The aggressive acts in the dreams were sometimes carried out by the scientists working in the sleep laboratory.[17] (This latter sounds a little like the plot of the classic horror film The Cabinet of Dr. Caligari.)

As these dreams appear similar in content to our list of what everyone dreams about at one time or another, we may again inquire about the differences between the seemingly ubiquitous anxiety dreams of humankind and the traumatized dreamers in Fisher's study. As we have indicated, one important difference is the intensity of the experience—the level of anxiety and physiological changes. A second difference seems to be in the frequency of these experiences. At some time or another, many of us may dream of being choked or strangled. But for most of us, nightmares are rare. In a survey of college students carried out by Dr. David Lester, most of the students indicated nightmares occurred infrequently, less than once a month.[18] Hartmann observed in a sleep laboratory that after some 400 REM awakenings, he had not come across a single dream report he would call a nightmare.[19] Contrast this with the experience of one of Fisher's subjects, who had a recurrent night terror thirty times in the sleep laboratory. He dreamed that he was being choked by the electrodes monitoring his REM movements. And before he came to the laboratory he dreamed of choking on nails and shirts.[20]

Third, there is a striking difference in dream recall. According to both Broughton and Fisher and his associates, there is very little recall for night terrors the following morning. Broughton sees these episodes much like sleepwalking, an experience followed by amnesia.[21] Contrast this failure of memory with the often detailed reports of the run-of-the-mill anxiety dream.

What causes these sudden night terrors? Fisher and his colleagues expressed the opinion that some of these dreams followed from nonanxious, innocuous thoughts occurring during NREM sleep. The innocuous thought brought up other ideas which were sources of tension. The effect was like striking an exposed nerve, flooding the person with terrifying perceptions.[22]

A different explanation was offered by Broughton. He believed that much of the ideational content of the night terror followed from hypersensitive physiological reactions. Persons experiencing night terrors were reacting during sleep to such physiological stimuli as marked tachycardia, respiratory changes and increased muscle tone. The dream or night terror was representation in fantasy of these physiological changes. In this view, increases in muscle tone would be the basis of the screams of night terrors; respiratory changes, the feelings of suffocation; and tachycardia, the intense anxiety.[23]

We will now turn to the nightmares of children. In writing about such nightmares, Dr. John Mack observes that only one of the cardinal features of the nightmare identified by Jones is usually present in children: intense dread. The sense of paralysis may or may not be present and the feeling of weight on the chest is not usually reported. The high level of anxiety, however, is clearly there.[24]

Over the years there have been a number of investigations of unpleasant dreams experienced by children. Cason interviewed children who were bothered frequently by nightmares. Most often the content of these nightmares concerned threatening animals or being chased. During these dreams the child reported feeling fear and helplessness. In most cases, the child woke up. He usually did not fall back to sleep immediately.[25]

The prominent role of threatening animals in children's nightmares is supported by other studies. In one study, for example, lions, tigers, bears, apes and snakes were villains. In another, there was a high incidence of wolves, dogs, horses and elephants as well as the lions and tigers. According to Dr. J. Louise Despert, these animals are destructive, biting and devouring the child.[26]

Threatening human figures included criminals and robbers, and there were monsters and supernatural creatures of various sorts, some of these following from fairy tales.[27]

An example of a nightmare involving the imagery of fairy tales was reported to me by a student:

> When I was a small child, I woke up screaming and crying from a terrible and horrifying dream about a witch. My sister, hearing my screams, asked me what the matter was. When I told her, she told me to say over and over again, "dreams are not true."[28]

Some of the dreams reported in a study carried out by Despert included being eaten by bears, an old woman sticking people's eyes out, seeing one's father eaten by a cannibal, and being threatened by owls and foxes.[29]

In his analysis of children's nightmares, Mack suggested that when anxiety was intense, disorientation and hallucinations persisted after awakening, and it was difficult to comfort the child, one might reasonably call the incident a *night terror*.[30]

Broughton has made some observations in the sleep laboratory of night terrors in children. These terrors occurred in NREM slow-wave sleep. According to Broughton:

> The child abruptly sits up in bed and screams. He appears to be staring wide-eyed at some imaginary object; his face is covered with perspiration and his breathing is labored. Consoling stimuli have no effect. After the attack, dream recall is rare and usually fragmentary.... The child has no recollection of the episode the following morning.[31]

The question of why children have nightmares has led to theorizing, particularly among psychoanalytic writers. One of the ideas proposed is that the nightmare or anxiety dream is an expression of a conflict over illicit sexual desires on the part of the young child. The conflict from a psychoanalytic perspective would be between the child's incestual desire for the parent and fear of punishment for this desire.[32]

It is instructive to see how a psychoanalytically oriented clinician, working from this framework, might deal with a child's nightmare. Mack provides us with some good case examples. The case we have chosen is one where members of the child's family seem clearly involved in the genesis of his nightmare. The child named Jim was three years old when the episode occurred. Jim was described as a gentle, unaggressive boy. He suffered from recurrent respiratory illness, which may reflect a state of anxiety related to the parents. The night terror that Jim experienced was recounted as follows:

> At 1 a.m., the mother awoke to hear Jim shrieking in terror. She found him cowering at the side of his crib, his eyes white with fear. He was not consoled by her turning on the lights and comforting him. Through his sobs he said he was trying to get away from "the thing." This he described as big, black, and like a man with an angry face with some red on it. He said it wanted to hurt him and had already hurt his hand, arm and leg with one of the father's radio wires. He slept no more that night, and for several nights feared going to bed and kept his parents up looking for "the thing," which he insisted was still under the pillow or in his room. He would not go to the bathroom alone. For a full week he thought "the thing" was somewhere in the apartment. During this time he was inseparable from his mother and would not go to nursery school. After the dream he put on his sister's sling because his arm was hurt "like hers." He hobbled about, complaining that his legs hurt and feared that little scratches would be fatal.
>
> In three weeks after the attack he was seen nine times by the child psychiatrist, during which time his fears diminished and then disappeared. At the same time his attitude toward his father changed from his usual mild acceptance. Speaking softly to his mother so his father, who was hard of hearing, could not hear him, he would say, "Mommy, when are we going to get a new Daddy? This one's all worn out. When's he gonna die?" Sometimes he would kick him. But despite this change, he maintained his loving relationship with his father.
>
> Jim was eager to begin treatment, for his mother had told him the doctor would "take the thing away."[33]

One technique Jim's therapist used was doll play. Here the child is able to act out his fantasies using dolls to represent real or imagined people. Mack describes Jim's play with the dolls as follows:

> In his play "the thing" was represented by one father doll, while another such doll stood for the "father himself." With considerable development and frequent restatement he played out his family drama. The little boy would go to the bathroom.... The father would order him back to bed, and on his way

he would bump into father's bed. The father reproached him angrily for this and sometimes fought with the boy. Sometimes the father got up, went to the mother's bed and got on top of her. Jim identified the father-thing doll with the words, "This is the thing that hurt the boy's leg in the night." He cooked, burned and killed the doll....[34]

One of the intriguing features of this particular case is that the child was able to make the identification between the "thing" of his night terror and the father doll. To assume, however, that all the bogey men, witches, strangers, and savage animals of nightmares are necessarily representations of the father or mother stretches the point considerably. An observation made by Dr. Arthur Jersild and his co-workers in an early study of children's dreams that the sources of children's nightmares are often things they have read or heard about, rather than events they have experienced, argues against blaming nightmares solely on the father and mother.[35] We must remember that the child is very small, vulnerable, with limited knowledge, and possesses a fertile imagination.

I can think of no better example of the influence of "stories" on the nightmares of children than Bourguignon's observations in Haiti. Bourguignon noticed that large numbers of children suffered from nightmares. While giving children Rorschach tests, she found that some of the children responded to the inkblots in ways such as, "This is a *zombi* ... the sort of thing I see at night." Or, "This is an animal ... an evil animal ... it's frightening ... an animal I've never seen ... an animal you see in dreams."[36] Zombis and night creatures were part of the cultural inheritance, transmitted to the child in stories, and then working their way into his dreams.

Given the discomfort caused by nightmares, and particularly by the night terror, one might wonder if there is anything one could do about them. Is there some way to prevent them? In addition to exploring the problem through psychotherapy, there are some new techniques that may have value. One of these involves the use of drugs. A clinical report suggests that the use of the antidepressant drug imipramine may be helpful in decreasing the occurrence of night terrors. Dr. John Marshall has been engaged in treating patients with post-traumatic syndromes. These are physical and psychological problems that follow a major injury or other traumatic experience. Marshall notes that severe and persistent nightmares were often part of the clinical picture. Marshall found that when he administered imipramine to one of his patients to help alleviate his depressive problems, there was also an effect on these nightmares.[37]

Marshall discovered this unanticipated benefit with a middle-aged patient who had developed psychological difficulties following cardiac bypass surgery for angina. When Marshall saw the patient he was suffering from dizziness, weakness, headaches, and severe night terrors.

Marshall described the patient's night terrors:

The patient described his night terrors as occurring two to three times a night, every night. He denied having nightmares of this type prior to surgery. He could not always recall the varying content of the nightmares, which included frightening dreams of the intensive care unit and, more frequently, of catastrophes. Examples of the dream content included finding himself mutilating a member of his family and terrible accidents or fires in which he or someone close to him was mangled or badly hurt. During these episodes, the patient became quite agitated; he often screamed, thrashed about, or leaped out of bed to cower in the corner. If he awoke, he found himself very anxious, frightened, and drenched in perspiration with his heart beating rapidly.[38]

Marshall went on to report the effects of the drug imipramine. "The patient was begun on 100 mg of imipramine at bedtime because it was felt that there was a considerable depressive component to this post-traumatic syndrome. One week later, he spontaneously noted that although he did not feel appreciably different, the night terrors had ceased on the first night of medication and he was sleeping through the night. The patient's wife corroborated his reports, stating that he had begun to sleep peacefully without screaming or thrashing about. The nightly dose of imipramine was increased to 300 mg over the next several weeks. There was no objective change in the patient's overall appearance, but he reported that he felt better, attributing this to his improved sleep. His wife also felt that while he did not show any significant improvement in his functioning, he was less irritable. The daymares also ceased. After several months on nightly doses of 150 mg of imipramine, the patient discontinued his medication for approximately six days because he had run out of money. He immediately noted a recurrence of the night terrors, although they occurred less often. When he resumed his medication, they ceased."[39]

Marshall then tried imipramine therapy on two new patients suffering from post-traumatic night terrors. In both cases there was a sharp decrease in the number of night terrors.[40] While Marshall's work should be considered exploratory because of the small number of subjects used, the use of drugs in the suppression of night terrors appears to be a promising approach.

Another experimental approach to the treatment of nightmares was reported by Dr. Norman Cavior and his associate, Anne-Marie Deutsch. This approach utilized a form of behavioral therapy called systematic desensitization. The procedure first teaches the patient deep muscle relaxation. Then, while the patient is relaxed, he begins to imagine the things which are bothering him, beginning with what is least troublesome, working up to what is most anxiety provoking. The patient stops whenever his level of discomfort becomes excessive. Repetition of the procedure tends to diminish anxiety.[41]

Cavior and Deutsch applied the technique to a sixteen-year-old boy living in a state correctional facility. The boy had a recurrent nightmare. The dream was about a violent argument between his mother and father, ending with his father holding a knife at his mother's throat. The boy reported being very disturbed by the dream.

After the patient was taught deep muscle relaxation, the dream was divided into twelve segments. The segments were ranked in terms of how upsetting they were. The least upsetting segment (the father coming home drunk) was presented first. The patient closed his eyes, visualized the scene without undue anxiety. Then the patient visualized the next segment, his mother yelling at his father, then his father shouting back, and so forth, until he was able to tolerate the entire dream. The whole procedure took three sessions.

The systematic desensitization procedure did not suppress the nightmares like the drug therapy. However, the procedure enabled the patient to experience the dream with much less resulting discomfort. He was now able to fall back to sleep almost at once.[42]

Additional case studies reported in the clinical literature have used systematic desensitization as a treatment for nightmares; larger controlled studies have also utilized the technique. In a recent study, for example, Dr. William Miller and Marina DiPilato evaluated the effects of systematic desensitization on the frequency and intensity of nightmares. These researchers found that following the treatment, their subjects reported fewer nightmares. Interestingly, the researchers reported that the muscle relaxation exercises were effective even without the added desensitization procedure. Perhaps simply teaching nightmare sufferers to relax may be helpful in dealing with their problem.[43]

What about the treatment of children with night terrors? Relaxation training and desensitization are, of course, possibilities. Dr. Erwin L. Taboada, who has worked with children, suggests the possible use of the anti-anxiety drug Valium. He has also tried psychotherapy aimed at uncovering possible traumatic experiences underlying the dream. In one case, he reported inducing a light hypnotic trance during which he asked the child to imagine himself successfully coping with the kind of experience that brought on the night terror. The therapeutic results were excellent: The night terrors disappeared.[44]

The studies we mentioned are too few in number to allow us to draw confident conclusions. What we can say is that there are promising approaches being studied for the treatment of night terrors and that there is hope for those troubled by them.

Chapter 11

Telepathic and Paranormal Dreams

We will remember that in the ancient Near East, there was widespread belief that dreams were the bearers of messages from the gods. The same belief is still held among some primitive peoples today. We may suppose that such beliefs grew out of ignorance of the nature of dreaming and a more general prescientific view of the world. The images and conversation of dreams must have seemed troubling and inexplicable. At the same time, the vagaries of the world—floods, famine, fortune—were explained in terms of the acts of gods, goddesses, and spirits. It seems reasonable that the puzzling phenomenon of the dream and belief in the working of gods and spirits were fused together into a relatively comfortable and coherent belief—that dreams were devices used by the gods to inform and misinform.

In modern times the theological element in this picture has not been entirely discarded. One still hears it preached that God appears to man in dreams. Along with these lingering ideas from our history and traditions, another question has arisen, one that is more researchable with the techniques of science. And that is, can men or women communicate ideas to other men or women in dreams? Does the altered state of consciousness of the dream increase the possibility of receiving telepathic communication?

When one even mentions the word *telepathy*, there is bound to be some kind of reaction in one's audience—perhaps a sudden show of interest. Far-out phenomena are very attractive to many people; such persons are readily disposed to believe in ESP, telepathy, clairvoyance, mind-over-matter, and a range of other paranormal, psychic, and supernatural events.

On the other side of the fence, there are hard-headed souls who will say, "Telepathy? It is an impossibility; therefore do not bother to show me your evidence, for if you have some, it is rigged—and if it isn't rigged, I won't believe it anyway."

I would suggest the attitude of keeping an open mind, but one tempered with scientific skepticism. This is the willingness to look at any phenomenon, but to demand that the utmost in scientific rigor be exercised in collection of facts and, whenever possible, that means be set up to replicate the study by independent investigators.

There are numerous reports of alleged telepathic dreams. In his book *New*

World of the Mind, Dr. J.B. Rhine described some dreams which are real mind bogglers. One of these took place during the Second World War. A mother dreamt that her son, stationed on a Pacific island, was suddenly endangered by a falling palm tree crashing over his tent. Frightened, she called out his name as if in a warning. Meanwhile, on the Pacific island, the son thought he heard in his sleep his mother's voice. Leaving his tent to find out where the voice was coming from, he turned around to see a tree fall behind him, demolishing the cot he had slept upon.[1]

In considering the possibility of dream telepathy, one could well begin by clearly recognizing the possible effects of chance in any observation. A certain number of seemingly remarkable coincidences will occur solely as a function of chance juxtaposition of events. Let us illustrate this problem by using a homey example. Suppose you dream about your grandmother five times during the year, and after one of these occasions, she calls up and says, "I was just thinking about you yesterday and was wondering how you were." You may exclaim, "How remarkable!" But what about the other four times you dreamt about her? She may have been thinking about baking a pie, or going to the supermarket, or your cousin Harold. It is also possible that your grandmother has thought about you on many days in which you had no dreams about her.

Whether you have experienced a coincidence or a genuine psychic phenomenon becomes in part a matter of probability. Fortunately there are statistical tests which can help us decide this. To illustrate, we will return to your grandmother. Let us suppose she thought about you on sixty-five days and you dreamt about her on five of those occasions. On the other 300 days, when she didn't think about you, you also dreamt about her five times. One could readily test these statistics against chance using probability tables worked out by statisticians.

If one were patient enough, one could actually run such an experiment. To keep the experiment kosher, we would have to make very sure you and your grandmother were not operating in collusion. Collusion and fraud may be suspected in successful paranormal experiments. (For some reason, collusion is rarely suspected in more conventional experiments.) Perhaps these suspicions are based on the showmanship of "mind readers" and other professed psychics. We know how clever magicians and other illusionists can be in making things look real that aren't real. In any event, tricks, collusion, and fraud must be ruled out. So in our research, we may have to put you and your grandmother in isolation wards for a couple of years.

Let us assume that both of you are sufficiently masochistic to cooperate in this mad experiment. We decide that she is supposed to transmit an image of herself on certain days unknown to you and you are expected to dream about her on those days. As we begin to collect your dreams, we find one of a little old lady who looks something like your grandmother, but isn't. You may say, "Well, that's close enough, isn't it?" If you are at all influenced by Freud, you might say, "Dreams aren't quite what they seem anyway, and how do you know that person wasn't a representation of my grandmother?" O.K. Being fair minded, we will allow this. But then you may push your luck and add, "Or for that matter, yesterday there was a *grand* piano in the dream, and couldn't. . .?" And so we also have a problem of figuring out what constitutes acceptable content in the dream.

Suppose that even after matching signal to reception, ruling out collusion, ruling out the effects of chance, and determining acceptable content, you come up with negative results? You might conclude only, "Perhaps I'm not psychic, or maybe my grandmother is a lousy sender; this doesn't prove that some pairs of people might not be able to communicate this way." And you could be right, for significant psychic abilities are said to reside in the few, not the many. As a prerequisite to doing anything, the parapsychologist believes one has to discover such persons.

Into this land of pitfalls, few have dared to tread. Until recently, few psychologists would have conducted a study of dream telepathy without wearing a ski mask to disguise their identity, for fear of being labeled as "one of those kooks." However, due to the efforts of Dr. Montague Ullman and his associates at Maimonides Medical Center, the problem has been brought into the scientific laboratory, where the issue could eventually be decided up or down on its merits. These investigators have developed an intriguing procedure which we shall now describe.

The materials to be communicated telepathically are paintings. This seems reasonable in view of the essentially visual nature of dreams. The particular painting selected for transmission is unknown to the subject, who remains in a sleep laboratory room throughout the night. The person directing the experiment is also unaware of which picture was selected. The "agent" concentrating on sending the picture to the sleeping subject is down the hall in another room, some ninety feet away from the subject. During REM periods, the subject is awakened by means of an intercom system, and his dream reports are recorded on tape. The tapes are transcribed, then given to three judges who have been kept away from the experiment altogether. The judges are given a number of possible target pictures, including the one that was really used. The judges are asked to rank these pictures in terms of how closely they resemble the dream report. Ullman reports that this matching task is by no means easy to do. When the judges have made their rankings, however, it is possible to calculate statistically whether there is a closer correspondence between what was depicted in the target picture and the content of the dream than one might expect from chance.[2]

When you take a group of people more or less unscreened for psychic abilities, no telepathic effect on dreams is apparent. In one experiment, Ullman's group tried twelve subjects and twelve different pictures, and the matchings were not above chance level.[3] In conventional psychological experiments, one would probably stop here, concluding there was nothing to show for one's efforts, and would move on to another problem. But parapsychology is different. It stresses the uniqueness of extra sensory capabilities and would consider the first experiment as only a screening experiment to pick out the potentially sensitive subject. Ullman's team picked out the best subject and tried the experiment again. This time, they reported significant results.[4]

Ullman presents some of these dream transcripts to illustrate these matchings. One of the paintings used as a target was Dali's *The Sacrament of the Last Supper*. The painting shows Jesus at a long table flanked by his disciples. There are bread and wine on the table, and a fishing boat can be seen in the background. While some of the dreams related by the sensitive subject have relatively little to do with the painting, two of them contain interesting correspondences.

One of the dream reports was concerned with boats. The subject indicated that the boats were fishing boats. As he described the boats, he thought of an unusually large painting that hung in the Sea Fare Restaurant. The painting showed a group of perhaps a dozen men, hauling a fishing boat ashore just after they had returned from fishing at sea.

In the other dream, the subject was examining a Christmas catalog.[5]

In the same paper, Ullman reports an attempt to replicate the two experiments with new subjects. Once again a cadre of twelve subjects produced nothing but chance results. Selection of the best subject and best agent this time failed to produce significant findings.[6] In a subsequent book, *Dream Telepathy*, Ullman and his colleagues describe continued experiments, with some apparent successes and some failures. An attempt to replicate these procedures in another sleep laboratory was not successful.[7] The ability to transmit information via dreams strikes me as having an illusive quality to it. In my judgment, a great deal of further research seems needed before one can say that dream telepathy has been consistently demonstrated.

Let us leave the question of dream telepathy with suspended judgment, and turn to the prophetic dream, the "pre-recognition dream" that predicts things to come. Once again, we will remember that the ancients thought that dreams could predict the future. And once again the idea dies hard; many people today believe this to be true. This belief could follow from the fact that many people have dreams which seem to come true. On the other hand, everybody has had dreams which have not come true. There are many more of these, but nobody tells about them or writes books about them. Reflect, for a moment, on the number of dreams experienced in any given night. Pick a figure of three billion dreamers, each dreaming perhaps four or five times a night; multiply these and you may have fifteen billion dreams among our human family in a single evening. In a year's time, the number of dreams would be of the order of fifty-four trillion, seven hundred and fifty billion! (Granted that poor recall will trim the figure considerably.) It is nearly certain that some of these dreams will be followed by events seemingly predicted in the dream, simply as a function of the chance juxtaposition of events. The only way to stop such coincidences is to stop the world and all activity on it. And when there are chance correspondences, human beings have been known to elaborate on what actually happened in relating a tale—and pretty soon fact and fiction may be interwoven into a rip-roaring story.

There is another reason why some dreams will appear to come true. Both the dream and the subsequent event may reflect the same concern in the individual. For example, a student might be concerned about an upcoming examination. He is not prepared for it and worries about how well he will do. As a source of unresolved tension, it becomes the subject of a dream. In the dream, he does poorly. If in reality, he does poorly also, which is always a strong possibility, the dream appears to be predictive. However, there is nothing mysterious about it.

We should also mention a concept which is sometimes relevant here: the self-fulfilling prophecy. If you believe something is going to come true, you may act in a way that helps bring it about. One can help make a dream come true by simply doing things consistent with the ideas of the dream.

How likely is it that dreams are accurate predictors of the unknown? A rather convincing study of the accuracy (or rather lack of it) of pre-recognition dreams was conducted by the distinguished psychiatrist Dr. Henry Murray, along with Dr. D.R. Wheeler. The study was carried out in March of 1932, a few days following the kidnapping of Colonel Charles Lindbergh's infant. This was a notorious case, a highly publicized crime that aroused great concern and sympathy among the American people. The Harvard psychological clinic had a notice printed in the newspaper, requesting any dreams concerning the kidnapping. Some 1300 dreams were mailed in to the clinic before the body of the child was discovered in a shallow grave, in a woods, not far from Lindbergh's home.

How accurate were these possible clairvoyant dreams in predicting the actual facts regarding the baby? In about 95 percent of the dreams, there was no report of the baby being dead. In only four out of the 1300 dreams was there a reasonably accurate depiction of the essential facts—that the child was dead, buried in a grave, located among trees. Typically the content of the dreams reflected erroneous theories promoted in the newspapers that the baby was being held prisoner on board a ship.[8]

Interestingly, some of these correspondents whose dreams were totally inaccurate claimed to have predicted past events like the sinking of the Titanic.[9] This study, then, tends to throw cold water on clairvoyant dreams.

What then is the case for pre-recognition dreams? A truly scientific basis in support of such dreams is very difficult to establish. Nonetheless, I think it is interesting to read through the parapsychological literature—keeping the provisos we have laid out in mind. One may be impressed, or one may not be. To illustrate the kind of materials one will find, we will excerpt a few of the cases here.

As one reads through the parapsychology literature, one finds many reports of pre-recognition dreams. Sometimes these are rather cheerful coincidences. Sometimes they are eerie, reminiscent of what one might find on the late night "chiller" movie. If you are looking for material for gothic novels, here is the place.

An example of a cheerful coincidence—a dream followed by the reality— was reported by a psychiatrist, Dr. Herbert Strean. One of his patients reported the following dream:

> I don't know why I dreamt of Annette. I haven't seen her or thought of her for three years when she left our company to get a much better job. Well, anyway, in the dream Annette comes back to our office and wants to work for us. I'm sore at her in the dream because this is a real comedown, financially and status-wise. . . .

Two weeks later Annette walked into the office. The two women embraced. Then the patient asked Annette what she was doing there. Annette replied, "I know you'll be against it, but I'm leaving my job and I am applying to come back here." The patient reported they argued about it very much like it had transpired in the dream.[10]

Our second example of a seemingly paranormal dream was reported by Czechoslovakian psychiatrist Dr. Hans Ehrenwald:

> The dreamer was a patient of mine, a highly educated woman of thirty-two, undergoing a short spell of psychological treatment. The dream goes back to her eighteenth year when she was spending her summer holidays with her parents in Carlsbad. Her father was a well-known publisher and in his company she met Mr. B., a noted painter, a married man of about her father's age. The artist suggested that he should paint a portrait of her, but she attributed this suggestion to his desire for publicity through her father and his social connexions. She was at that time intensely opposed to any forms of what she regarded as mercenary strategems, particularly in art and literature, and she resented very much a similar attitude she believed she noticed in her father. Yet Mr. B. persuaded her to agree to his plan and she posed for him for a couple of weeks in his studio—it was actually a rather prosaic hotel room—with his wife regularly present at the sittings. Mrs. B. was a beautiful woman in her thirties, and she and her husband seemed quite happy together. Yet the patient disliked her somewhat condescending manner towards her, although she could not complain of lack of kindness in her behaviour.
>
> Returning to Prague from her holidays she lost sight of the artist and his wife for several weeks. It was at that time—in September 1926— that she dreamed that she came into a hotel room where she found the painter in a state of complete despair, sitting in a chair. "My wife has died," said the painter in tears. The room all around was in great disorder and the dreamer felt she had come to console him and put things right in the room. On awakening she was greatly upset by the dream. Yet she did not speak about it to anybody until the following evening, when the telephone rang and a friend told her that Mrs. B. had died unexpectedly the night before in a Prague nursing home from a septic tooth. Now the patient revealed the dream to her relatives, and it is by them that her account has been corroborated for me.[11]

Dr. Louisa Rhine has collected a very large number of apparent paranormal dreams. In her presentation of these cases, one can see that these dreams frequently dealt with death or injury. In some instances, the dreams were actually followed by death or injury to the persons dreamt about. In other instances death or injury befell other persons known to the dreamer.

A few of Dr. Rhine's cases are here presented to illustrate some of these macabre events:

> He was pastor of the Church for more than thirty years. Several years before his death, he dreamed one night that he himself died; they took him to the cemetery: he saw the grave and just before they let him down into the grave, he woke up. Of course, the dream lingered with him for a long time. In the meantime, his son, James, went to New York to study banking. He took pneumonia and died. His father and mother were with him when he died, and his father wired one of his Elders to prepare the burial the next day. Those were all the instructions he gave. When they reached the cemetery the grave was on the identical spot where his own grave was in his dream months before.[12]

> In the fall of '38, I dreamed I read on the inside page of our newspaper a story titled "Billy Smythe Killed." The article stated that while riding his bicycle my son had been hit by a car and killed.
> Naturally when I woke I was worried and told Billy, 14, to be very careful when he rode his bike. However, nothing untoward occurred until Feb. 28, 1939, when my son, for no definite reason we can find killed himself with a 22 rifle. This occurred about 7 in the morning. In the paper that night in the same position as in my dream was the article telling of his death.[13]

> I dreamed that I was traveling along a lonely stretch of road. Suddenly a heavy black car loomed up ahead of me in the early morning light. A woman and child were in the front seat. Suddenly she lost control of the car, swerved into mine, causing a head-on collision. We were thrown against a lone tree and I saw all of us, hanging as if dead from its limbs.
> Soon after, my brother's wife decided to accompany him on a trip. They set out early in the morning. They were on a lonely highway with few trees. Suddenly a black, heavy car loomed out of nowhere. A woman and child were alone in it. She lost control and the car headed toward my brother's . . . .

Unlike many cases, this last report had a happy ending. The sister-in-law grabbed the wheel, the cars swerved apart and no one was hurt.[14]

There have been paranormal dreams reported by public figures. One of the grimmest of these is attributed to Abraham Lincoln. Our source is an article by Dr. George Wilson, who in turn cites the statement of a friend of the President, a Mr. Robert Lamon. Lamon said he was present when the dream was related, along with Mrs. Lincoln and one or two others. According to Lamon's recollection, Lincoln said the following:

...but the other night I had a dream which has haunted me ever since. I am afraid that I have done wrong to mention the subject at all, but somehow the thing has got possession of me and, like Banquo's ghost, it will not down. About ten days ago, I retired very late; I was weary, fell into a slumber and soon began to dream. . . .

There seemed to be a death-like silence about me; then I heard subdued sobs as if a number of people were weeping. I thought I left my bed and wandered downstairs. There the silence was broken by the same pitiful sobbing, but the mourners were invisible. I went from room to room; no living person was in sight, but the same mournful sounds of distress met me as I passed along. It was light in all the rooms; every object was familiar to me; but where were all the people who were grieving as if their hearts would break? I was puzzled and bewildered; what could be the meaning of all this? Determined to find the cause of a state of things so mysterious and so shocking, I kept on until I arrived at the East Room, which I entered. There I met a sickening surprise. Before me was a catafalque on which rested a corpse wrapped in funeral vestments. Around it were stationed soldiers who were acting as guards; and there was a throng of people, some gazing mournfully upon the corpse whose face was covered, others weeping pitifully. "Who is dead in the White House?" I demanded of one of the soldiers. "The President," was his answer. "He was killed by an assassin!" Then came a loud burst of grief from the crowd, which awoke me from my dream. I slept no more that night; and although it was only a dream, I have been strangely annoyed by it ever since.[15]

This dream was reported to have occurred in the second week of April, 1865. He was assassinated within the week!

Pre-recognition of catastrophe? The long arm of coincidence? The Civil War was bloody. Death was all around, weighing heavily on Lincoln's mind. That he, himself, was hated by many people was a fact of life. The dream itself, then, would not be that unusual under these circumstances. The timing of the dream, however, is enough to make one wonder, even if ever so slightly.

II. The Analysis of Dreams

Chapter 12
The Many Faces of Dreams

Dreams have many faces. Some appear very commonplace, looking in some ways like a recapitulation of one's everyday experience. For example, the following dream was reported by a student who had been seeking part-time work around the campus. She tried the college library and was told there were typing jobs available. The student said she would brush up on her typing to see if she could pass the typing test. The dream recapitulating these events provides some interesting twists:

> I dreamt about going to the library for a book. And I was on the second floor by the depository catalogue and there was a desk with two typewriters on it. I told a man that was there I was looking for a job and he told me to type what was written on a pencil as a test. I tried to put the pencil in the typewriter as if it was a piece of paper and then took it out and started typing. I was nervous and did horribly. While I was typing, the man left to see what kind of job he could find. Then two people came by, one a man I didn't know and another guy who is in my English class. Then the man came back and told me that he didn't have anything, so I told him I had seen the librarian and she told me to come back after she returned from her vacation.

Some dreams seem compensatory, pointing to problem areas that have not been adequately addressed in reality. In the way of background for our illustrative case, the dreamer, a young woman, was involved in the theater. She had a close friend, an actor, who had worked with her on several plays. The young woman believed her actor friend was having marital difficulties. This bothered her. She would have liked to help, but he would not open up to her about his troubles, so she put the problem out of mind. The following dream suggested this concern was still very much alive:

> I dreamt that I was working with a friend of mine whom I know and we were working on a play. He had gotten into some kind of trouble which I don't remember and I tried to help him. We were in the country and I was at the house of the man who was trying to capture my friend. I ran out after my friend on foot; he had gone riding and I reached him just after I crossed a road and ran into some woods. I told him what was happening and he said that that was all right as he knew it was going to happen and there was no way to stop it. He told me I could have the horse he was riding to keep and

I thought at the time this was rather strange. He got down and started to walk back to the house and I stood there and watched him go, feeling very helpless. I so did want him to get away because I knew he was being punished for something he hadn't meant to do but there was nothing I could do.

Other dreams look like fulfillment of wishes, providing in fantasy what has not taken place in reality. In the following illustration, the subject, a young man, had been trying for the past six months to get his parents' permission to buy a motorcycle. He said this desire was continually on his mind.

It started off with me finally getting a cycle. I hopped on it and start[ed] thru L.A. I had a girl as my riding partner. I was either heading South or North because it was dark and the sun was low in the sky. I seemed to be traveling towards some hills, but they never got any closer. I was going at top speed thru regular city streets. I had no face guard on but me and my rider looked like the cycle was stopped. I mean our clothes weren't rippling or her hair flowing in the wind. The motorcycle was big, probably over 500 cc.

Some other examples of clear-cut wish fulfillment dreams that come to mind are of a man on a diet who dreamt of eating fattening foods, and a student who dreamt of meeting an exciting girl at a party only to wake up the next morning wondering who she was. I might also mention a dream reported by a patient I had been seeing whose husband had recently died. She had become very depressed by his loss. In her dream she saw him leaving the hospital, all dressed up. He gave her the keys to the house, saying he would meet her there in a little while.

Some dreams express feelings and behaviors which are of doubtful acceptability in waking life. This seems particularly true for acts of violence and aggression. In the following example, the violence (stabbing) is legitimized by dehumanizing the objects and making the aggressive action one of protecting others. The dream is also replete with Freudian sexual symbolism.

I was given two jobs caring for little girls—while their mothers took care of the younger children. In a large meadow, I taught the girl diving or some sort of sport off a high structure like life guards use. There was no water anywhere around us; then some monsters attacked us. I was put upon to save us all from the monsters. The girl and I took a train with very steep turnings and places where the track went straight up into the air to the den of the monsters. I stabbed them all to death with a penknife.

Finally, some dreams express feelings of anxiety—ranging from apprehension to outright terror. In this example, the subject was about to undergo some diagnostic tests on a chronic knee condition:

I dreamt I was in an army hospital. They had just performed some diagnostic tests. The doctor came up and said, "I have good news for you. It's only in one place." I was curious. I asked, "What's only in one place?" "Cancer," he replied. "It's in your larynx. But it has not metastasized." "Will it have to come out?" I asked. He replied, "Yes." Then he said, "You have diabetes." He took out a needle and started jabbing me in the buttocks, giving me insulin shots. Suddenly I felt panicky. I couldn't stand the thought of having cancer and diabetes. I was feeling overwrought. Then my mother was standing there trying to reassure me, but it was to no avail. I woke up suddenly in a fright.

Freud attempted to place all types of dreams under one rubric; he said underlying all dreams are wishes. It taxed even Freud's ingenuity to explain anxiety dreams in terms of wish fulfillment, but that is what he did, more or less successfully. In taking a point of view for this book, we will put aside Freud's view as too restrictive. In our view, the theory of wish fulfillment forces meanings out of dreams which may not be there. In its place, we shall use the broader language that *dreams tend to deal with unresolved problems*. We are not saying that this statement applies to all dreams, but we are assuming it applies to most dreams. The research finding by Drs. Rados and Cartwright that what is on the minds of subjects as they prepare to sleep tends to be similar in theme to the content of their subsequent dreams[1] supports this thesis.

When we adopt this view of dreams, it enables us to look at dreams which appear to rehash everyday events, and say there may be some lingering dissatisfaction or tensions relating to these events. Perhaps analyzing such dreams might help us sharpen our notions of what we want and don't want, suggesting needed changes in our behavior or interpersonal relations.

Dreams of wish fulfillment fit under this theme of unresolved problems very nicely. Not only are the problems defined clearly in such dreams, the desired solutions are also depicted.

Jung's notion that many dreams are compensatory dovetails with the view of dreams we are proposing here. The meanings of "unresolved problems" and "compensation" seem very close. In adopting this view of dreams, however, we are ignoring Jung's other theories about dreams, such as the collective unconscious, which seem very speculative.

That dreams may call attention to feelings and actions that we might not want to admit—e.g., sexual impulses and aggressive acts and feelings—falls within our conception of unresolved problems. Such needs have been subjected to more than usual defensive pressures. They are frequently labeled as unacceptable during the process of child development. Society attempts to limit their expression throughout life to carefully circumscribed conditions. As a result of such pressures, these impulses may be inhibited, suppressed, and even forced out of awareness. Let us consider anger. Every day we are subjected to frustrations, sometimes causing a build-up of angry feelings. We may deny this anger; it may show itself in somatic complaints such as headaches or skin problems; or we may let it out, lessening (with luck) our tensions. If we act carelessly in the way we express these feelings, however, all we may achieve is making other people angry, ultimately increasing our tensions. Angry feelings are difficult to deal with in a civilized order which demands restraint, yet deal with these feelings we must. In our view, dreams may act to call attention to the presence of such feelings and the need to deal more effectively with them.

The simpler anxiety dreams—fear of being late, of failing examinations—fit clearly under our rubric of unresolved problems. The dream is expressing a clear concern about impending events, or revealing unresolved tensions about something past. The more profound night terror seems to point to deeper disturbances.

In proposing this view of dreams, we offer an answer to a question asked much earlier: What is the function or value of dreaming? We now see that dreams can be useful in bringing up problems that have not been adequately dealt with.

If we accept this view of dreams as a working model, another question follows: How can we analyze dreams so we can identify these problems? My answer is that while the manifest content of dreams is of obvious value in telling us something about the problems that may be bothering us, one can learn a good deal more by using the manifest content as a starting point and trying to probe deeper.

There have been a number of techniques developed which attempt to probe beyond the surface of the dream. These include drawing the dream, visualizing the dream, dramatizing the dream, and associating to the dream. We shall discuss some of these methods, then describe in detail a new association procedure, called the *Dream Incident Technique*, showing how this can be used in the unraveling of dreams.

Chapter 13

Drawing, Visualizing,
and Dramatizing Dreams

Drawing what one has experienced in a dream enables one to project something additionally of oneself into the meaning of the dream. In the size, shape, posture and coloring of figures and background, one could reveal clues about one's perceptions of the characters and their relationships, and the emotional tone of the dream. A therapist could then ask questions about the picture which might lead to further clarifications about the meaning of the dream.

This is at present a speculative possibility because little systematic work has been done with the idea. I believe Freud is credited with inventing the idea of drawing dreams, though he did not ordinarily use it in his practice. Jung and his followers have used the technique more frequently. N.D.C. Lewis and Max Stern are among the psychoanalysts who have written about the use of this technique in therapy.

While the drawing technique has potential value as a diagnostic and therapeutic tool, the procedure does pose a number of problems. The drawing, like the dream, is still difficult to interpret. The subject's ability to draw or paint enhances or limits what he can do. The dream, too, is more akin to a motion picture than a painting as there are a number of sequences. Does one sketch them all? Still, the approach has hardly been exploited.

To illustrate some of the possibilities inherent in the technique, I will present some data from two students who have rendered some of their memories of dreams into picture. The students volunteered to try the experiment after attending university lectures I had given on dreams. Both students reported that drawing dreams was not a comfortable task—that it aroused anxiety.

The first student, Celeste, grew up in a metropolitan area, San Francisco. She now attends a university in the Midwest. Celeste's three pictures were painted in color.

Celeste's first painting (Figure 1) is expressive and modernistic. It is based on a recent dream. Our conversation about the dream went as follows:

DR. ROBBINS: Let's take a look at this painting.
CELESTE: All right. I had this dream a couple of weeks ago. It's really weird.

This is a lamp we have in our hallway. It sits on the table (*Celeste points to parts of the painting*). There are the doors to the living room; we have stairs coming down here. And this is really strange. This leg is supposed to be behind this person, who is my stepmother, who is standing at the top of the stairs. She said, "he's dead! he's dead!" That was my father. And I was standing at the bottom of the stairs. I remember feeling really sick, really frightened, like everything at once. It was really strange . . . very, very vivid.

DR. ROBBINS: Let me reconstruct it. You're saying that your stepmother is at the top of the stairs, you're at the bottom of the stairs, and she's saying that he's dead, he's dead—about your father.

CELESTE: Yeah.

DR. ROBBINS: Is your father in the picture?

CELESTE: That one leg.

DR. ROBBINS: (Pointing) This is your stepmother. What is the protrusion?

CELESTE: That's blood. It's really bizarre. She was standing at the top of the stairs—I don't remember the body, I remember the blood . . . and I remember the leg, and I just remember these disparate objects—like the lamp. I don't remember any other part of my body . . . just the head—like it was swimming, and the whole thing was effluent.

DR. ROBBINS: Tell me about the colors. Were they colors you visualized in the dream or were they colors you felt as you painted?

CELESTE: Both. A lot of the grey area [below the stairs] I remember in the dream. The yellow [background] and the green [face at the bottom of the stairs]—it was the way I felt. Those colors were also in the dream. I can't explain it exactly.

DR. ROBBINS: What do yellow and green mean to you as colors?

CELESTE: That particular shade of green to me is very vile. The yellow—I normally like. It's the color of my bedroom. It's very outgoing and cheery.

DR. ROBBINS: What went on in your mind as you painted it?

CELESTE: I had a rough time working on it. It was rough getting down to work.

DR. ROBBINS: What about it was rough?

CELESTE: Just rendering it. I knew what I had to put down—but I just couldn't make myself sit down and work on it. I'd work on it for twenty minutes and just have to get up and leave the room.

DR. ROBBINS: Did you feel resistance to it?

CELESTE: Yeah. That's what I mean.

DR. ROBBINS: What were these thoughts?

CELESTE: They were very disturbing. The dream to me was very disturbing. I am very close to my father. Until about six years ago, I really didn't know him. My real mother is dead, and he's the only one left. And the fact that she was standing there saying he's dead! he's dead! it upset me. It's a creepy feeling when you wake up.

DR. ROBBINS: Tell me about your stepmother.

CELESTE: Well, that says it right there. She's a wonderful person, but we do things differently. I never think of her as my mother.

DR. ROBBINS: Are you living with your father and stepmother now?

CELESTE: Yes. I moved in with them six years ago.

DR. ROBBINS: In the dream, is that your father's blood?

CELESTE: No. That was hers. She was sick from the idea too. She was very upset. And I was really upset. It was like I had just come home. It was sort of like an accusation too—not like why did you kill him—but why weren't you

Figure 1 (original in color).

home when he died? That's because I always get this jive at home—like this is not a hotel—this is your home—why aren't you ever here. (*Laughter*).

DR. ROBBINS: What do you think you learned from this dream yourself?

CELESTE: That I'm very guilty. I felt very guilty when I woke up for not being there—with all those accusations.

DR. ROBBINS: The accusations your stepmother makes?

CELESTE: Yeah.

DR. ROBBINS: How about your father, does he make the accusations?
CELESTE: No. She's the voice. He likes to stay neutral. He's in sort of a tenuous position—I'm his daughter, but she's his wife. That puts him right in the middle.
DR. ROBBINS: Do you see any possible relationship between the fact that he takes this neutral position and she does all the talking and in your painting here that the blood flows from her mouth and he's dead?
CELESTE: I think that probably has a great deal to do with it and the fact that I felt so guilty and sick when I woke up. Usually when I have a nightmare and I awake, I feel physically ill.
DR. ROBBINS: Do you think you have any resentment about this passive role your father plays between you and your stepmother?
CELESTE: I might. I don't really know. My father and I have a strange relationship. It's like a love affair. It's not because he's my father, but because he's the only one I have left. But we don't talk, because I really don't know what to say to him . . . we don't have anything in common.
DR. ROBBINS: And in the picture he's dead.
CELESTE: Yeah, right!
DR. ROBBINS: The painting seems to mirror some aspects of the home relationship. The consequence of it is you're guilty. You paint yourself with a color you call vile.
CELESTE: Yeah.

Celeste's second picture (Figure 2) was of a series of tornados. In explaining the background of these pictures, Celeste said she had never been in a tornado, but she had a kind of fascination with them and at the same time, she was terrified of them. When there were tornado watches she would sit in the corner of the room, feeling very shaky. She said that after her mother died, she had frequent dreams of being chased by tornados. The only concrete experience she has of seeing a tornado was watching the motion picture *The Wizard of Oz*.

The first of the four sections in the picture was described as a combination house and boat. She was out in the water and every time she stuck her head out, the tornado would "come to get her." The second section depicted the storm cellar of a neighbor of her mother's. Once again the tornado was waiting for her, if she came out. The third section showed her being chased by the tornado. The final section showed a fully formed tornado in the background with Celeste running toward a house—"with a door that was much too small," and she was "much too big to get through the door." There were stairs leading underground to a tiny place. Her father was down there, and she eventually made it there.

In discussing these pictures with Celeste, one thing became very apparent: the intense and overwhelming nature of the threat presented. In looking at the last caption showing the tiny space she must penetrate to save herself from the onrushing tornado, she said, "One moment I was outside, and it was like if I didn't get in there in two seconds, I couldn't get through. But if I didn't get in I would be killed . . . and the next moment I was down here. I kept coming

Figure 2

out to see if everything was clear. Everytime I walked out, one of these damn things was following me."

Our discussion also shed some more light on the relations between Celeste and her father. In the last caption, we learned that her father was waiting for her in safe enclosure. Celeste viewed her father's presence as protective. "I remember him saying, 'don't go out; don't go out, it's not safe.'" I asked Celeste whether her father was a comforting, protective type of person, and she replied that "I never saw him. My parents were divorced when I was six. My parents split up on very bad terms. I lived with my mother. The stuff my mother used to feed me was anti-father."

Celeste made an observation, and I think an important one, that these dreams occurred during a very rough year of her life – the year her mother died and when she was having a difficult time at school.

Celeste's final painting was of a pair of red lips. She reported that she had a recurrent dream of these lips as a very young child, possibly as early as two years old. She saw the lips as vibrating, hanging near her bed as she went to sleep. In our inquiry, we were not able to elucidate the meaning of these lips, except that they scared her. The dream ceased to occur when she was still a little girl.

In looking through the three dreams Celeste depicted in her paintings, we can see some emerging features. One is that the paintings suggest she has at times experienced considerable anxiety. The recurrent tornado suggests a feeling or fear of being swept away. In one dream, safety and reassurance are viewed in her father, but he is generally perceived as less than a safe anchor. His limitations as helper and comforter are clear; he was absent during her childhood and seen as somewhat ineffectual in her current life. Moreover, Celeste's needs for him seem to be truncated, if not blocked, by the presence of a stepmother. Celeste's needs for her father's support and affection and her fear of losing these (her father is the only family she has left) are a major theme suggested by the dreams. These needs and anxieties may be related to the guilty feelings that emerge.

One interesting aspect of the paintings is the disembodied characters. In one picture, there are only vibrating lips, in another only heads and a leg. One wonders what the absence of bodies means. Perhaps it mirrors the absence of viable relationships in the home.

All of these are impressions, of course, derived from the paintings and the follow-up inquiry. These are hypotheses—questions raised, not substantiated clinical findings. To confirm or revise these views, hours of additional conversation would have to be spent with Celeste. Here we are seeking only to demonstrate the potentialities of a method of dream analysis, as a way of opening up areas for study relating to personality.

The dreams of our second subject, Laura, present something of a contrast to the clear-cut anxiety dreams of Celeste. Like Celeste, Laura attends college in the Midwest. She, however, was born and raised on a tobacco farm in rural North Carolina. As with Celeste, I knew very little about Laura before the interview. She brought along three sketches, representing three different dreams. The first picture (Figure 3) was drawn in pencil, the latter two (Figures 4 and 5) in pen and ink.

LAURA: (Pointing to first sketch) I had this dream about three weeks ago. An old girl friend of mine from high school named Arlene and I got together for some strange reason. Now I haven't seen Arlene in five years, but in the dream we were going out west. We were in my car and the car breaks down. We didn't know where we were going. So, we just stopped at this old restaurant. It was called "The Thatched Roof Restaurant." I remember that no one could tell us where we were going. It was very frustrating. I remembered just walking around the building. That (points to the woman in the drawing) is Arlene. I was behind the building, with my car. I tried to draw my car there (again pointing to the sketch). We couldn't get directions there. And we couldn't get anyone to fix my car. And I don't remember exactly what happened toward the end. I remember it was frustrating and I remember this particular restaurant—and it was very woodsy. It was in a forest type area. But, I don't know what happened. I just remember us walking around the building. It seemed very strange because I hadn't seen Arlene in all this time.

Figure 3

DR. ROBBINS: What's she like?

LAURA: She's a very strange girl. It isn't that she's strange but her family background is strange. Her mother has a thing about dogs and keeps all these cages full of dogs around the house. Her mother had a thing against men. She told Arlene that dogs are better than men. She would take Arlene to bars to try to meet men, and yet she would tell her how bad they were. I would come home and tell my mother all these things. She would get very upset. She didn't want me to see Arlene any more. So now I'm seeing Arlene and we're going on a trip. I don't know where we are. We're going out west . . . where I didn't know. We were lost and no one would help us. There were people in the restaurant, but they ignored us. So we were walking round and round the restaurant.

DR. ROBBINS: Round and round the restaurant?

LAURA: Yes. Like we were trying to find the answer.

DR. ROBBINS: Find the answer to what question?

LAURA: To where we were going and what was wrong with our car. I remember being really scared. I kept thinking, why am I with Arlene? Why am I seeing Arlene? It was so real!

DR. ROBBINS: Let's turn our attention to the restaurant. Do you have any recollection of a place like that?

LAURA: I've never seen a place like that. Yes I have in a museum exhibit of an African exhibit. There were huts with thatched roofs. That's the only thing I've ever seen like that.

DR. ROBBINS: Let's talk about you and Arlene again. I would think that would have to be kind of important. You haven't seen her for a number of years. Have you had any communication with her?

LAURA: I've tried to get in touch with her about three years ago. She worked at a bar, as a barmaid. She wasn't there. They said she left with some guy. So I called her mother. She gave me all this jibberish about Arlene not being her daughter any more . . . she's disowned her. So that's the last time I tried to reach her.

DR. ROBBINS: What does Arlene mean to you?

LAURA: She's a symbol of wrong. Mother didn't like her. I was sixteen at the time. I liked her. I wanted to be with this girl. She's fun. She's exciting. She'd take me places I would never get to go. But I never did go anywhere with her.

DR. ROBBINS: But now you are with Arlene in the dream and you are lost.

LAURA: Yeah. So, maybe she isn't really that good. Well I guess my mother was right. Arlene isn't good. She didn't have direction. She didn't know where she was going. She wasn't the kind of person who has direction.

DR. ROBBINS: In the dream, was it you or Arlene who was the person who was driving? Do you remember?

LAURA: I think Arlene was driving. We took the wrong road. I don't know how we got to this little restaurant. I remember it so well.

DR. ROBBINS: What was it like inside?

LAURA: It was brown. It had a bar, with all these purple lights on the side. The people seemed stupid.

DR. ROBBINS: Purple lights? Have you ever seen a place with purple lights?

LAURA: Yeah. One time I looked at a house with my parents to buy. The people had decorated their garage. They had a bar with lights on one side. They decorated the whole place in purple and black. I have never seen that combination. I guess it stuck in my mind.

DR. ROBBINS: Did you find it attractive?

LAURA: No. It was horrible.

DR. ROBBINS: There were purple lights in this place (*pointing to the drawing*).

LAURA: In fact this place was very much like that room. It was dark . . . purple bubble lights were there. And the people were sort of dumb . . . they really didn't know what was going on either.

DR. ROBBINS: In a sense, this lodge was a kind of transformation of this house in some respects. . . . So there you are with Arlene who was the rejected girl by your parents and her parents—who represented something glamorous to you.

LAURA: She was. She wore the shortest skirts, the most makeup, the longest hair, and here I am—church every Sunday.

DR. ROBBINS: So there you are with her. She takes you out some place going west and you end up in this place that reminds you of a rather unhappy spot—that you didn't think had the highest taste in the world—that turned you off.

LAURA: It sure did.

DR. ROBBINS: And now you're trying to figure out how to get away from this place.

LAURA: Of course.

DR. ROBBINS: Running around in circles.

LAURA: (*Laughter*)

DR. ROBBINS: Let's leave this drawing and let's go to the next one.

LAURA: This is a dream I had as a child. My dad's a tobacco farmer. We lived on a farm in North Carolina. I had to walk to school. I remember it was early in the morning and it was late. My dad had a strict rule that you did not run through his tobacco crop. So I remember being late and remember saying I'm not going to listen to my dad. I'm going to run through the tobacco field because I'm in a hurry. I remember doing it and I couldn't get out of it. There was tobacco everywhere. The more I ran, the more it was there. It wouldn't stop growing. I kept knocking the leaves over. It was gummy. And I remember getting all this stuff on my school clothes. I knew my mother would get upset. I got it on my arm, my hair started getting sticky. The more I ran, the stickier I got. And that was the dream. It was just crazy. I couldn't get out of it.

DR. ROBBINS: What kind of emotions were you feeling during the dream?

LAURA: I was scared. I didn't know what to do. I didn't have anyone to yell to. No one was there. And this barn was there. The barn kept getting farther away. It was very strange.

DR. ROBBINS: This is definitely your home situation?

LAURA: Yes. It's exactly like it. (*Points to the drawing.*) This is my house. Here is the road I should have taken. . . . These are trees. It's exactly the way it was. I could have even put it in color.

DR. ROBBINS: Did you ever get stuck in any place when you were a kid? That you couldn't get out of?

LAURA: The barn—one time.

DR. ROBBINS: What happened then?

LAURA: I had to crawl under the barn. And I remember it took me a long time to figure how to get under there, but eventually I did.

DR. ROBBINS: Were you scared then?

LAURA: Yes, I was crying. I was yelling for my mother. I was about five or six.

DR. ROBBINS: What would have happened to you if your father had caught you in the tobacco field?

LAURA: He would have beat me. He would have taken a broom or a limb off the tree. It hurt. I remember telling my grandmother to beat him. (*Laughter.*) See, I used to run away. I was the only child for a long time; I didn't have anyone to talk to. So I talked to the dog. So he probably figured if I was going to run away I would run across the field. Someone might see me on the road. They wouldn't see me in the field. At that age I didn't have anything to do. There were no other kids . . . just my dog. I remember running away one time. He got me. He beat me, and it hurt. I yelled I was going to run away again. So I went to my grandmother's house.

DR. ROBBINS: What was your grandmother like?

Figure 4

LAURA: She is a great woman. The momma of the area. Everyone who has a problem goes to her.
DR. ROBBINS: What was your father like?
LAURA: He is a quiet man. He wouldn't hurt you unless he's very upset.
DR. ROBBINS: Why do you think he gave you a beating as a child?
LAURA: Because he didn't want me to run away. And that's the only thing I understood at that age.

Figure 5

DR. ROBBINS: It wasn't punitive. It was to protect you?
LAURA: Right.
DR. ROBBINS: All right, tell me about your third picture.
LAURA: There am I running away—there I am with my little dog. I'm getting tired and it's getting dark. That's my bed, the one I used to have in my bedroom ... at home.
DR. ROBBINS: Back in the farm?
LAURA: Yes. But it's where I want to be now. In the woods. Because I'm tired. I remember walking around for hours and hours. It's getting dark and

I wanted to find a place to rest. I remember being so shocked when I saw the bed. I walked out and there was the bed!

DR. ROBBINS: You recognize the woods?

LAURA: That's the same woods.

DR. ROBBINS: You notice as you look at the two pictures of the representa-tions of you, they are very different. In this one (the preceding picture) you're much more grown up . . . you look about five or ten years older.

LAURA: Because in this one I'm not running away. Now I know the effects of running through the field. In this one I do not. I'm bored. I want to get away from the farm, so I go wandering through the woods with my dog.

DR. ROBBINS: Tell me about the woods. What kinds of experiences did you have there?

LAURA: Very nice. We had a monkey vine in the woods . . . a vine you swing on. We had a stream back there. We would watch the fish and go wading in it.

DR. ROBBINS: On the whole, your experiences in the woods were very pleasant?

LAURA: Very, very much. I loved it. I used to go out there quite a bit.

DR. ROBBINS: When you were in the woods, were you leaving something in the house that you wanted to get away from?

LAURA: Um hum.

DR. ROBBINS: What were you trying to get away from?

LAURA: My parents.

DR. ROBBINS: Why did you want to get away from them?

LAURA: Because, I didn't want to stay there. All they wanted to do was stay in the house and watch television. If I'd go outside I was restricted to a certain area. And I told them, I didn't want to stay in.

DR. ROBBINS: Did your parents know you were out there in the woods?

LAURA: No. Never. It wouldn't have been any fun if they knew.

DR. ROBBINS: It was kind of a clandestine adventure.

LAURA: Exactly. It was the most exciting thing I could do. And then when I felt like that—it was good. I could stay out here. And now that I had my bed here, this was my home, and I didn't have to go back.

DR. ROBBINS: When we consider the three paintings, one thing you're tak-ing here (the third painting) is a clandestine adventure. You're walking in the woods, escaping something you might call boredom or restriction. In the other painting, the first one, there you are taking what amounts to a clandestine adventure with your friend, Arlene. She is a kind of symbol of the more glamorous, escape-type life—and there you're going with her, only it doesn't end up in a bed of roses. It ends up where you're going around in circles—something like here in the second drawing where you are in the tobacco patch—running and running and not quite getting anywhere. There are some common elements here: trying to get out of a rut, looking for something more exciting, looking for something a little clandestine—but not finding it except in the woods dream. This is the one dream you seem to find something in. There's your bed all safe and secure in the woods. In the second dream, you never quite reach your goal—while in the first dream, you are go-ing around in circles. Your destination turned out to be a bust. I wonder if you can relate that at all to what might be going on with you now? Do you see any relationships with anything in your current life?

LAURA: Well, it's not very exciting, I'll tell you that now. I work full time. I have a very good steady job. I go to school at night because I want a four-year degree. After I get my degree, I want another job. It's very structured. Sometimes I get uptight with wanting to do something different ... not necessarily wrong, but something. ...

DR. ROBBINS: A little more impulsive?

LAURA: Exactly. Not something as well thought out. My life has been completely structured.

DR. ROBBINS: In a sense, your dreams might be saying, "Let's take a vacation. Let's go out and break loose."

LAURA: Yes—live as you are now. Enjoy life for today—instead of for ten years from now. That's the way I've always been geared—for ten years from now. Don't do anything now, because it will hurt you later.

DR. ROBBINS: Just like what your parents are saying. "Don't go anywhere, remain in the house," or, "Be careful where you walk, because if you go in the wrong place, you'll get caught." And in the first dream, you did go to the wrong place, and you ended up going in circles. It looked like you have an approach and a little avoidance built into the same thing. You want to go somewhere, and your dreams are saying it's not quite clear [that] if you get there it'll be good. In none of these things do you see your parents, but they seem to be in the background of everything, admonishing you not to do things. Once again, these are speculations. We don't know these things to be true, but there is a certain consistency which is interesting.

In commenting briefly on Laura's drawings and our subsequent inquiry, there are recurrent themes suggesting some tensions relating to autonomy. We have seen instances of attempts to leave confining circumstances and resistance to parental authority. Stresses relating to autonomy are a frequent problem for persons of college age, relating in part to the normal development of independence from one's parents. In our discussion of the Dream Incident Technique, we shall encounter this problem repeatedly and will discuss its implications in some detail.

We shall now turn our attention to the technique of "visualizing" dreams. This technique shares some elements with drawing dreams inasmuch as both involve perceptual processes. The procedure also shares elements in common with the association procedures we shall discuss in the next two chapters.

Dr. Joseph Reyher, who has been working with the technique at Michigan State University, began his experiments in a therapeutic situation. His patients were told to lean back in their chairs, close their eyes, and relate everything that came into their minds. While feelings and physical sensations were sometimes reported, the therapist was mainly concerned with the patient experiencing images and ultimately intense visual fantasies. During the procedure, the therapist remained silent except for questions designed to elicit images. Some patients had difficulty with the procedure. In these instances, the therapist continued to ask questions such as, "Now just tell me what images come to mind."

As the patient becomes familiar with the procedure, he is able to describe the images visualized; these images tend to shift from one to another. Sometimes the images elicit anxiety. Reyher terms these images *hot images*.

Sometimes images that seem at first to be neutral become connected with conflict. For example, "the image of an automobile for one student subject turned
into her father's car and subsequent imagery of (her) father was distressing."[1]

Reyher reports that the procedure often arouses anxiety in the patient. For
severely repressed patients, the procedure may elicit rather acute reactions.
Therefore, it is not something to be undertaken in the absence of a therapist
experienced with the procedure. According to Reyher, the advantage of the
procedure is that it leads the patients to rapid confrontation with their problems, hence speeding up therapy.

In subsequent studies, Reyher and his colleague, Dr. Howard Morishige,
applied the procedure to visualization of dreams. The subject was instructed
to close his eyes and visualize scenes from a vivid dream. In the laboratory, the
subject's physiological reactions were monitored, including EEG and pulse
readings. We have already described one of their EEG findings: that the alpha
rhythm was desynchronized during dream visualization.[2]

Morishige and Reyher illustrated the visualization procedure applied to
dreams in a clinical excerpt. In the dream, the subject, a woman, was very anxious, unable to move or wake up. "Somehow she found herself in the bathroom
standing before the sink trying to splash water on her face, but she could not
get her cupped hands to her face. She then looked up into the mirror and saw
a photographic negative of herself. She awakened in reality feeling very
anxious...."[3]

The experimenter began the visualization procedure by asking her to
describe the dream again, making "a note of any images that happen to come
into your mind's eye."

She repeated the dream, stating how she couldn't move her hands,
couldn't wake up, then thinking that if she could only get some water on her
face, it would wake her up. Then she said, "I'm having different visions."

The experimenter asked her to describe these. She replied that the scene
was once again in the bathroom, but her vision was now of a male standing
there with his penis exposed. Later, she saw herself again. She looked into the
mirror and there was nothing there. "I was just a negative." She tried to
visualize the man again. The experimenter asked what he was wearing. She
responded, "Plaid shirt, but I don't necessarily know if it's a man. I think it
could have been me." Continuing to visualize, she reported, "I saw myself looking down into the sink basin ... and moving my hands to cup the water. All
of a sudden I saw the hands moving towards the penis. I saw the figure."

The subject became uncomfortable, saying she wanted to open her eyes.
The procedure had apparently targeted in on basic psychosexual conflicts.[4]

As Reyher's procedure is experimental and seems to arouse anxiety, it is
not something to recommend for the novice dream analyst to try on himself
or others. Nonetheless, it is an interesting approach to dream analysis that
warrants increased attention, particularly in the context of psychotherapy.

The technique of dramatizing the dream is associated with Gestalt therapy. The method is described in detail in Dr. Frederick Perls' stimulating book *Gestalt Therapy Verbatim* and briefly in a paper by Lewis Alban and Dr. William Groman.[5] Underlying the technique is the assumption that dreams deal with parts of our personality that have become alienated from one's central self, and in a real sense disowned. The dreamer does not want to recognize these aspects of himself. Because such avoidance is felt to be psychologically crippling, Gestalt therapy is aimed at integrating these various facets of self.

As in other methods of dream analysis, the subject begins by relating a dream. The therapist listens, but does not interpret. Rather the therapist asks the dreamer to act as if he were different parts of the dream. These parts might be any persons, objects, events or moods described in the dream content. The dreamer first takes the role of one party in the dream, speaks and acts as if it were that party, entering into a dialogue with the other components of the dream. As he does this playacting, the patient is seated in one chair and speaks to an empty chair. The part of the dream he speaks to is imagined to reside in the empty chair.

To facilitate the dialogue, the patient may then move to the empty chair, take the role of that part of the dream, and rebut the part he had just played.

Judging from examples in Perls' book *Gestalt Therapy Verbatim*, a great deal of emotion can be generated by this procedure—as various aspects of the personality "have at" one another. If the technique is handled skillfully by the therapist, the patient becomes more aware of fragmented parts of his personality, and should be able to assimilate these formerly avoided aspects of his personality. In theory, this should mean less intrapsychic conflict, improving the ability of the person to function effectively in everyday life.

Let us look at some brief examples of how this works in practice.

One young woman, Liz, had recurrent dreams of tarantulas and other spiders crawling on her. Perls asked her to talk to the spider. Liz asked the spider to go away. Liz then took the role of the spider, responding that it wanted to go somewhere, and she was in the way . . . and that it was going to crawl over her. As the dialogue continued, Liz asked the spider why it crawled on her. The answer given was that she wasn't important. Then, Liz contradicted the spider, saying, yes, she was important. As the dialogue continued, it began to bring out Liz's conflicts relating to her own worth.[6]

A second example was of a man, Carl. Carl's dream was also recurrent. The dream happened in a desert at night. Mainly visible were a train track and an oncoming train with a high-pitched whistle. Carl reported a feeling of fear during the dream.

Perls began by asking Carl to play the part of the desert—inquiring what would it be like to be a desert. Carl responded that he had no solidity, he was blown about by the wind, and went on without beginning or end. Later Carl played the train. Here again, he felt he would be going on and on, with enormous energy, but never accomplishing anything. Then Carl played the tracks.

Here he felt he was flat on his back with life running over him. All of these roles led to a self perception of drifting, of lack of purpose and control over his destiny.[7]

While one may gain a sense of the Gestalt therapy approach to dreams in these excerpts, one can best appreciate the dynamics of the technique by reading verbatim dialogue (e.g., *Gestalt Therapy Verbatim*) or by viewing films of Gestalt therapy. A number of such films were made by Perls before his death. My impression of the technique is that it requires imagination and fluency on the part of the dreamer. The acting out of the dream should be carried out with the aid of a therapist who is skilled in the procedure, and who is trained to deal with the strong emotions that may arise in the process.

Chapter 14

Dream Association

Freud discovered the method of free association while treating patients in psychotherapy. These patients came to him with problems such as phobias, hysterical symptoms, and obsessive ideas. Working with his colleague, Joseph Breuer, Freud believed that if he could trace these symptoms back to their points of origin in the patient's psychological structure, the symptoms would disappear.

According to Ernest Jones, Freud's method of tracing the origin of these symptoms developed gradually. In the beginning, he tried a concentration technique. The patient, a certain Fraulein Elizabeth Von R., was asked to relax, think about a specific symptom, and try to remember anything that might reveal clues about how the symptom came into being. Initially, Freud touched the patient's forehead with his hand, thinking this might help her to associate.

Freud probably questioned Fraulein Von R. frequently, because she told him to quit interrupting her flow of thought. Freud must have sensed that his probes were counterproductive, for his technique became more and more one of listening to emerging chains of ideas. As he explored the possibilities of free association, Freud began to ask his patients "to communicate . . . every idea or thought that occurred to them in connection" with a given subject.[1] In this way he felt he could uncover the conflicts underlying the symptoms.

Freud noticed that while free-associating ideas, some patients began to bring up their dreams. These dream reports were apparently stimulated by thoughts relating to the symptoms. Freud began to accept the idea that a dream could be part of the association of ideas leading back from the symptom to the origin of the conflict. And then he hit upon a creative notice (what some have called an "ah ha!" experience): If dreams are part of the chain of thought leading to the origin of the problem, why not use dreams as a beginning point – treat them as he would symptoms, and let associations flow from them. The idea opened up new vistas into his explorations of unconscious processes, for now he had a multitude of beginning points from which to launch his probes.

The objective of the free-association method was to circumvent or bypass the critical faculty which sifts ideas emerging into consciousness. The subject was told to report "whatever comes into his head" and not to suppress a thought "because it strikes him as unimportant or irrelevant or because it seems to him meaningless."[2]

In using the free-association technique with dreams, Freud did not ask the patient to associate to the dream as a whole. Rather, he would cut the dream into pieces, and ask for associations to each piece separately.

Freud presented illustrations of how the free-association method works, using material from his own dreams. For example, he related a dream he had that included one of his patients, Irma. In a segment of the dream, he was examining her for a physical complaint:

> I took her to the window to look down her throat. She showed some recalcitrance, like women with false teeth. I thought to myself that really there was no need for her to do that.[3]

In point of fact, Freud was treating her for emotional symptoms and had never had occasion to examine her throat. His free associations, however, led to events that could have given rise to this segment of the dream:

> What happened in the dream reminded me of an examination I had carried out some time before of a governess: at a first glance she had seemed a picture of youthful beauty, but when it came to opening her mouth she had taken measures to conceal her plates. This led to recollections of other medical examinations and of little secrets revealed in the course of them — to the satisfaction of neither party.[4]

And further:

> The false teeth took me to the governess whom I had already mentioned; I then thought of someone else to whom the features might be alluding. She again was not one of my patients, nor should I have liked to have her as a patient, since I had noticed that she was bashful in my presence and I could not think she would have been an amenable patient. . . . Thus I had been comparing my patient Irma with two other people who would also have been recalcitrant to treatment.[5]

Free association, then, may produce a chain of connected thoughts, an outpouring of ideas, that may suggest certain conclusions. One of the analyst's tests is to interpret this emerging material, using Freud's principles of psychoanalysis as a guideline. Success would seem to depend on the ability of the patient to allow involuntary ideas to flow from his mind and the skill of the analyst in interpreting these materials.

The use of dream association in psychotherapy is illustrated in a clinical excerpt provided by Dr. Ralph Greenson. The patient, a male, was suffering from a depressive problem and anxiety concerning sexual relations. In one of his dreams, he was in a huge department store. He noticed "shiny orange and green plastic raincoats on display." Also he saw "a middle aged Jewish woman," and "a female mannequin dressed in a gray flannel dress." There was also a third woman, waiting eagerly for him, near a small surrey. She was "putting clothes in it." He remembered feeling sorry for the horse. He lifted the surrey to hitch it and was surprised by how light it was. Then he reacted by thinking "I was silly to feel sorry for the horse."

In associating to the dream, the patient commented on how different the three women in the dream were. The older woman reminded him of his mother, while the mannequin suggested "beautiful, pure and cold" women—like his wife. His train of thought then went into his unsatisfying sexual relationship with his wife. Following her pregnancy, their sex life was "nil." The patient thought he was like the horse in the dream, having to pull the financial load. The analyst began to comment, referring to the surrey as a buggy. The patient then interrupted. "That buggy is so light," he said. "It's a baby buggy, it's a baby carriage. No wonder it was so light, it was so tiny, and the woman was putting clothes on it, like diapers." This revelation was followed by a train of thought leading back to his childhood memories, when he was pushing his baby sister in a carriage.

The patient's associations to the green and orange raincoats suggested a link between raincoats, rubbers and condoms. He recalled finding condoms among his father's belongings. He said he took some, hoping for a chance to use them. However, the opportunity never arose; the condoms disintegrated in his wallet.

Some of these associations, like the mannequin and the condoms, seemed clearly related to the unresolved sexual difficulties faced by the patient. Some of the associations, like the surrey, seemed related to his feelings about his wife's pregnancy. The train of thought leading to earlier unresolved problems of his childhood served to open up new possibilities in the treatment of the patient. Dr. Greenson reported that the hitherto quiet course of therapy now changed into "tearful and angry hours," as the patient's psychological defenses had been penetrated with the aid of dream analysis.[6]

We will present one more example, the dream and associations of a young woman who is a psychotherapist. She volunteered the following account to me.

The dream: Her ex-husband, Joe, had been missing for two days. After this time had elapsed, she became very anxious, almost frantic that some misfortune had happened to him. She organized a search party to look for him. After a while, the search party discovered a body that had been killed by a lion. She identified it. It was Joe.

The scene then shifted. She found herself with her brother, Chris. Chris had acquired a pride of lions as pets. The lions came up to her one by one, half friendly, half menacing, licking her hand. Chris said not to worry about these lions, but warned her about one of the lions that looked like a horse; this was the one that killed Joe, and it was out to get her.

The scene changed again. She was trying to return home. The lion, now in the form of a horse, was after her. Once she encountered it and stabbed it. Then she tried to run home. Her legs moved rapidly, but her motion was more like treading water. She became lost. She tried asking her way from some passersby. They were evasive. Then, suddenly, she awoke.

Her associations: That afternoon she had seen a patient, a middle-aged woman, who was in deep emotional trouble. The patient's problems seemed almost hopeless. The patient's resources to cope with her problems were limited, and all the efforts of the therapist had thus far produced little observable effect.

In the evening, she turned the patient's problems over in her mind, but could come to no conclusions. She was troubled by the situation, but finally decided to put the problem out of mind. She turned on the television set to watch a movie, *The Heartbreak Kid*. It was about an amoral young man who jilted his bride of a few days in favor of a more attractive woman. Later, she turned on another show. The story concerned a wife who was plotting to murder her husband.

Her associations about her husband led her to a recent meeting in New Orleans which she attended, where her ex-husband was also in attendance. She knew Joe was there, but she was ambivalent about seeing him. Although their marriage had been a bad one, she knew she was still attracted to him. If she saw him, she was afraid of getting involved again, which she knew would be a mistake. Besides, she had met a man that she liked a great deal and was hoping to marry. It would be unfair to him to see her ex-husband. During the meeting, she felt her emotions churned up with memories of her marriage, but she avoided seeing Joe. She felt she had maintained a morally sound position. How different her behavior was from the two programs she had turned on. Yet it now seemed clear that her self-denial had not erased the conflict, and in her dream, her procrastination in looking for Joe had proved disastrous.

In thinking about Joe, she reflected that he was very interested in wildlife. In fact, he had once considered deserting her for a career in this field. She mused, how fitting it was that he was killed by a lion. In interpreting this dream fragment, she felt that this was no death wish; only a wish to have this problem out of her life. Her marriage had been an insurmountable problem, a complete failure. And now, she reflected about her patient. The problem also seemed insurmountable, and she was failing at this, too.

What was her brother, Chris, doing in the dream? That morning, she recalled, she had sent a letter to Chris. His former fiancée wanted to get back in touch with him and had asked her to be an intermediary. The correspondence with the other dream association seemed perfect.

She thought further about Chris. In both appearance and manner, he reminded her of a colleague, a psychotherapist. It was the very colleague who had referred the troubled woman to her for therapy. She remarked, it was as if her colleague had thrown her into the lion's den.

It appears that the therapist's dreams were highlighting some difficult problems the therapist had been facing; the one concerning her ex-husband, the other a difficult patient. In the first instance, there were the stirrings of old feelings and the memory of failure; in the second, there was the expectation of a new failure. The dream combined these problems in interesting ways and, adding the intensity of anxiety, almost forced the issues into the therapist's awareness. Free association helped unlock some of the pieces of the puzzle. The therapist reported that the insights she obtained helped her cope with her own feelings and the objective problems more effectively.

As we indicated, the use of free association calls for spontaneity on the part of the patient and some brilliance on the part of the analyst. It is not possible for many patients to free-associate to the degree Freud wished. Indeed, Eissler, writing many years after Freud, voiced the opinion that it was doubtful whether anyone had completely fulfilled Freud's dictum.[7] Even when the patient is able to free-associate effectively and the analyst is highly skilled, there still remains a problem. Each analyst may interpret the dream associations somewhat differently. One may place weight on a given idea; another may minimize its importance. As Dr. Martin Bergmann points out, the analyst's theoretical bias can influence his interpretation.[8]

If you went to two therapists, free-associated to dreams, and received two different interpretations, how would you know which one was more correct? Is it possible to introduce some order into the free-association technique, to make it more reliable, more objective, yet still retain its seemingly enormous potential for probing into the meanings of dreams?

We will discuss three different approaches that try to use dream associations in a more objective manner. The first approach was developed by Drs. Edith Sheppard and Bertram Karon, the second by Dr. John Tokar and his colleagues, and the third is my own Dream Incident Technique which will be presented in the following chapter.

Sheppard and Karon worked out a procedure for therapists or researchers to rate dream association materials objectively. In developing their techniques, they collected dreams and associations from hospitalized psychiatric patients. Following Freud's suggestion, these associations were obtained in response to each element in the dream. Any associations that referred directly to the dream content were selected, typed up on cards and given to an independent analyst. The analyst rated these associations for the presence or absence of certain psychological and psychoanalytic concepts. For example, ratings were made for the presence of hostility. This was indicated by destructive behavior, bad interpersonal relations, unpleasant feelings, etc. Another example would be ratings for ego weakness. Indications for this would include mutilation of the body, illness, and unusual body image.

The authors found it was possible to rate both dreams and associations on these psychological characteristics. In some cases, such as hostility, the ratings for the dreams and associations were frequently very similar; the associations revealed little more than the manifest content of the dream. In other instances, there was no relationship at all between the ratings for the dreams and the associations. The associations revealed a different picture from the dreams.[9]

The Sheppard and Karon procedure is an application of content analysis. It relies on a trained outside analyst to interpret the dream associations, given some guidelines. These associations, however, may mean one thing to the analyst and quite possibly something else to the dreamer who produced them. Much as he would like to, the analyst cannot put himself into the mind of the dreamer. Is there a way to more fully utilize the experience and knowledge of the dreamer?

One procedure attempting to do this was developed by John Tokar and his associates. In Tokar's approach, the investigators begin by choosing a limited number of key words from dream reports—and to this extent a subjective clinical judgment is required. Then the dreamer is asked to make up sentences from these key words. Making up sentences from words or sentence stems is a useful technique in itself in revealing personality problems and has been formalized in such tests as the Rotter Incomplete Sentence Blank Test. The Tokar procedure picks key words from the dream, which presumably adds a link to current troubling concerns. The procedure then gets quite involved, for the key words are deleted from the sentences and the subject is asked to supply new key words. The procedure leads to further links between sentences and the substitute key words. While this may appear something like a word game, an associative process seems to be involved that could delve into areas of concern for the person.

Tokar's research group illustrated the procedure with a patient who was undergoing psychotherapy. The patient reported several dreams. One of these dreams (which I have slightly edited to delete pauses in the verbatim account) was as follows:

> Well, I think the dream that was frightening was the man that was involved in the dream was a man that I had gone with for quite a few years, who was married, and in this dream he was always with other women. Their backs were turned to me, it was always the backs; and I could never see their faces; and they were all dark-haired women, and they were not making love, but they were being very affectionate toward one another, and I was witnessing this and I felt myself become intensely jealous and anxious, and yet I realized that I could interrupt the situation by breaking into the pair of them, and that this man would go with me (I could get him away, but I was compelled not to) and the intensity of the jealousy and anxiety I felt wasn't applicable to the individual himself so I guess he was symbolic of some, of someone else. And I guess that was the scary, frightening dream. And it concluded, and also what I thought was significant is the fact that all these women had dark hair, and his wife was a blonde. And as I, well, discovered later, well, my mother had dark hair so it was that type of association, and I think the feeling was frightening more than the actual action that was taking place in the dream.[10]

This dream and two others were submitted to a number of psychotherapists, who picked out what they thought were the "key words" in the dreams. In the dream presented here, key words included "jealous," "frightening," and "dark-haired women." The patient was then asked to construct sentences using these key words. Her sentences dealt with important areas such as home, father, and men. For example, one sentence was "Home was a very frightening place."

The key words were then deleted. In their place were substituted a variety of other words that the patient felt were related to it. For "frightening," the words substituted included "lousy," "difficult," "uncomfortable" and "miserable." The patient rated the various sentence stems dealing with home, father, men, etc., in terms of whether the substitute key words made sense in the sentences. The patient agreed with the idea that home was a very lousy place, that father was a very miserable man, and that many men are difficult.

When further substitutions had been carried out, an analyst looked at the data concluding that "the subject appears to have a negative relationship with her father and very negative feelings about him. She feels he was domineering, austere, cold, frightening, and jealous. She projects these negative feelings onto her relationships with other men." Other conclusions were offered about the patient's perceptions of her mother and women, of her home, her self image, and her interpersonal relationships. There was a substantial degree of agreement between these conclusions from the dream association technique and the views of the patient's therapist.

The patient responded to the procedure by saying, "Well, it's sort of a diagnosis of myself through construction of sentences and words. It's like a picture of myself that I have of myself—that I would like to keep to myself . . . I don't like the picture I've painted of myself, I'm uncomfortable with it . . . I'm sure it's the truth, but you know, you just don't like to see it in blue and white." The investigator used a blue pen.[11]

Chapter 15

The Dream Incident Technique

The *Dream Incident Technique* is a method of dream analysis. It is an association technique following upon the basic idea of Freud. Whereas Freud argued for totally free association, leaving the burden of interpretation up to the skill of the analyst, the *Dream Incident Technique* (DIT) is more circumscribed in its procedures and can be used with as much objectivity as any personality test.

Like Freud's procedure of free association, the DIT begins with the manifest content of the dream. The objective is to unscramble the real events that were involved in the formation of the dream. We assume that dreams are constructed from past experiences (things that actually happened to oneself, things that one has read, heard about, seen on television or in the movies). In dreams, these raw ingredients are transformed into minidramas. If one can isolate the ingredients that went into the dream—particularly those events which involve one's own past behavior and social interactions—one can then take a close look at these events and see what was going on. In these events, what were you trying to accomplish? Was there strife or conflict? Was it a pleasant memory? Was it a situation of better times, now lost? One could ask many questions, but looking at the meaning of these real experiences (the ingredients underlying the dream) should tell you something about the meaning of the dream itself.

The Dream Incident Technique specifically addresses this problem. The technique is designed to isolate past experiences related to the dream and to examine their meaning.

The basic assumptions of the technique are that (1) dreams deal with unresolved problems—areas of current tension—and that (2) associations can help identify the nature of these tensions. As we indicated, these assumptions generally follow from the psychoanalytic school, though our use of associations is very different. The technique assumes that current tensions may deal with many facets of daily life—problems relating to achievement, self-assertion, aggression, love, play, etc. The technique places no special emphasis on sexual tensions, though measures of these are included. The Dream Incident Technique assumes that dream content is generated in large part by past incidents that happened to the person, and that associations of this genre would be the most useful to obtain. Finally, the technique assumes that these associated incidents can be rated by the dreamer to assess their meaning. These ratings are then treated like psychological test data, giving us information about the kinds of tensions currently pressing the individual.

But all of this is somewhat abstract. Let's look at how the technique actually works.

The first problem is to obtain a dream specimen. Preferably one would obtain this with the aid of a sleep laboratory, but in the absence of this, we have used the following instructions:

> In the morning, as soon as you wake up, try to recall whether you dreamt during the night. If you did dream, and remember the dream, write it down immediately, as recall for dreams tends to become poorer later in the day. If you had several dreams during the night, just write down the one you remember best.

The second step is to obtain the dream-related incidents (associations). To do this, we used the following instructions:

> 1. Read your dream over. Think about it for a while. Then go back and read over the sentences of the dream, very slowly, one by one. Then relax, and let your mind drift freely over the dream thoughts.
> 2. As you think about the dream, do any incidents or events which *actually* happened to you come to mind? These could be incidents from any time in your life, but it must be something you, yourself, were involved in. Participants in the incident might have included members of your family, friends, chance acquaintances, or perhaps no one other than yourself. Some incidents may come up which seem directly connected to the dream. Other incidents may pass through your mind that don't seem too related to the dream. However, we are definitely interested in *all* incidents that come into your mind while you think about the dream.
> 3. If an incident occurs to you, write it down on one of the sheets provided. Write down as many different incidents as occur to you – up to a total of seven incidents for the dream. Write each incident on a separate sheet.
> 4. When you have trouble thinking of incidents, try reading the dream over again. You may read the dream over as many times as you wish.
> 5. If fifteen minutes go by and you can think of no new incidents, stop.

On the small sheet used for writing down the incident, we added the following note:

> Be sure to describe only *specific events*, something that happened at a given time and place.
> In your description, please include where the incident occurred, approximately when it happened, and what you and the other participants were doing.

Each completed incident sheet is then attached in a blank space on a specially devised form. On the form, there is a series of items. A few of the items are presented below to give an idea as to what they are like:

> To share an experience with a friend.
> To go to new places: to do new things.
> To give comfort, sympathy.
> To excel; to attain a high standard.
> To have my ideas, my way of doing things prevail.
> To avoid trouble or unpleasantness.
> To feel close to someone of the opposite sex.
> To resist attempts by others to tell me what to do.
> To express anger; to tell someone off.
> To have a good time; to enjoy myself.
> To fulfill an obligation; to live up to a commitment or promise.
> To attract attention; to be noticed, talked about.

The directions on the form stated that this was a list of hopes, wishes or desires that most people felt at one time or another. The subject was asked to think about the incident described. If he felt any of these hopes or wishes before or during the incident, he was to check the item.

When all the incidents have been rated, the data can be scored using specially developed keys. The keys were developed with the aid of computers and factor analysis, the data analysis procedure mentioned earlier. The scores indicate tension levels in various areas of interpersonal relations, and it becomes possible to compare the scores of an individual with the average scores of his peers.

The DIT as used to date includes measures of tensions relating to:

affection	(seeking love and warmth from others)
achievement	(the desire to attain, produce, excel)
dominance	(to control, exert power and influence)
autonomy	(to act as one wishes, to exert one's individuality, to be free from control)
adventure	(to seek different and unusual experiences)
sex	(to experience erotic physical contact and sensations)
aggression	(feelings of anger, acts of violence, verbal hostility)
social recognition	(being noticed and admired by others)
nurturance	(giving comfort and emotional support)
play	(social and recreational enjoyments)
infavoidance	(avoidance of embarrassment and social unpleasantness)
guilt avoidance	(behaving according to conscience, acting responsibly)

These concepts are based on Murray's system of personality description which is detailed in his book *Explorations in Personality* (New York: Oxford University Press, 1938). We have been working on an updated version of the DIT, adding several broader measures such as tensions relating to emotional closeness and self-actualization.

To illustrate how the Dream Incident Technique works, we will present a few cases. The subjects were all attending a college on the East Coast. I never met any of the subjects personally. The interpretations advanced about the persons and their problems are based on the Dream Incident Technique, some questionnaire data and scores on the Edwards Personal Preference Schedule.

The first case, Betty, is a twenty-one-year-old woman. At the time our data were obtained, Betty was a college student in her junior year. From our questionnaire data, we learned she was an active person who played tennis, swam, bowled, and hiked. Betty had a half dozen close friends, including a special boyfriend, whom she dated frequently. They had a warm, affectionate relationship that included frequent sexual experiences. She was active socially, often going to parties. She was elected chairman of an organization. While she could feel irritated at people, she was not inclined to express anger openly or get into arguments. Betty's grades in school were average. She lived at home with her parents. Her scores on a personality test (the Edwards Personal Preference Schedule, a test that measures the strength of various personality needs—as one views oneself) indicated that she was in the average range for all of the personality needs assessed on the scale. She evidenced no unusually strong needs. Betty reported the following dream:

> I asked my mother for some log paper and we were in a room similar to her bedroom but not in our house. Somehow I was next walking across my grammar school playground and met three bridesmaids dressed in pink crepe and the maid of honor in a mulberry empire dress with a tweed skirt. The dresses were long. Then I came around the corner now by the bookstore wearing a long dress and passed the bridesmaids and had trouble with my dress—I kept stepping into the hem. As I passed the girls, one of my sister's friends called me corpulent. I went into the theater with a gentleman—my brother—who would not give me my beaded purse which he said contained his driver's license. I was angry with him and walked down the hall to the kitchen and took something from the old fashioned refrigerator. (The theater had given way to the old house I was in before.) I talked to my mother about "my brother"—he was getting married and my parents weren't at the wedding. I didn't go either; I was mad at him about my purse and wanted to work on my graph. Next I was alone with "my brother" who was no longer my brother, his new wife had gone away and we were talking. We talked about his going to bed with me before his wife came back and I laughed and said something about the fact that she wouldn't appreciate it. During our conversation I was combing my hair and he was sewing; at the end of the conversation I noticed that it was my pink nightgown that he was sewing on. Then I woke up.

In thinking about the dream content, Betty reported the following incidents:

The night before I went to put on my pink nightgown and discovered that I still hadn't mended it. It has been quite a while since I tore it. I don't remember when or how it was torn. I went to put it on in my bedroom and it was late. I didn't wear a nightgown that night.

In June of this year a friend of the family got married and her maid of honor was a girl who I had gone to grammar school with. This girl had moved away to New York some years ago. At the wedding she wore pale green or pale lavender. (At first I thought green—but on thinking, I believe it was lavender.) She looked very attractive but we hardly spoke to each other. The wedding was at the chapel.

I bought some log paper to write up my physiology laboratory report during that day. I bought it in the afternoon in the pharmacy near the campus. I didn't like the log paper. The color was a displeasing avocado green.

A friend's husband picked me up after work one evening and took me out for a cocktail. When he was driving me home, he decided to take a ride. He stopped the car where there was a nice view and we talked. He thought I was rather sexy and would make a good marriage partner. He suggested I should relieve my tensions. Later he kissed me and tried to run his hands over me. I was irritated and told him to take me home. This occurred in June.

I went to the city with my sister and her friend (who called me corpulent) to the flower show last month and then went to dinner. The waiter walked out of the restaurant and escorted me in; he gave us outstanding service. In the meantime, I was giving my sister's friend some advice about her boyfriend and every time we were discussing something private, the French waiter would come over and ask if there was something he could help me with.

Four years ago I was at the annual ball. I was wearing a candlelight colored ball gown which is my favorite. My hair looked quite dark and I had used different make-up than usual. I attracted a lot of attention.

Betty rated each incident on our cheklist sampling different personality needs. When we summed her responses to the several incidents and averaged them, we derived a percentage figure which we could compare with our case file of other students. The results are interesting, suggesting a compensating kind of dream in the Jungian tradition. Her dreams seem to be calling attention to those areas of her life she was not effectively dealing with. In real life, Betty has warm and affectionate relationships, and her dream incident score in this area was low, indicating little psychic pressure in this regard. Likewise for her needs for play and adventure; in real life Betty is very active and her dream incident scores are again low. In her behavior, she is not inclined to express anger, and her dream incident score for aggression was high, suggesting unresolved problems here. The same was true for autonomy. Her dream incident scores indicate she is experiencing conflict about her level of freedom. This might possibly reflect problems living at home with parents and siblings. Finally, Betty's grades in real life are only fair, while her dream incident scores for achievement are high.

This technique of dream analysis, then, yields a different conclusion from the one that might be drawn simply on the basis of the manifest content. The manifest content included a strong emphasis on sexuality. The Dream Incident

Technique suggested that concerns about personal freedom, anger, and achievement were motivations underlying the dream—perhaps even some of its sexual content. It may be that the sexual content served as a vehicle for the working out of these other needs.

The dream analysis of our first case, Betty, appeared to show rather clear evidence of compensation. The analysis of our second case, Sheila, also points this way, though perhaps less clearly. Compensation here is more in the order of sharpening what appears to be an already reasonably well-balanced life style. Sheila is a twenty-one-year-old woman, also a college junior. Unlike Betty, Sheila was doing very well in school; her grade average was B-plus and was getting still higher. A professor had recently taken special notice of some of her work. Sheila lived in a rooming house that included both young men and women residents. Perhaps it was the nature of this environment that led her to report she had many close friends and frequent casual dates, though relatively few formal dates. She had one boyfriend she preferred, but described the relationship as friendly rather than warm and affectionate. There appeared to be only limited sexual contact in the relationship.

During the past year, Sheila seemed active physically, playing tennis, bowling, and doing some swimming and hiking as well.

Her scores on the Edwards Personal Preference Schedule indicated that she saw herself as a person who wanted to be in the center of attention and admired by others, and who also had strong needs to be nurturant (comforting and sympathetic) to others.

Sheila reported the following dream:

> I was wandering about some dockyards (I think someone was with me) looking at crates. I was looking for arms shipments to the wrong countries. There was a crate for Yemen and I commented to a man (who was now accompanying me) that wasn't Yemen a small country on the western tip of the Arabian Peninsula. He agreed that it was. I think something else was said too. I wanted to know what was in the crate without having to ask. Turned out that it supposedly contained fruit. Then I was concerned that it would spoil. There was also a bunch of grapes going somewhere but they were in the shade and so wouldn't spoil. Good. Then the scene switched to the produce section of a supermarket. I was wandering about with an old lady. There were some peas (in pods) and a man was eating them. I wanted some too, but didn't take any. Then I was alone. There was some sort of game played with the customers. Various numbers were called out over the loudspeaker and pasted on a bulletin board. If you had these numbers, you won. I didn't know how you acquired these numbers (I had none) nor what the prize was. I didn't win. Then there was a mass exodus of people. Don't know where they went, but I went somewhere too, with or without the crowd, I don't know, and I entered a rather large modern building—somehow connected with the market. In a rather huge room were just a few people and we were all going to have drinks, so we sat around a table and at one end was my English professor, an elderly man. Then something was said about saying grace (the drinks had been poured), and I inquired as to the propriety of saying grace for drinks. The professor said that one definitely should. The alarm rang.

Sheila wrote out the following incidents when reflecting upon her dream:

Last fall I went on a skin-diving trip. I had a wretched trip out, for I got horribly seasick even before we got out of the bay. There were four other people on the trip—two men and two boys. I got over being sick after I got into the water and had a good time. One of the fellows saw a shark. We scooted back to the boat, but soon went back in. On the way back, I didn't get sick. The owner even let me steer the boat.

When I was in first grade, I was very fond of my teacher and she of me. I was also very fond of avocados and one day she gave me a whole avocado. Happiness is having one whole avocado of your very one. I think it was that day that I kissed her goodbye and called her mommy—I'm not sure. My girl friend teased me about it later, but not meanly.

One night not long ago, a friend (boy) and I went to have dinner with a woman who used to live with us (boarding house). We brought the wine and stuff for making tacos. Before dinner we had sherry and yakked and then proceeded to construct the tacos—much fun. For dessert there was pie and ice cream. I had too much wine and was slightly drunk—more so than the other two. We left around midnight.

When I was quite young, I stole a candy bar from a supermarket and felt guilty about it for years. A little later I had every intention of snitching a bag of peanuts, but a checker came over and asked me what I was doing. Waiting for my mother. Sure. I never tried anything again.

About three months ago, two fellows, another girl and I went downtown to a movie. During intermission they had a bingo game. None of us won anything. Playing was kind of fun, but watching everyone else in the place was more interesting. Oh—the movies were good.

Sometime last school year—mid-winter I think—I went to see an old teacher/friend whom I hadn't seen in a couple of years. I met her at school and we went to her place, where we chatted over a drink for forty-five minutes or so when I left, so that she could get ready to go out somewhere.

Her DIT ratings showed a very high score for affection, and high scores for adventure, play and achievement and social recognition. In interpreting these scores, we remember that she had no shortage of casual dates, but did not have a close relationship with the boy she liked. The incident recalled about her teacher and the avocado in her early years further suggests this lack in the affectional area, and the possibility of it being longstanding.

The high dream incident scores for adventure and play suggest that her casual college-based activities are not sufficient for her needs in this area. The need to experience new things with more sense of excitement comes through in the dream analysis.

The most puzzling feature of her DIT profile is the high need for achievement. This seems inconsistent with a compensation theory, because she is already doing extremely well in school. Could she be driven by a compulsive need to achieve? When we look at her Edwards PPS score for achievement, we find it is not unduly high; she does not perceive herself as an achiever.

It seems possible that this achievement tension is not academic in nature, but relates to social relationships—perhaps her needs to be closer to people, which are not being met, or her needs to be admired by them.

We ran an analysis of a second dream on Sheila. The manifest content of the dream was quite different, but the patterns for the dream incident scores were very similar. Once again, there were high scores for affection, adventure, play, and achievement. These consistent findings, then, suggest that while Sheila's life style seems ostensibly balanced with academic success and much sociality, there are important missing ingredients—perhaps relating to the intensity or vitality of her experiences.

Our third case is Doris, a twenty-year-old sophomore. Doris is more of a "loner" than the first two subjects. She had recently traveled abroad alone. She is less intimate with her friends, not involved in organizations, not much given to parties. Her interest and affection seem to be completely concentrated on one person: her fiancé, Bob. At the time the dream was reported, Bob was away for the summer.

Doris is only a fair student. She has only a modest interest in athletics, and no particular hobbies. She is a more assertive person than the previous subjects. She "gets mad" when irritated, disagrees with her professors in class, and has tried to get school requirements waived. Her self-perception on the Edwards test suggests she has rather high needs for autonomy and little need to be dependent on others.

Her dream was as follows:

> Although I can only seem to remember a dream back to the point where I was semi-conscious, I know I was in Montpellier, France, and I was on my way to a voluntary event of some sort. I arrived but they wouldn't let me in because I didn't have my reg-card! from college. I was angry and upset so I left this building and walked right into the adjoining one which "felt" like the home I stayed in in France, but, in actuality, was our apartment here in town. No one there. I tried to take a tranquilizer—couldn't swallow it—tasted horrible. I was falling asleep. I heard a woman come into the other room and lie down, also to sleep. Then I heard a man (my fiancé) in the bathroom taking a shower. I was very upset about my volunteer work rejection. It was raining outside; and I was wearing pants and one of my brother's shirts. I don't remember changing as I was quite dressed up before I fell asleep. I went into the bathroom. He kissed me—our faces were all wet from the shower and steam. He smiled and swatted me on my backside to "go get ready." I was happy again but very cold—the window in our room was open. I woke up, and closed it.

She wrote out these incidents in response to the dream:

> Walking through the streets of Montpellier at the beginning of the dream was quite comparable to a scene in the movie, "The Umbrellas of Cherbourg"—I believe my hair was even combed the same way as the girl's, and I had a trench coat on and it was raining. I saw the movie two or three months ago on T.V. I was in France this August.

Not having my reg. card for school: Last Friday I wasn't allowed to pick up my ushering card, because I didn't have my reg. card. I was quite angry, but not as upset as I was in the dream.

The building I went into to volunteer for work was very similar in furnishings to a house I was in last night on a date with a friend from class. He wasn't there at all, but the furnishings and feelings were much the same. I didn't belong there and was quite uncomfortable.

Taking the tranquilizer: I did take one or two as I was fairly nervous about meeting so many friends and family, but I never had trouble taking it – can't figure out why I'd ever dream this. Perhaps I was a little tense, because so many people were appearing whom I couldn't recognize.

My wearing pants: Quite significant! Ever since I've known this fellow (my fiancé) I've become quite accustomed to wearing only dresses and skirts (and even enjoying it) as he hates pants or bermudas. This is no easy task, but is adhered to strictly in the name of love, but in the dream, I had on my worst pants and old shirt. His kiss was very tender and understanding. He wasn't about to get angry – the swat on my seat was accompanied with one of our affectionate terms and a hearty yell – that I'd better change before we went out, but that I could do and wear what I wanted. This whole scene is very much like how such incidents in our lives go. He teases me, but then all of a sudden takes me tenderly and I'm no longer angry. There was a scene exactly like this, except for the furnishings, in France.

The woman asleep in the other room: His mother whom I was never sure when she'd pop into a room, but we were never bothered by it, just as I wasn't in the dream. The recurrent coughing in the dream (hers) kept reminding me the more awake I became, that I owe her a letter. Also, one evening she allowed us to spend the night together in their home. She was marvelous about it, but was at all times quite audible in the next room.

Cold air through window: The room I stayed in in Reims was always accompanied by a cold blast of air in the morning. I felt I was in this room and could hear French being spoken outside when I woke up.

Doris' dream incident scores are highest in the areas of autonomy and sex. Both of these issues probably reflect strains in her relationship with Bob. It is the all-important relationship, yet is a source of tension. Her normally assertive, independent personality appears to have been blunted somewhat in the relationship. She has had to accommodate herself for the sake of her love, and it has not been easy. Her dreams and associations suggest this struggle, and the difficulties in adjustment she faces.

Our fourth case, Margaret, is a twenty-two-year-old senior. She is an average student academically, but she has a distinct artistic flair. She writes poetry, etches and does other graphic art projects. Margaret is not much for parties, but she likes to camp and hike. She is active in a hiking club; recently she went camping in the mountains. She has a steady boyfriend. Their relationship was described as warm and affectionate on both sides. Her Edwards test profile suggests only one strong need, in the area of autonomy.

The two dreams I have collected from this young woman are very different. One seems to mirror her experiences in the outdoors. The other, which is given below, reflects another aspect of her personality and seems compensatory in that it deals with what for her are unusual issues.

> I dreamed that a very close male friend of mine, the hiking companion I mentioned previously, had been killed in a mountaineering accident. I saw him on the snowfield, just before he went off to do a hard peak. Then for some reason, I had to leave on a trip of some sort, or I could have climbed with him. When I returned from this trip, I saw a newspaper, and the headline mentioned an accident on the mountain he'd been climbing. A friend of mine came up and said, "Don't you know? Tony is dead." I cried and cried. (Really!) But then I had to go and manage his affairs, distributing property to relatives, friends, etc. It was awful. But when I went to his house (apt.) to begin the task, the place wasn't his actual residence at all, but the residence of a painter friend of mine who is now in New York. And the manager had barred and bolted the door, not admitting anyone. Yet I absolutely *had* to get in, to start settling matters. So I broke in, and listed everything, called people, etc. Everyone I called was very nasty to me, asking what right *I* had to be doing this. I went outside when I finished, to sleep in the back of his car (a station wagon). But a lot of rock climbers were out there plotting how to steal the pitons, hammers, carabiners and other climbing equipment he has around. I was very frightened, but too sad to care. I went to "sleep," and the dream ended. I woke up so convinced it was real, I halfway believed he was dead until I heard from him a week later.

The following incidents were written in connection with this dream:

> There have been a lot of deaths in my family and among my friends. In the past six years I have lost my grandfather, an aunt I dearly loved, my step-father (of cancer), my father, and a close girl friend who was decapitated in an auto accident in front of me. I feel pretty shaky about close personal attachments. Also my grandmother could die soon. She is sick and sort of on the verge at all times and my mother suspects she has cancer.
> The stairway and room that appeared in the dream are involved with another person, a close friend who moved away to New York. I have not heard from or about him since (nor did I expect to). But I am very curious as to how he is faring in graduate school. I would like him to succeed; I think he is a talented painter. We were close friends.
> The person involved in the dream has asked me to be executor of his will. I don't like it at all, but I will do it, for a friend. This occurred about one month before this dream. This involved contacting his family, strict Catholics from New England—probably wouldn't approve of me if they knew I existed, and carrying out certain property instructions.

The DIT scores for this dream which stand out are nurturance and guilt avoidance. The nurturant feelings—the desire to care for and protect—are not paramount in her everyday concerns. Her self-perceptions on the Edwards test show this to be an area of little importance for her. But there has been much anguish about recent death, and her sense of concern and desires to help have become more important and are highlighted in the dream analysis.

The guilt avoidance, too, seems to have stemmed from this rash of recent deaths among friends and family members.

Reactions to death are complex, involving not only feelings of loss, but sometimes feelings of self-recrimination. Questions are bound to arise, such as, "Could I have done more?" The dream incidents suggest Margaret may be struggling with such questions.

These cases illustrate the use of the Dream Incident Technique. The examples demonstrate the possible usefulness of the technique as a means of learning more about the concerns of the dreamer. When we begin to add background information about the subject, it becomes possible to advance some clinical interpretations. In some instances we have seen indications of the process Jung termed compensation.

There are a number of technical questions about the procedure which have to be answered. These are questions psychologists pose about any measuring technique. One of these questions has to do with *reliability*. For example, if you took DIT readings one night and you took them again a month later, would you find essentially the same picture or would it be radically different? Since the DIT deals with "current tensions" and these will increase or decrease over time, depending on what happens in one's life, we would not expect perfect correspondence. For example, if a student has a great deal of achievement tension before his exams and gets good grades, his tensions for achievement would probably diminish.

We have made several studies of the consistency of dream incident scores over time, finding that the correlations between scores taken from dreams about six weeks apart were in the moderate (+.5) range. That is to say, there is consistency between DIT readings over time despite the fact that the manifest content of the two dreams used as sources for the scores might be very different.

If we increase the time interval between dreams, we should expect that more events would intervene to alter the picture of current tensions levels. We would therefore expect the DIT correlations between dreams to be somewhat lower. Looking at Dream Incident scores taken at intervals of about nine weeks, we found this to be true.

There is another aspect of reliability that measures the internal consistency of the items making up a scale. We have checked out the consistency of the items in our new version of the DIT. The correlations we obtained were in the .8 to .9 range, indicating the scales are highly reliable.

The other major question concerns the *validity* of the technique. What evidence is there that dream incident scores really provide measures of unresolved problems or areas of tension?

I would like to summarize some of this evidence. Most of the data were collected in studies carried out in collaboration with my colleagues, Drs. Roland Tanck and Arnold Meyersburg.

In one study, we asked students to fill out the Edwards Personal Preference

Schedule. This test includes a measure of one's achievement motivation—that is, how important one feels it is to "achieve" compared to other things one could be doing in life. We also asked students for their recent grade averages—their grade index for the preceding semester. We predicted that students whose motivations to achieve were high and whose actual grades were low would show high achievement tension scores on the DIT. The prediction was borne out, and we replicated this finding in a subsequent study.[1]

The next study included a laboratory experiment. In the study we used a pupilometer, an instrument which repeatedly photographs the pupil of the eye while one looks at a stimulus such as a slide or motion pictures. Dr. Ekard Hess has found that when one looks at an interesting stimulus (e.g., males looking at pictures of nude females) the pupils tend to dilate.[2]

We wondered what would happen if subjects with high DIT scores indicating tension in a given area (such as sex) viewed sexual stimuli while their pupils were being photographed. We hypothesized that their pupils ought to dilate.

We decided to make up some videotapes of scenes depicting several areas measured by the DIT. These scenes would portray sexual, aggressive, affiliative, nurturant, achieving, and dominant behavior. With the help of our colleagues at George Washington University Hospital, David Touch and Carlee Weston, and some students from the university's drama department, we launched into a brief career of television production. For an aggression scene, we televised one girl slapping another one across the face. In another aggressive scene, one of our student actresses was televised looking very grim, holding a pistol in her hand. Our achievement scenes included a young woman in a cap and gown receiving a diploma. One of our nurturance scenes was of a woman comforting a crying child. Our erotic scenes included a young woman looking through an illustrated sex manual, and a man and woman (in apparent nudity) caressing each other in bed.

When we finished making up these tapes, we showed the scenes (each ten seconds in length) on a television monitor. Each scene was preceded by ten seconds of blank material.

Subjects for our study were undergraduate students. While the students viewed these scenes, their pupils were photographed by Tanck's camera. When the viewing was over, we asked each student to look at still shots representing the various scenes they had just watched. The students were asked to judge how much they had felt stimulated by the scene as they watched it. Interestingly, there was no relationship whatever between the subjects' estimates of how much they had been stimulated and the actual dilation of their pupils. The subjects were not conscious of their physiological reactions.[3]

We related the dream incident scores and the pupillary responses to the videotapes. As predicted, our subjects with DIT scores indicating higher sex tension were more likely to show pupillary dilations when viewing the sex-related scenes. The same finding was true for dream incident scores for nurturance; those with higher scores in this area dilated more to the mother and child scene. The findings for achievement were also positive, but fell just short of statistical significance.

The findings for aggression, however, were surprising. Our subjects with dream incident scores indicating unresolved problems relating to aggression did not react with pupillary dilations; instead there was a very strong tendency for these subjects to contract their pupils while viewing the aggressive scenes. It seemed like a defensive reaction, like turning off the stimulus.[4]

We had also given our subjects the Edwards Personal Preference Schedule, measuring psychological needs based on self-perceptions. This test has nothing to do with dreams. The EPPS measurements for achievement, sex, nurturance, etc., did not relate to pupillary activity. Rather, the EPPS correlated with our postexperimental assessments of how much the person *thought* he had been stimulated.

These results are interesting in that they suggest that a measure based on dream associations, presumably linked to materials below the level of conscious awareness, correlated significantly with an unconscious measure—pupillary reactions. At the same time, a personality test using as its base conscious self-perceptions predicted only the postexperimental conscious evaluations.[5]

One, of course, has to be cautious in interpreting these results. We would like to see the study replicated by other investigators.

In another study, we looked at the possible relationship of dream incident scores and certain kinds of physical symptoms that are believed to be tension-related. Our rationale was that if the DIT does indeed measure tensions, or something closely related, then persons scoring high on these measures should be more vulnerable to stress-related symptoms. We further felt that persons who had such *high DIT scores and did not handle stress well* would be the most likely to report such symptoms.

We collected DIT data on students and also gave them the Minnesota Multiphasic Personality Inventory (MMPI), a widely used psychological test which contains a scale called "Ego Strength." Ths Ego Strength measure was used as a rough index of a person's ability to cope with stress.

As we planned on using a college-age sample, we selected three DIT measures which we felt would be highly relevant in this group: achievement, autonomy, and sex. College students frequently experience problems in all of these areas.

To obtain our medical data, several senior medical students at the university were enlisted to interview our subjects, using a standard history-taking procedure. The medical students inquired about a variety of current complaints, such as headaches, weakness, dizziness, and digestive problems.

In analyzing the data, we found pretty much what we had predicted. Subjects who showed high dream incident scores in any of the three areas studied (achievement, autonomy, and sex), and who also showed less capability of dealing with stress, reported a higher number of physical complaints.

We subsequently found in our analyses that tensions in the areas of autonomy and sex related to the number of physical complaints, even if we disregarded the measure of the Ego Strength. Tensions relating to autonomy seemed particularly sensitive to health-related measures. We found out that students with unresolved problems relating to autonomy were more likely to visit physicians and use medicines of various kinds.

Tensions relating to autonomy were not only reflected in the presence of physical symptoms, but were also correlated with drug use. We found incident scores for autonomy were associated with increased use of marijuana and hallucinogenics.[6]

We have run additional studies with the Dream Incident Technique. For example, we found that the scores have practically no relationship to the scores of the MMPI, a test that points up neurotic and psychotic tendencies.[7] Judging from these results, tensions indicated by the DIT for the most part seem to fall within what we think of as the normal range of human problems, not the unusual.

One addendum to this, however, seems worth noting. We found a tendency for people with high dream incident scores to be somewhat more depressed in the way they respond to projective techniques. We used the Thematic Apperception Test, a projective test consisting of a series of pictures usually portraying one or two persons in various scenes. For example, one picture is of a pensive-looking boy with a violin. The subject given this test is asked to make up stories about each picture. These stories are assumed to reflect the person's own emotions and experiences. In our study, we found that stories coming from our subjects with high dream incident scores had a depressed quality to them. Things were sad; they weren't going right; the endings were bleak.[8] Since both the DIT and the Thematic Apperception Test presumably reflect a person's experience, we might anticipate some relationship. In this case, it seems to be a relationship of unresolved problems suggested by the dreams and sadness suggested by the pictures.

Chapter 16

Using Dreams in Your Life

One of the basic ideas advanced in this book is that dreams are a source of information about an individual's concerns or problems that have not been fully resolved in waking behavior. If this assumption is true, then a person who understands his dreams should be in a better position to take actions to deal with his problems. The possible rewards are less tension, increased self-understanding, and from this, we would hope, more satisfying interpersonal relationships.

It is this assumption—that dreams are a key in unlocking unresolved problems—that has led to the use of dream analysis as a technique in psychotherapy. We have seen how in psychoanalytic practice, free association to dreams is used to uncover unconscious pressures believed to be crucial in the formation of uncomfortable and disabling symptoms. We have also seen how in Gestalt therapy, acting out the dream is used to help the patient to get more in touch with various aspects of himself. Dream interpretation even has a place in group therapy where the focus may be on interpersonal relations, rather than on intrapsychic conflicts. Interestingly, one of the dreams that is sometimes reported in group therapy sessions is a dream about the group itself.

In a limited sense, the therapist who utilizes dream analysis has a function something like the diviners of ancient time who were said to have the skill to understand the meaning of dreams and their implications for the life of the dreamer. Both the diviner and the therapist are professionals equipped with theory and technique. The modern therapist, obviously, holds a considerable advantage over the ancient diviner of dreams, as he has a large store of scientific information available to draw on in shaping his ideas.

Dream interpretation, of course, is but a small facet of psychotherapy. Traditionally, psychotherapy is a long-term process that builds up and maintains a special relationship between therapist and patient, a relationship that facilitates the working through of emotional problems. If you merely want a dream interpreted, you do not ring the doorbell of a psychotherapist and say, "Tell me what this means," as you might have with the diviners of old.

What about the person who is curious about his dreams—wants to know what they may indicate about his life—yet has no interest or need to undergo therapy? What does he do to learn the meaning of his dreams? There are psychics, fortune tellers and others claiming to have knowledge of dream interpretation. There are friends who may have read a bit of Freud and may feel they know more than they do. I might also mention that there are "dream books" which offer translations of the meaning of dreams. In my view, these books represent the high point of absurdity in dream analysis.

Back in the 1940s, Harry Weiss rummaged through libraries and antiquarian collections, discovering a wide variety of dream books. There was an Oriental dream book, an Italian dream book (which claimed to be the greatest authority on dreams ever published), *The Complete Fortune-teller and Dream Book*, *The Witch Doctor's Illustrated Dream Book*, the *Universal Dream Dictionary*, and one written by King John of the Gypsies.

According to one book, if you dreamt of money, you were due for a loss. If you dreamt of hanging, you would become rich and respected. According to another book, if you dreamt you heard a clock strike, you would be speedily married. One book stated that dreaming of knives foretold lawsuits, disgrace, and an unfaithful, shrewish wife.

If you were the betting type, there were dream books designed especially for you, for it was assumed that dreams were linked to numbers. According to one book, if you dreamt about beans, your lucky numbers were 72, 18, and 11. Five years later, a different book came out, suggesting what they really had in mind was 2, 20, and 25. This was later changed to 3, 1, and 62, and still later to 2, 4, 11, and 20. Fortunately, dreams about beans are rare, and probably few fortunes were lost trying to keep abreast of the ever-changing lucky number.

If one is inclined to distrust such advice relating to dream interpretations, then one is thrown on one's own resources and possibly some books from the library. One might ask at this point whether it is a good idea for the individual to try to understand his dreams without the assistance of a trained psychotherapist. My answer is that I would prefer to see dream analysis undertaken with the assistance of someone skilled. Not only does one have the advantage of drawing on professional training, one may also cross-check his own ideas with another's and may avoid unwarranted conclusions. However, the question as to whether it is a good idea for people to interpret their dreams may be irrelevant. People have been doing it for thousands of years and will continue to do so. Therefore, some guidance may be in order.

The first and most important guideline I would offer is to maintain a healthy skepticism about what people say or have written about dreams. If someone offers you an explanation for your dream, don't believe it without some reasonable evidence that it is so. Much nonsense has been written about dreams. It is one thing to speculate and another to provide evidence; the two should not be confused.

Secondly, it is important to obtain good data from yourself. Dreams differ from night to night. Rather than depend on a single dream, it makes sense to collect a series of dreams. With a number of dreams, you can look for common features and recurring ideas. You may possibly discover some revealing patterns.

To obtain the most accurate data, it makes sense to write down or tape record your dream just as soon as you awaken. Cohen's study of the effects of early morning interference clearly indicates how much even trivial distractions may weaken dream recall. In my own initial experiments with the Dream Incident Technique, I found a tape recorder very helpful.

Many people have difficulty remembering dreams and ask how they can improve their ability to do so. One thing that might help is making a systematic effort in this regard. Put a tape recorder or notebook by your bedside and make a commitment to yourself that you are going to try to recall a dream in the morning. Keep this up for a couple of weeks and you should get some results. I recommend setting up a systematic sleep log or diary, with an entry for each day of the week where you can record whether you recalled a dream. The following diary, similar to the dream logs used in research on dream recall, may be helpful. Just place a check in each box where appropriate; describe the dreams you recall on a separate sheet. (Note: the diary page shown should of course be extended to the end of the month; space limitations here required that we show only a portion.)

Month _____

Day of Month	1	2	3	4	5	6	7	8	9	10	11	12	13	14
Did not recall having a dream														
Remembered dreaming, but could not recall details enough to describe														
Dream recalled— described on a separate sheet														

The other component of a systematic effort to recall dreams I mentioned was commitment. This is a reflection of your level of interest in dreams and your desire to find out what they might show about yourself, your needs and your problems. Motivation or commitment, of course, is an individual matter, but it can make a difference in your ability to recall dreams.

Dr. Henry Reed has gone a step further in the effort to improve memory for dreams. He actually organized a course to help people try to remember dreams. The course included not only the elements of commitment and effort, but readings and discussions as well. The course seemed effective. The students' evaluations indicated that the quality of dream recall was improved. There was increased visual detail, more memory for color, more auditory recall, and more report of emotion.[1]

Another demonstration of how being motivated can help recall dreams was provided by Drs. David Redfering and Jack Keller. Upon questioning their students before the experiment, they found that on the average, the students felt they recalled only three to four dreams a month. The experimenters then gave the students some special instruction sheets. The instruction sheet was partly motivational, emphasizing the value of remembering dreams, and partly informational, telling about the capacity to recall dreams. The experimenters also provided a log on which to keep a record of the number of dreams re-corded. For further encouragement, subjects were telephoned once a week and given a pep talk "to keep at it." The results were dramatic. The students reported they recalled more than one dream a night.[2]

A third guideline is not to take dreams literally. Dreams are constructed out of past experiences and what one reads and sees. What emerges is a produc-tion the mind has pieced together. You may not have done or may never do what is depicted in your dream. An acquaintance of mine was once troubled by homosexual dreams. He had always been heterosexual and as far as I know continues to be so. Whatever the meaning of the dreams were, they did not portend that he was about to engage in homosexuality.

When it comes to the time to interpret the dream, one may go through three processes or stages. I would call these stages association, integration, and confirmation. The first stage, association, is a means to uncover the network of experiences that the dream is based upon. One may try Freud's technique of free associating—taking each element of the dream one at a time—and let-ting one's mind drift over whatever thoughts emerge, letting the chain of ideas develop; or one might utilize the instructions for association we developed for the Dream Incident Technique. As a beginning point, I would suggest using the DIT instructions, for we have found with over two hundred subjects that the procedure can be used fairly easily. Moreover, you can be relatively more certain that the associated incidents have a direct connection with the dream.

Once you have written out some of the asociations to the dream and have developed some idea of the kind of experiences that were drawn on in con-structing the dream, the next step is asking *why*. Why were these particular ex-periences selected? What does this tell you about your current life? Or stated another way, does this point to any deficits in your activities, interpersonal relations, or overall life style?

This comparison of the dream and its associated experiences with your current life situation is what I called *integration*. It is working back and forth between the dream and the experiences underlying it and your present situation, looking for similarities and differences. Perhaps something has changed. Perhaps something has gone out of your life. Is the dream pointing to any deficits, or as Jung conceived it, imbalances?

Your efforts at integrating the facts of your present life as you see them with the experiences evoked by the dream may lead you to a hypothesis that some aspects of your life could stand sharpening up. These aspects may deal with your work or school situation, with the important interpersonal relationships in your life, with unmet needs for diversion or recreation, with problems relating to the expression of your feelings of anger or love, or with the need to more fully express yourself in life. Deficits or problems in any of these areas may be suggested by your dream analysis.

I used the word hypothesis to describe the result of your attempt to contrast the dream-related materials with your current life experiences. A hypothesis is an educated guess; it is far from a statement of fact. In science, a hypothesis may be confirmed by setting up careful studies using controls and objective measurements. The hypothesis you derive from your dream analysis cannot be confirmed or discounted by such experiments. Confirmation cannot be as clear-cut in everyday experience.

One source of support for your hypothesis may come from additional dreams and associated experiences which lead to the same general conclusion. It is also possible to see if the notions you develop about yourself make sense in the light of your daily activities. Basically, this is simply taking a look at what you are doing and experiencing in the light of your hypothesis and seeing where and when it seems to explain things—and where it does not. If your hypothesis makes no sense, forget it, or at least put it on the back burner. On the other hand, if your hypothesis seems supported by your observation and experience, it may be a useful starting point from which to consider adjustments in your life pattern.

As a final word, I urge caution in both trying and using dream analysis. Whatever conclusions you come to should always be viewed as tentative. Acting on the basis of erroneous ideas about oneself can do mischief not only to oneself but to others as well. With this proviso, I close with an invitation and a warm welcome to the fascinating realm of dreams!

Notes

Chapter 1. *A Look at Dreams in the Ancient World and Primitive Cultures*

1. Penelope's dreams of the eagle and the geese occur toward the conclusion of the *Odyssey*, shortly before the slaying of the suitors. Homer, *The Odyssey of Homer*. See trans. by S.H. Butcher and A. Lang (New York: Macmillan, 1930), pages 301–302.

2. *The Odyssey*, page 302.

3. Homer, *The Iliad of Homer*. See the translation by E. Rees (New York: Modern Library, Random House, 1963), page 23.

4. *The Odyssey*, page 306. This dream of Penelope brings to mind Freud's theory that wishes underlie dreams. See Chapter 2 of this book.

5. Aeschylus, *The Libation Bearers*, in D. Grene, and R. Lattimore (eds.), *The Complete Greek Tragedies*, Vol. 1 (Chicago: University of Chicago Press, 1953), page 112.

6. *The Libation Bearers*, page 113.

7. M.G. Papageorgiou, "Incubation as a form of psychotherapy in the case of ancient and modern Greece," *Psychotherapy and Psychosomatics*, 1975, **26**, pages 35–38.

8. S. Cohen, "Aristedes: A second century case report," *Psychosomatics*, 1972, **13**, pages 200–202. See in particular page 201.

9. Numbers 12: 5–6 (Revised Standard Version).

10. Numbers 12: 7–8.

11. The dialogue dream of Abimelech is related in Genesis 20: 3–7. Abimelech is warned not to approach Sarah, the wife of Abraham. Abimelech replies that he did not know she was Abraham's wife, but was told she was his sister. The dream of Solomon is in 1 Kings 3: 5–14. In this dream Solomon is asked what he wishes God to give him and replies that he desires an understanding mind with which to govern.

12. In Jacob's dream (Genesis 31: 11–13) Jacob is told by an angel to return to the land of his birth. Laban (Genesis 31: 24) is told not to say a word to Jacob, good or bad.

13. These dreams of Joseph which provoked the anger of his brothers are related in Genesis 37: 5–10.

14. The fulfillment of Joseph's prophetic dreams is related in Genesis 42 and specifically in Genesis 42:6.

15. Nebuchadnezzar's dreams are related in Daniel 2: 31–35. Daniel's interpretation is in 2: 36–45.

16. The second dream, Daniel's interpretation and the king's subsequent misfortune are related in Daniel 4: 4–33. Daniel foretold that the king would be driven from the company of men and would live with the beasts of the field. The Bible relates that in twelve months, the prophecy was borne out.

17. A.L. Oppenheim, "Mantic dreams in the Ancient Near East," in G.E. von Grunebaum and R. Caillois (eds.), *The Dream and Human Societies* (Berkeley: University of California Press, 1966). See pages 347–349.

18. Oppenheim, page 347.
19. Oppenheim, page 346.
20. This tale is one of many fascinating accounts collected by Herodotus during his travels and researches. Herodotus: *The Persian Wars* (New York, Modern Library, Random House, 1942), pages 20–23.
21. *The Persian Wars*, pages 60–73.
22. M.L. Kurland, "Oneiromancy: An historical review of dream interpretation," *American Journal of Psychotherapy*, 1972, **26,** page 412. The idea is suggestive of Freud's theories (see Chapter 2 of this book).
23. G.M. Foster, "Dreams, character, and cognitive orientation in Tzintzuntzan," *Ethos*, 1973, **1,** page 109.
24. Foster, pages 110–111.
25. Foster, page 111.
26. S.G. Lee, "Social influences in Zulu dreaming," *Journal of Social Psychology*, 1958, **47,** pages 265–283. See page 266 for his observations on the gender and sexual orientation of dream diviners.
27. Lee, page 268.
28. V. Crapanzano, "Saints, Jnun, and dreams: An essay in Moroccan ethnopsychology," *Psychiatry*, 1975, **38,** pages 145–159. See page 148.
29. Crapanzano, page 149.
30. See Crapanzano, page 147, for a more detailed account of 'A'isha Qandisha.
31. Crapanzano, page 148.
32. Crapanzano, page 149.
33. E.E. Bourguignon, "Dreams and dream interpretation in Haiti," *American Anthropologist*, 1954, **56,** pages 262–268.
34. Bourguignon, page 268.
35. See J. Piaget, *The Child's Conception of the World* (New York: Harcourt, Brace, 1929). In Chapter 6, Piaget presents many illustrations showing changes in children's concepts of dreaming as they mature intellectually. Piaget distinguishes between three stages: (1) the dream comes from outside the body and is a real external event; (2) the dream arises in our thought, but still is external; and (3) the dream is internal and arises internally.
36. M. Laurendeau and A. Pinard, *Causal Thinking in the Child* (New York: International Universities Press, 1962).
37. R.A. Shweder and R.A. LeVine, "Dream concepts of Hausa children: A critique of the 'doctrine of invariant sequence' in cognitive development," *Ethos*, 1975, **3,** pages 209–230. See pages 219–220.
38. Shweder and LeVine, page 222.

Chapter 2. Some Modern Theories of Dreaming

1. S. Freud, *The Interpretation of Dreams* (New York: Basic Books, 1955). This book, Freud's major statement on dreams, was first published at the turn of the twentieth century. The quotation describing the dream censor is on pages 143–144.
2. The *dreamwork*, Freud's name for the process that transfers unconscious ideas into dream content, occupies a key position in Freud's theory of dreams. Freud discusses the dreamwork in detail in Chapter 6 of *The Interpretation of Dreams*, describing the various devices used by the dreamwork, and illustrating these devices with discussions of dreams.
3. See pages 350–384 of *The Interpretation of Dreams* for Freud's treatment of symbols in dreams.

4. The idea of *manifest* and *latent*, or observable and hidden, is an important idea in Freudian psychoanalysis and has been utilized by theorists in other fields as well. Sociologist Robert K. Merton used these terms in discussing the functions of social institutions. See R.K. Merton, *Social Theory and Social Structure* (New York: Free Press, 1957).

5. *The Interpretation of Dreams*, pages 396–397.

6. R.A. Clark, "Jungian and Freudian approach to dreams," *American Journal of Psychotherapy*, 1961, **15**, pages 89–100.

7. See Clark, pages 91–92.

8. C.G. Jung, *The Development of Personality*, Vol. 17 of the *Collected Works*, translated by R.F.C. Hull, Bollingen Series XX (Princeton, N.J.: Princeton University Press, 1954), pages 67–68.

9. See Jung, *Development of Personality*, page 117.

10. See Jung, *Development of Personality*, page 59.

11. See Jung, *Development of Personality*, page 100.

12. See Jung, *Development of Personality*, page 103.

13. See Jung, *Development of Personality*, page 157.

14. See Jung, *Development of Personality*, page 163.

15. H.L. Ansbacher and R.R. Ansbacher (eds.), *The Individual Psychology of Alfred Adler* (New York: Basic Books, 1956). See pages 359–360.

16. See Ansbacher and Ansbacher, page 360.

17. See Ansbacher and Ansbacher, pages 362–363.

18. See Ansbacher and Ansbacher, page 360.

19. J. Dallett, "Theories of dream function," *Psychological Bulletin*, 1973, **79**, pages 408–416. See page 409 for discussion of these themes.

20. L. Breger, I. Hunter, and R.W. Lane, "The effects of stress on dreams," *Psychological Issues*, 1971, **7** (3). See page 11.

21. L. Breger, "Function of dreams," *Journal of Abnormal Psychology Monograph*, 1967, **72** ((5, whole No. 641). See page 19.

22. See Breger, "Function of dreams," page 24.

Chapter 3. *The Scientific Study of Dreaming*

1. See *The Complete Greek Tragedies*, Volume 1, page 47. The context of the passage is the loss caused by Helen's flight to Troy.
There are a number of sources of error contributing to inaccurate data in dream research. Inaccuracies of memory can be a prime source of error, particularly in studies conducted outside the sleep laboratory. In addition, the study of dreams is subject to the problems and errors common to most psychological investigations, which rely on the self-reports of subjects. People differ in the extent to which they are able and willing to reveal sensitive material about themselves. Another source of error that dream studies share with other areas of psychological research is the "demand characteristics" of the experimental situation. Subjects often attempt to do what they can to comply with the perceived intent of the experimental situation, and this attempt could influence what is reported.

2. W. Dement and E.A. Wolpert, "Relationships in the manifest content of dreams occurring on the same night," *Journal of Nervous and Mental Disease*, 1958, **126**, pages 568–578. See page 569.

3. H. Trosman, A. Rechtschaffen, W. Offenkrantz, and E. Wolpert, "Studies in psychophysiology of dreams," *Archives of General Psychiatry*, 1960, **3**, pages 602–607. See page 604.

4. B. Domhoff and J. Kamiya, "Problems in dream content study with objective indicators (III. Changes in dream content throughout the night)," *Archives of General Psychiatry*, 1964, **11**, pages 529–532. See the data presented in the table, page 530.

5. W. Dement, "The physiology of dreaming," doctoral dissertation, University of Chicago, 1958. See page 25.

6. Dement, "The physiology of dreaming," page 23.

7. R. Gardner, Jr., W.I. Grossman, H.P. Roffwarg, and H. Weiner, "The relationship of small limb movements during REM sleep to dreamed limb action," *Psychosomatic Medicine*, 1975, **37**, pages 147–159.

8. F.J. McGuigan and R.G. Tanner, "Covert oral behavior during conversational and visual dreams," *Psychonomic Science*, 1971, **23**, pages 263–264.

9. E. Aserinsky, "Periodic respiratory pattern occurring in conjunction with eye movements during sleep," *Science*, 1965, **150**, pages 763–766. Note in particular page 764.

10. G. Rosenblatt, E. Hartmann, and G.R. Zwilling, "Cardiac irritability during sleep and dreaming," *Journal of Psychosomatic Research*, 1973, **17**, pages 129–134. The authors suggested the possible use of the drug propranolol, a beta blocker, which slows heart rate (see page 133).

11. C. Fisher, J. Gross, and J. Zuch, "Cycle of penile erection synchronous with dreaming (REM) sleep," preliminary report, *Archives of General Psychiatry*, 1966, **15**, pages 29–45. I. Karacan, D.R. Goodenough, A. Shapiro, and S. Starker, "Erection cycle during sleep in relation to dream anxiety," *Archives of General Psychiatry*, 1966, **15**, pages 183–189.

12. W. Dement, "The effect of dream deprivation," *Science*, 1960, **131**, pages 1705–1707. The psychological changes are noted on page 1707.

13. D.A. Chernik, "Effect of REM sleep deprivation on learning and recall by humans," *Perceptual and Motor Skills*, 1972, **34**, pages 283–294. Comparisons between REM-deprived and NREM-deprived subjects are presented on page 292.

14. D. Foulkes, T. Pivik, J.B. Ahrens, and E.W. Swanson, "Effects of 'dream deprivation' on dream content: An attempted cross-night replication," *Journal of Abnormal Psychology*, 1968, **73**, pages 403–415.

15. W.C. Dement, *Some Must Watch While Some Must Sleep* (San Francisco: Freeman, 1974), page 91.

16. Differences between REM and NREM reports are discussed in D. Foulkes, "Theories of dream formation and recent studies of sleep consciousness," *Psychological Bulletin*, 1964, **62**, pages 236–247. Note in particular the discussion beginning on page 240.

17. See Foulkes, "Theories of dream formation," page 241.

18. P. Bakan, "Dreaming, REM sleep and the right hemisphere: A theoretical integration," *Journal of Altered States of Consciousness*, 1977–78, **3**, pages 285–307. See page 286.

19. D.B. Cohen, "Sources of bias in our characterization of dreams," *Perceptual and Motor Skills*, 1977, **45**, page 98.

Chapter 4. *The Manifest Content of Dreams*

1. E.A. Gutheil, *The Handbook of Dream Analysis* (New York: Liveright, 1951). Gutheil's discussion of symbols is in Chapter 3.

The approach to content analysis we described is basically an empirical one. As we indicated, one can also approach the content of analysis of dreams from a particular theoretical position—Freud, Jung, Breger, etc. The choice of a theoretical framework influences what facets of dreams one pays particular attention to.

2. P. Hauri, J. Sawyer, and A. Rechtschaffen, "Dimensions of dreaming: A factored scale for rating dream reports," *Journal of Abnormal Psychology*, 1967, **72,** page 18.

3. See Hauri et al., "Dimensions of dreaming," page 18.

4. See Hauri et al., "Dimensions of dreaming," page 21.

5. See Foster, page 116.

6. These statistics suggest a surprisingly high incidence of dreaming in color. The two studies cited: E. Kahn, W. Dement, C. Fisher, and J.E. Barmack, "Incidence of color in immediately recalled dreams," *Science*, 1962, **137,** pages 1054–1055. See page 1055. J. Herman, H. Roffwarg, and E.S. Tauber, "Color and other perceptual qualities of REM and NREM sleep," *Psychophysiology*, 1968, **5,** page 223.

7. A. Grey and D. Kalsched, "Oedipus east and west: An exploration via manifest dream content," *Journal of Cross-Cultural Psychology*, 1971, **2,** pages 337–352. See page 344.

8. D. Foulkes, J. Larson, E.M. Swanson, and M. Rardin, "Two studies of childhood dreaming," *American Journal of Orthopsychiatry*, 1969, **39,** pages 627–643. See in particular pages 630–631.

9. See Foulkes et al., "Two studies," page 630. Also note D. Foulkes, "Children's dreams: Age changes and sex differences," *Waking and Sleeping*, 1977, **1,** page 172. Typical dream settings for young children are home and recreational settings.

10. R.M. Griffith, O. Miyagi, and A. Tago, "The universality of typical dreams: Japanese vs. Americans," *American Anthropologist*, 1958, **60,** pages 1173–1179. The percent of dreams of various kinds are presented in Table 1, page 1177.

11. See Griffith et al., page 1177. Gutheil's interpretations of typical dreams are found in Chapter 3 of *The Handbook of Dream Analysis*.

12. See Griffith et al., page 1177.

13. See Griffith et al., page 1177.

Chapter 5. *The Stimulus and the Dream*

1. E. Hartmann, "The day residue: time distribution of waking events," *Psychophysiology*, 1968, **5,** page 222.

2. See Hartmann, "The day residue."

3. These data are presented in W. Dement, "The physiology of dreaming," Table 8 (page 40).

4. Dement presents a number of illustrations showing the incorporation of external stimulation into dream content. See "The physiology of dreaming," page 19.

5. R.D. Cartwright, N. Bernick, G. Borowitz, and A. Kling, "Effect of an erotic movie on the sleep and dreams of young men," *Archives of General Psychiatry*, 1969, **20,** pages 262–271. The data presenting actions in the dream incorporated from the film and from the laboratory are reported in Table 6 of the article.

6. D.R. Goodenough, H.A. Witkin, D. Koulack, and H. Cohen, "The effects of stress films on dream effect and on respiration and eye movement activity during rapid-eye-movement sleep," *Psychophysiology*, 1975, **12,** pages 313–320. See page 316.

7. J.M. DeKoninck and D. Koulack, "Dream content and adaptation to a stressful situation," *Journal of Abnormal Psychology*, 1975, **84,** pages 250–260. See in particular page 255.

8. P.C. Walker and R.F.Q. Johnson, "The influence of presleep suggestions on dream content: Evidence and methodological problems," *Psychological Bulletin*, 1974, **81,** pages 362–370. The description of Schroetter's experiments is on pages 362 and 363.

9. C.T. Tart and L. Dick, "Conscious control of dreaming: The posthypnotic dream," *Journal of Abnormal Psychology*, 1970, **76,** pages 304–315.

10. See Walker and Johnson, page 363.

11. R. Ogilvie, K. Busby, L. Costello, and R. Broughton, "The effects of pre-sleep suggestion upon REM sleep," *Canadian Journal of Behavioral Science*, 1975, **7**, pages 139–150. See page 145 for findings on REM density.

12. R. Ogilvie, K. Belicki, and A. Nagy, "Voluntary control of dream affect?" *Waking and Sleeping*, 1978, **2**, pages 189–194. K. Belicki and P. Bowers, "The role of demand characteristics and hypnotic ability in dream change following a presleep instruction," *Journal of Abnormal Psychology*, 1982, **91**, pages 426–432.

13. D. Foulkes, T. Pivik, H.S. Steadman, P.S. Spear, and J.D. Symonds, "Dreams of the male child: An EEG study," *Journal of Abnormal Psychology*, 1967, **72**, pages 457–467. P. Hauri, "Effects of evening activity on subsequent sleep and dreams," doctoral dissertation, University of Chicago, 1967.

14. P.R. Robbins and R.H. Tanck, "Community violence and aggression in dreams: An observation," *Perceptual and Motor Skills*, 1969, **29**, pages 41–42.

15. Y. Rofé and I. Lewin, "The effect of war environment on dreams and sleep habits," *Series in Clinical and Community Psychology: Stress and Anxiety*, 1982, **8**, pages 67–79.

16. See DeKoninck and Koulack, pages 251 and 258.

17. P. Wood, "Dreaming and social isolation," doctoral dissertation, University of North Carolina, 1962.

18. J.L. Singer and B.F. Streiner, "Imaginative content in the dreams and fantasy play of blind and sighted children," *Perceptual and Motor Skills*, 1966, **22**, pages 475–482. Note in particular pages 479 and 480.

19. D. Kirtley and K. Cannistraci, "Dreams of the visually handicapped: Toward a normative approach," *American Foundation for the Blind, Research Bulletin*, 1974, **27**, pages 111–133. See pages 114, 116, and 118.

20. E.S. Tauber, H.P. Roffwarg, and J. Herman, "The effects of longstanding perceptual alterations on the hallucinatory content of dreams," *Psychophysiology*, 1968, **5**, page 219.

21. J.H. Mendelson, L. Siger, and P. Solomon, "Psychiatric observations on congenital and acquired deafness: Symbolic and perceptual processes in dreams," *American Journal of Psychiatry*, 1960, **116**, pages 883–888. The percent of dreams reported in color by the congenital deaf (92 percent) is markedly higher than for persons with normal hearing. See page 886. The dreams included both standard signing and gestural communications (page 886).

22. J.H. Ryan, "Dreams of paraplegics," *Archives of General Psychiatry*, 1961, **5**, pages 286–291.

23. See Ryan, page 287.

24. See Ryan, page 290.

25. A.E. Comarr, J.M. Cressy, and M. Letch, "Sleep dreams of sex among traumatic paraplegics and quadriplegics," *Sexuality and Disability*, 1983, 6, pages 25–29.

26. J. Money, "Phantom orgasm in the dreams of paraplegic men and women," *Archives of General Psychiatry*, 1960, **3**, pages 373–382. See page 376.

27. Money's findings recall both Freud's thinking in regard to wish fulfillment and Jung's thinking relating to compensation (Chapter 2, this book).

28. S.Y. Choi, "Dreams as a prognostic factor in alchoholism," *American Journal of Psychiatry*, 1973, **130**, pages 699–702. After presenting his statistical findings, Choi indicated that all of the patients in the sample expressed this feeling of relief (page 702).

Chapter 6. *Dream Recall*

1. D.B. Cohen, "Toward a theory of dream recall," *Psychological Bulletin*, 1974, **81**, pages 138-154. The paper reviews evidence for various theories concerning dream recall. The interference hypothesis is discussed on pages 146 and 147.

2. See Freud, pages 525-526.

3. A. Shapiro, D.R. Goodenough, I. Binderman, and I. Sleser, "Dream recall and the physiology of sleep," *Journal of Applied Psychology*, 1964, **19**, pages 778-783.

4. The subject's experience was described in a paper by D.R. Goodenough, H.A. Witkin, H.B. Lewis, D. Koulack, and H. Cohen, "Repression, interference and field dependence as factors in dream forgetting," *Journal of Abnormal Psychology*, 1974, **83**, page 34.

5. E. Kahn and C. Fisher, "Dream recall in the aged," *Psychophysiology*, 1968, **5**, page 222.

6. M. Kramer and T. Roth, "Dreams and dementia: A laboratory exploration of dream recall and dream content in chronic brain syndrome patients," *International Journal of Aging and Human Development*, 1975, **6**, pages 169-178.

7. See B. Barber, "Factors underlying individual differences in rate of dream reporting," doctoral dissertation, Yeshiva University, 1969; and S.S. Anish, "The relationship of dream recall to defensive mode," doctoral dissertation, University of Pittsburgh, 1969. In addition to studying the influence of individual differences in memory on dream recall, researchers have explored the possible role of differences in personality and attitudes about dreams on dream recall. For examples of such research see D.R. Cann and D.C. Donderi, "Jungian personality typology and the recall of everyday and archetypal dreams," *Journal of Personality and Social Psychology*, 1986, **50**, pages 1021-1030. Also see Z.Z. Cernovsky, "Dream recall and attitude toward dreams," *Perceptual and Motor Skills*, 1984, **58**, pages 911-914.

8. T.L. Cory, D.W. Ormiston, E. Simmel, and M. Dainoff, "Predicting the frequency of dream recall," *Journal of Abnormal Psychology*, 1975, **84**, pages 261-266. See Table 1, page 263, for the statistical findings comparing recallers and nonrecallers of dreams.

9. R.F. Martinetti, "Cognitive antecedents of dream recall," *Perceptual and Motor Skills*, 1985, **60**, pages 395-401. See page 399.

10. D.B. Cohen and G. Wolfe, "Dream recall and repression: Evidence for an alternative hypothesis," *Journal of Consulting and Clinical Psychology*, 1973, **41**, pages 349-355. The findings cited are presented in Study No. 4, page 352.

11. G.L. Gerber, "Coping effectiveness and dreams as a function of personality and dream recall," *Journal of Clinical Psychology*, 1978, **34**, pages 526-532. General estimates of "how often one dreams" are not particularly accurate predictors of how frequently one will report dreams when asked to do so using a morning diary procedure. Gerber's results for the dream diary are presented on page 531. See also Cory et al., and P.R. Robbins and R.H. Tanck, "The Repression-sensitization scale, dreams and dream associations," *Journal of Clinical Psychology*, 1970, **26**, pages 219-221.

12. Goodenough found the increase in contentless dreams only in a subgroup of subjects identified by a personality measure. The meaning of contentless dreams is still far from clear. See Goodenough et al., "Repression, interference and field dependence."

13. See Goodenough et al., "Repression, interference and field dependence," page 34.

14. See Dement, "The physiology of dreaming," page 23.

15. See Cohen, "Toward a theory of dream recall," pages 142-145.

16. See Cohen, "Toward a theory of dream recall," pages 144-145.

17. C.A. Meier, H. Ruef, A. Zeigler, and C.S. Hall, "Forgetting of dreams in the

laboratory," *Perceptual & Motor Skills*, 1968, **26,** pages 551–557. See page 554 for the findings relating to dream intensity.

18. See Goodenough et al., "Repression, interference and field dependence," pages 42–43.

19. See Goodenough et al., "Repression, interference and field dependence," page 34.

20. E.A. Wolpert and H. Trosman, "Studies in psychophysiology of dreams (I. Experimental evocation of sequential dream episodes)," *Archives of Neurology and Psychiatry*, 1958, **79,** pages 603–606. The investigators found that the percent of dream reports was lower when they waited for indications of bodily movement before awakening the subject (See Table 2, page 606).

Chapter 7. *Dreams and Mental Illness*

1. A.N. Fleiss, "Psychotic symptoms: A disturbance in the sleep mechanism," *Psychiatric Quarterly*, 1962, **36,** page 728.

2. G.W. Vogel, "Dreaming and schizophrenia," *Psychiatric Annals*, 1974, **4,** pages 63–77.

3. See Vogel, page 64.

4. See Vogel, page 66.

5. See Vogel, page 65.

6. S.C. Chang, "Dream-recall and themes of hospitalized schizophrenics," *Archives of General Psychiatry*, 1964, **10,** pages 121–122.

7. P. Carrington, "Dreams and schizophrenia," *Archives of General Psychiatry*, 1972, **26,** page 349.

8. See Carrington, pages 346–347.

9. See Carrington, page 347.

10. See Carrington, page 348, for examples of mutilation dreams in the schizophrenic sample.

11. See Carrington, page 348.

12. See Carrington, page 350, for theoretical implications of the study.

13. M. Kramer and T. Roth, "A comparison of dream content in laboratory dream reports of schizophrenic and depressive patient groups," *Comprehensive Psychiatry*, 1973, **14,** pages 325–329. See pages 326–329.

14. R.J. Langs, "Manifest dreams from three clinical groups," *Archives of General Psychiatry*, 1966, **14,** page 639.

15. See Chang, page 121.

16. J.B. Miller, "Dreams during varying stages of depression," *Archives of General Psychiatry*, 1969, **20,** page 561.

17. See Miller, page 562.

18. R. Baer, R. Ebtinger, I. Israel, and T. Kammerer, "A propos des rêves de déprimés," *Annales Médico-Psychologiques*, 1967, **2,** page 812.

19. See Langs, page 639.

20. A.T. Beck and C.H. Ward, "Dreams of depressed patients," *Archives of General Psychiatry*, 1961, **5,** pages 462–467. See page 462.

21. P. Hauri, "Dreams in patients remitted from reactive depression," *Journal of Abnormal Psychology*, 1976, **85,** pages 1–10. These relatively brief dreams were found during REM period awakenings. See page 6.

Chapter 8. *Symbolism*

1. *The Odyssey*, pages 301–302.

2. Daniel 4:4–33.

3. Freud, page 353.
4. Freud, page 354.
5. Freud, page 354.
6. Freud, page 354.
7. Freud, page 355.
8. See Gutheil, Chapter 3, particularly page 136.
9. P.R. Robbins and R.H. Tanck, "Sexual gratification and sexual symbolism in dreams: Some support for Freud's theory," *Bulletin of the Menninger Clinic*, 1980, **44,** page 51.
10. See Robbins and Tanck, "Sexual gratification and sexual symbolism," page 51.
11. See Robbins and Tanck, "Sexual gratification and sexual symbolism," pages 51–52.
12. See Robbins and Tanck, "Sexual gratification and sexual symbolism," pages 53–54.
13. R.A. Clark and M.R. Sensibar, "The relationship between symbolic and manifest projections of sexuality with some incidental correlates," in J.W. Atkinson (ed.), *Motives in Fantasy, Action and Society* (Princeton, N.J.: Van Nostrand, 1958).
14. Wallach, M.A., "Two correlates of symbolic sexual arousal: Level of anxiety and liking for esthetic material," *Journal of Abnormal and Social Psychology*, 1960, **61,** pages 396–401.
15. P.R. Robbins, R.H. Tanck, and F. Houshi, "Anxiety and dream symbolism," *Journal of Personality*, 1985, **53,** pages 17–22. See pages 19–20.
16. G. Roheim, "The song of the sirens," *Psychiatric Quarterly*, 1948, **22,** pages 18–44. While Freud urged restraint in using symbols in dream interpretation, some of his followers have used these ideas in highly speculative ways. A case in point is Dr. Geza Roheim's interpretations of folklore and mythology. Roheim analyzed myths relating to water spirits from such countries as Hungary, Russia, Germany and Greece. Referring to Homer's narrative of Odysseus and the sirens, she has the following to say: "The figure of Odysseus tied to the mast suggests the penis in erection." And later, "Odysseus is tied to the mast, erect, while his men are rowing. . . . The dream, in the first layer, must be of coitus with the mother. Her voice is irresistible, it means 'go to sleep and dream of having intercourse with the sirens.' And the song of the sirens is a mother's lullaby." (See pages 25–26.) Another example: "We suspect, therefore, that the water spirits' long tresses are the dreamer's pubic hair and that all the spirits' activities, combing, sewing, patching, counting, represent masturbation." (Page 34.)
17. K. Lessler, "Sexual symbols, structured and unstructured," *Journal of Consulting Psychology*, 1962, **26,** pages 44–49. The directions given to Lessler's subjects are on page 45.
18. See Lessler, page 45.
19. R.A. Schonbar and J.R. Davitz, "The connotative meaning of sexual symbols," *Journal of Consulting Psychology*, 1960, **24,** pages 483–487. The authors concluded that "in general, culture rather than form determined the sexual meaning of objects." (Page 487.)
20. R.A. Richardson, "The cross-cultural validity of Freudian sexual symbolism," *International Journal of Symbology*, 1971, **2,** pages 1–7. Note the discussion on page 6.
21. W.W. Meissner, "Affective response to psychoanalytic death symbols," *Journal of Abnormal and Social Psychology*, 1958, **56,** pages 295–299. In discussing his results, Meissner makes the point that his subjects were a selected religiously trained group and that parallel studies with other groups were needed (page 298).

Chapter 9. *Dreams and Creativity*

1. R. Dreistadt, "An analysis of how dreams are used in creative behavior," *Psychology*, 1971, **8,** pages 24–50. Wagner is discussed on page 25; Coleridge, on page 27; Stevenson, on page 43.

2. See Dreistadt, page 31.

3. S. Krippner and W. Hughes, "Genius at work," *Psychology Today*, 1970, **4,** pages 40–43. Bohr is discussed on page 41; Agassiz and Howe, on page 42.

4. See Dreistadt for a very impressive list of creative people.

5. See Dreistadt, page 28.

6. J. Adelson, "Creativity and the dream," *Merrill-Palmer Quarterly*, 1960, **6,** page 93.

7. W.H. Sylvia, P.M. Clark, and L.J. Monroe, "Dream reports of subjects high and low in creative ability," *Journal of General Psychology*, 1978, **99,** pages 205–211. See in particular page 209.

8. N. Schechter, G.R. Schmeidler, and M. Staal, "Dream reports and creative tendencies in students of the arts, sciences, and engineering," *Journal of Consulting Psychology*, 1965, **29,** pages 415–421. The differences between the art students and the other groups are presented on pages 417 and 418.

9. See Schechter et al., page 420.

10. See Schechter et al., page 420.

11. G. Domino, "Primary process thinking in dream reports as related to creative achievement," *Journal of Consulting and Clinical Psychology*, 1976, **44,** pages 929–932.

12. Domino's observations recall Jung's view that the unconscious offers potentially useful materials for creative expression (See Chapter 2 of this book).

13. R.D. Cartwright, "Problem solving: Waking and dreaming," *Journal of Abnormal Psychology*, 1974, **83,** pages 451–455. See results, page 453.

14. See Cartwright, page 454.

15. See Cartwright, pages 453–454.

16. R. Davé, "Effects of hypnotically induced dreams on creative problem solving," *Journal of Abnormal Psychology*, 1979, **88,** page 296.

17. See Davé, page 298.

Chapter 10. *Nightmares*

1. E. Jones, *On the Nightmare* (New York: Grove, 1959). The three characteristics of the nightmare are discussed on pages 74–75.

2. See Lee, page 268.

3. See Foster, page 109.

4. See Griffith et al., page 1177.

5. See Hall and Van de Castle, Table 14–29 (Summary of Emotions).

6. The studies on recurrent dreams are: P.R. Robbins and F. Houshi, "Some observations on recurrent dreams," *Bulletin of the Menninger Clinic*, 1983, **47,** pages 262–265; R.B. Lacoursiere, K.E. Godfrey, and L.M. Ruby, "Traumatic neurosis in the etiology of alcoholism: Viet Nam combat and other trauma," *American Journal of Psychiatry*, 1980, **137,** pages 966–968. In the study by Gentil and Lader, the dreams of persons diagnosed as anxious neurotics were compared with normal controls: L.F. Gentil and M. Lader, "Dream content and daytime activities in anxious and calm women," *Psychological Medicine*, 1978, **8,** pages 297–304. Note page 301.

7. H. Morishige and J. Reyher, "Alpha rhythm during three conditions of visual imagery and emergent uncovering psychotherapy: The critical role of anxiety," *Journal*

of Abnormal Psychology, 1975, **84**, pages 531–538. The investigators found that the desynchronization of alpha was greater for dreams than for free imagery, page 534. See also J. Reyher and H. Morishige, "Electroencephalogram and rapid eye movements during free imagery and dream recall," *Journal of Abnormal Psychology*, 1969, **74**, pages 576–582.

8. C. Winget and F.T. Kapp, "The relationship of the manifest content of dreams to duration of childbirth in primipare," *Psychosomatic Medicine*, 1972, **34**, pages 313–320.

9. M.J. Feldman and E. Hyman, "Content analysis of nightmare reports," *Psychophysiology*, 1968, **5**, page 221.

10. H. Cason, "The nightmare dream," *Psychological Monographs*, 1935, **46**, No. 5 (whole No. 209), page 30.

11. See Cason, page 30.

12. See Cason, page 30.

13. See Cason, pages 30–31.

14. See Cason, page 31.

15. C. Fisher, E. Kahn, A. Edwards, D.M. Davis, and J. Fine, "A psychophysiological study of nightmares and night terrors," *Journal of Nervous and Mental Disease*, 1974, **158**, pages 174–188. This report is the third in a series of papers. The descriptions cited are on page 186.

16. See Fisher et al., "A psychophysiological study," page 181.

17. See Fisher et al., "A psychophysiological study," page 179.

18. D. Lester, "The fear of death of those who have nightmares," *Journal of Psychology*, 1968, **69**, page 246.

19. E. Hartmann, "A note on the nightmare," *International Psychiatry Clinics*, 1970, **7**, page 193. Hartmann has been interested in studying the personality characteristics of persons who are lifelong nightmare sufferers. His research team has reported that such persons appear to score higher on the psychotic scales of the MMPI than control subjects. See E. Hartmann, D. Russ, M. Oldfield, I. Sivan, and S. Cooper, "Who has nightmares: The personality of the lifelong nightmare sufferer," *Archives of General Psychiatry*, 1987, **44**, pages 49–56.

20. See Fisher et al., "A psychophysiological study," Case S1.

21. R.J. Broughton, "Sleep disorders: Disorders of arousal?" *Science*, 1968, **159**, pages 1070–1078. See page 1071 for discussion of recall of night terrors.

22. See Fisher et al., "A psychophysiological study," pages 184–185, for a discussion of this possible line of explanation of night terrors.

23. Broughton stresses the role of physiological changes in his paper "The incubus attack," which is included in E. Hartmann (ed.), *Sleep and Dreaming* (Boston: Little, Brown, 1970). See page 190.

24. J.E. Mack, "Nightmares, conflict, and ego development in childhood," *International Journal of Psycho-Analysis*, 1965, **46**, pages 403–427. See page 404.

25. See Cason's monograph. It is well to keep Cason's observations in perspective. While these disturbing nightmares are realities for children, Foulkes' REM studies (See Chapter 5, this book) indicate that the large majority of children's dreams are pleasant.

26. J.L. Despert, "Dreams in children of pre-school age," in A. Freud, H. Hartman, and E. Kris (eds.), *The Psychoanalytic Study of the Child* (New York: International Universities Press, 1949). Note in particular pages 153, 162.

27. See Despert, pages 154, 161.

28. This was a dream report collected during research I carried out with Dr. Roland H. Tanck.

29. See Despert, page 161, for examples.

30. See Mack, page 404.

31. See Broughton, "Sleep disorders," page 1071.

32. See, for example, Mack, page 405.
33. See Mack, pages 413–414.
34. See Mack, page 414.
35. A.T. Jersild, F.V. Markey, and C.L. Jersild, "Children's fears, dreams, wishes, daydreams, likes, dislikes, pleasant and unpleasant memories," *Child Development Monographs*, No. 12 (New York: Teachers' College, Columbia University, 1933).
36. See Bourguignon, page 263.
37. J.R. Marshall, "The treatment of night terrors associated with the post-traumatic syndrome," *American Journal of Psychiatry*, 1975, **132**, pages 293–295. See Case I, page 293.
38. See Marshall, Case I, page 293.
39. See Marshall, Case I, page 293.
40. See Marshall, Case I, page 294.
41. N. Cavior and A. Deutsch, "Systematic desensitization to reduce dream-induced anxiety," *Journal of Nervous and Mental Disease*, 1975, **161**, pages 433–435. The systematic desensitization procedure has been used primarily as a clinical procedure in the treatment of phobias.
42. See Cavior and Deutsch, page 434.
43. W. Miller and M. Dipilato, "Treatment of nightmares via relaxation and desensitization: A controlled evaluation," *Journal of Consulting and Clinical Psychology*, 1983, **51**, page 873.
44. E.L. Toboada, "Night terrors in children: Causes and treatment," *Texas Medicine*, 1974, **70**, page 71.

Chapter 11. *Telepathic and Paranormal Dreams*

1. J.B. Rhine, *New World of the Mind* (New York: Morrow, 1953), page 25.
2. M. Ullman, "Telepathy and dreams," *Experimental Medicine and Surgery*, 1969, **27**, pages 19–38. The procedures and statistical tests are described on page 26. In the author's judgment, these experiments display both innovative thinking and scientific care. Nonetheless, judging from a review of Irvin Child, the studies have been misrepresented in the psychological literature. See I.L. Child, "Psychology and anomalous observations: The question of ESP in dreams," *American Psychologist*, 1985, **40**, pages 1219–1230.
3. See Ullman, page 26.
4. See Ullman, page 28.
5. These dream reports are described in Ullman, pages 28–29.
6. See Ullman, page 30.
7. E. Belvedere and D. Foulkes, "Telepathy and dreams: A failure to replicate," *Perceptual and Motor Skills*, 1971, **33**, pages 783–789.
8. H.A. Murray and D.R. Wheeler, "A note on the possible clairvoyance of dreams," *Journal of Psychology*, 1937, **3**, pages 309–313. The descriptions of the typical dream reports are on pages 309–310.
9. See Murray and Wheeler, page 313.
10. H.S. Strean, "A paranormal dream," *Psychoanalytic Review*, 1969, **56**, page 143.
11. H. Ehrenwald, "Telepathy in dreams," *British Journal of Medical Psychology*, 1942, **19**, pages 313–323. See Case 2, beginning on page 319.
12. L.E. Rhine, "Psychological Processes in ESP experiences (Part II. Dreams)," *Journal of Parapsychology*, 1962, **26**, page 177.
13. See L.E. Rhine, page 178.
14. See L.E. Rhine, page 186.

15. G.S. Wilson, "A prophetic dream reported by Abraham Lincoln," *American Imago*, 1940, **1,** page 47.

Chapter 12. The Many Faces of Dreams

1. R. Rados and R.D. Cartwright, "Where do dreams come from? A comparison of presleep and REM sleep thematic content," *Journal of Abnormal Psychology*, 1982, **91,** pages 433–436.

Chapter 13. Drawing, Visualizing, and Dramatizing Dreams

1. See Morishige and Reyher, page 535.
2. See Morishige and Reyher, page 534.
3. See Morishige and Reyher, page 536.
4. See Morishige and Reyher, page 536.
5. F.S. Perls, *Gestalt Therapy Verbatim* (Moab, Utah: Real People Press, 1969). L.S. Alban and W.D. Groman, "Dreamwork in a Gestalt therapy context," *American Journal of Psychoanalysis*, 1975, **35,** pages 147–156.
6. See Perls, chapter entitled "Dreamwork Seminar," Case 3, Liz.
7. See Perls, chapter entitled "Dreamwork Seminar," Case 4, Carl.

Chapter 14. Dream Association

1. See Freud, page 100.
2. See Freud, page 101.
3. See Freud, page 109.
4. See Freud, page 109.
5. See Freud, page 110.
6. R.R. Greenson, "The exceptional position of the dream in psychoanalytic practice," *The Psychoanalytic Quarterly*, 1970, **39,** pages 519–549. This dream began on page 540.
7. K.R. Eissler, *Goethe, A Psychoanalytic Study, 1775–1786*, Vol. I (Detroit: Wayne State University Press, 1963), page 198.
8. M.S. Bergmann, "Free association and interpretation of dreams: Historical and methodological considerations," in E.F. Hammer, *Use of Interpretation in Treatment* (New York: Grune & Stratton, 1968). Bergmann highlights this problem on the last two pages of his essay.
9. E. Sheppard and B. Karon, "Systematic studies of dreams: Relationship between the manifest dream and associations to the dream elements," *Comprehensive Psychiatry*, 1964, **5,** pages 335–343. See Table 2 for the relations between manifest dream content and dream associations which were significant.
10. J.T. Tokar, A.J. Brunse, P. Castelnuovo-Tedesco, and V.J. Stefflre, "An objective method of dream analysis," *Psychoanalytic Quarterly*, 1973, **42,** pages 563–578. The dream reports for the patient begin on page 565.
11. See Tokar, pages 574–575.

Chapter 15. The Dream Incident Technique

1. These findings are reported in the following articles: P.R. Robbins, "An approach to measuring psychological tensions by means of dream associations," *Psycho-*

logical Reports, 1966, **18**, pages 959–971; P.R. Robbins and R.H. Tanck, "The Dream Incident Technique as a measure of unresolved problems," *Journal of Personality Assessment*, 1978, **42**, pages 583–591.

2. See, for example, E. Hess, "Attitude and pupil size," *Scientific American*, April 1965, **212**, pages 46–54.

3. R.H. Tanck and P.R. Robbins, "Pupillary reactions to sexual, aggressive, and other stimuli as a function of personality," *Journal of Projective Techniques and Personality Assessment*, 1970, **34**, page 279.

4. See Tanck and Robbins, page 280, for the findings relating to aggression.

5. See Tanck and Robbins, Table 2.

6. The data relating to physical symptoms are reported in P.R. Robbins, R.H. Tanck, and H.A. Meyersburg, "A study of three psychosomatic hypotheses," *Journal of Psychosomatic Research*, 1972, **16**, pages 93–97. The findings relating to drug use are reported in P.R. Robbins, R.H. Tanck, and H.A. Meyersburg, "Psychological factors in smoking, drinking, and drug experimentation," *Journal of Clinical Psychology*, 1971, **27**, pages 450–452.

7. These are previously unpublished findings.

8. These are previously unpublished findings.

Chapter 16. *Using Dreams in Your Life*

1. H. Reed, "Learning to remember dreams," *Journal of Humanistic Psychology*, 1973, **13**, pages 33–48. The findings and self-evaluations of the subjects are presented on page 40.

2. D.L. Redfering and J.N. Keller, "Influence of differential instructions on the frequency of dream recall," *Journal of Clinical Psychology*, 1974, **30**, pages 268–271. These calls by the experimenters would tend to heighten the "demand" characteristics of the experimental situation and may have contributed to the increased dream reports.

Bibliography

Adelson, J. Creativity and the dream. *Merrill-Palmer Quarterly*, 1960, **6**, 92–97.

Alban, L.S., and Groman, W.D. Dreamwork in a Gestalt therapy context. *American Journal of Psychoanalysis*, 1975, **35**, 147–156.

Anish, S.S. The relationship of dream recall to defensive mode. Doctoral dissertation, University of Pittsburgh, 1969.

Ansbacher, H.L., and Ansbacher, R.R. (eds.). *The Individual Psychology of Alfred Adler.* New York: Basic Books, 1956.

Artemidorus. *The Interpretation of Dreams: The Oneirocritica of Artemidorus.* Translated by R. White. Park Ridge, N.J.: Noyes Classical Studies, 1975.

Ascrinsky, E. Periodic respiratory pattern occurring in conjunction with eye movements during sleep. *Science*, 1965, **150**, 763–766.

Baer, R.; Ebtinger, R.; Israel, I.; and Kammerer, T. A propos des rêves de déprimés. *Annales Médico-Psychologiques*, 1967, **2**, 812.

Bakan, P. Dreaming, REM sleep and the right hemisphere: A theoretical integration. *Journal of Altered States of Consciousness*, 1977–78, **3**, 285–307.

Barber, B. Factors underlying individual differences in rate of dream reporting. Doctoral dissertation, Yeshiva University, 1969.

Beck, A.T., and Ward, C.H. Dreams of depressed patients. *Archives of General Psychiatry*, 1961, **5**, 462–467.

Belicki, K., and Bowers, P. The role of demand characteristics and hypnotic ability in dream change following a pre-sleep instruction. *Journal of Abnormal Psychology*, 1982, **91**, 426–432.

Belvedere, E., and Foulkes, D. Telepathy and dreams: A failure to replicate. *Perceptual and Motor Skills*, 1971, **33**, 783–789.

Bergmann, M.S. Free association and interpretation of dreams: Historical and methodological considerations. In Hammer, E.F. *Use of Interpretation in Treatment.* New York: Grune & Stratton, 1968.

Bourguignon, E.E. Dreams and dream interpretation in Haiti. *American Anthropologist*, 1954, **56**, 262–268.

Breger, L. Function of dreams. *Journal of Abnormal Psychology Monograph*, 1967, **72**, (5, whole No. 641).

_____; Hunter, I.; and Lane, R.W. The effect of stress on dreams. *Psychological Issues*, 1971, **7**, (3).

Brenneis, C.B. Developmental aspects of aging in women: A comparative study of dreams. *Archives of General Psychiatry*, 1975, **32**, 429–435.

Broughton, R.J. Sleep disorders: Disorders of arousal? *Science*, 1968, **159**, 1070–1078.

_____. The incubus attack. In Hartmann, E. (ed.). *Sleep and Dreaming.* Boston: Little, Brown, 1970.

Bryne, D. The repression-sensitization scale: Rationale, reliability, and validity. *Journal of Personality*, 1961, **29**, 334–349.

Cann, D.R., and Donderi, D.C. Jungian personality typology and the recall of everyday and archetypal dreams. *Journal of Personality and Social Psychology*, 1986, **50,** 1021–1030.

Carrington, P. Dreams and schizophrenia. *Archives of General Psychiatry*, 1972, **26,** 343–350.

Cartwright, R.D. Problem solving: Waking and dreaming. *Journal of Abnormal Psychology*, 1974, **83,** 451–455.

————; Bernick, N.; Borowitz, G.; and Kling, A. Effect of an erotic movie on the sleep and dreams of young men. *Archives of General Psychiatry*, 1969, **20,** 262–271.

Cason, H. The nightmare dream. *Psychological Monographs*, 1935, **46,** No. 5 (whole No. 209).

Cavior, N., and Deutsch, A. Systematic desensitization to reduce dream-induced anxiety. *Journal of Nervous and Mental Disease*, 1975, **161,** 433–435.

Cernovsky, Z.Z. Dream recall and attitude toward dreams. *Perceptual and Motor Skills*, 1984, **58,** 911–914.

Chang, S.C. Dream-recall and themes of hospitalized schizophrenics. *Archives of General Psychiatry*, 1964, **10,** 119–122.

Chernik, D.A. Effect of REM sleep deprivation on learning and recall by humans. *Perceptual and Motor Skills*, 1972, **34,** 283–294.

Child, I.L. Psychology and anomalous observations: The question of ESP in dreams. *American Psychologist*, 1985, **40,** 1219–1230.

Choi, S.Y. Dreams as a prognostic factor in alcoholism. *American Journal of Psychiatry*, 1973, **130,** 699–702.

Clark, R.A. Jungian and Freudian approach to dreams. *American Journal of Psychotherapy*, 1961, **15,** 89–100.

————, and Sensibar, M.R. The relationship between symbolic and manifest projections of sexuality with some incidental correlates. In J.W. Atkinson (ed.). *Motives in Fantasy, Action and Society*. Princeton, N.J.: Van Nostrand, 1958.

Cohen, D.B. Toward a theory of dream recall. *Psychological Bulletin*, 1974, **81,** 138–154.

————. Sources of bias in our characterization of dreams. *Perceptual and Motor Skills*, 1977, **45,** 98.

————, and Wolfe, G. Dream recall and repression: Evidence for an alternative hypothesis. *Journal of Consulting and Clinical Psychology*, 1973, **41,** 349–355.

Cohen, S. Aristedes: A second century case report. *Psychosomatics*, 1972, **13,** 200–202.

Comarr, A.E.; Cressy, J.M.; and Letch, M. Sleep dreams of sex among traumatic paraplegics and quadriplegics. *Sexuality and Disability*, 1983, **6,** 25–29.

Cory, T.L.; Ormiston, D.W.; Simmel, E.; and Dainoff, M. Predicting the frequency of dream recall. *Journal of Abnormal Psychology*, 1975, **84,** 261–266.

Crapanzano, V. Saints, Jnun, and dreams: An essay in Moroccan ethnopsychology. *Psychiatry*, 1975, **38,** 145–159.

Dallett, J. Theories of dream function. *Psychological Bulletin*, 1973, **79,** 408–416.

Davé, R. Effects of hypnotically induced dreams on creative problem solving. *Journal of Abnormal Psychology*, 1979, **88,** 293–302.

DeKoninck, J.M., and Koulack, D. Dream content and adaptation to a stressful situation. *Journal of Abnormal Psychology*, 1975, **84,** 250–260.

Dement, W. The physiology of dreaming. Doctoral diss. University of Chicago, 1958.

————. The effect of dream deprivation. *Science*, 1960, **131,** 1705–1707.

————. *Some Must Watch While Some Must Sleep*. San Francisco: Freeman, 1974.

————, and Wolpert, E.A. Relationships in the manifest content of dreams occurring on the same night. *Journal of Nervous and Mental Disease*, 1958, **126,** 568–578.

Despert, J.L. Dreams in children of pre-school age. In Freud, A.; Hartman, H.; and Kris, E. (eds.). *The Psychoanalytic Study of the Child*. New York: International Universities Press, 1949.

Domhoff, B., and Kamiya, J. Problems in dream content study with objective indicators. (I. A Comparison of home and laboratory dream reports.) *Archives of General Psychiatry*, 1964, **11**, 519–524.

————, and ————. Problems in dream content study with objective indicators. (III. Changes in dream content throughout the night.) *Archives of General Psychiatry*, 1964, **11**, 529–532.

Domino, G. Primary process thinking in dream reports as related to creative achievement. *Journal of Consulting and Clinical Psychology*, 1976, **44**, 929–932.

Dreistadt, R. An analysis of how dreams are used in creative behavior. *Psychology*, 1971, **8**, 24–50.

Ehrenwald, H. Telepathy in dreams. *British Journal of Medical Psychology*, 1942, **19**, 313–323.

Eissler, K.R. *Goethe, A Psychoanalytic Study 1775–1786*. Vol. I. Detroit: Wayne State University Press, 1963.

Feldman, M.J., and Hyman, E. Content analysis of nightmare reports. *Psychophysiology*, 1968, **5**, 221.

Fisher, C.; Gross, J.; and Zuch, J. Cycle of penile erection synchronous with dreaming (REM) sleep. Preliminary report. *Archives of General Psychiatry*, 1965, **12**, 29–45.

————; Kahn, E.; Edwards, A.; Davis, D.M.; and Fine, J. A psychophysiological study of nightmares and night terrors. *Journal of Nervous and Mental Disease*, 1974, **158**, 174–188.

Fleiss, A.N. Psychotic symptoms: A disturbance in the sleep mechanism. *Psychiatric Quarterly*, 1962, **36**, 727–733.

Foster, G.M. Dreams, character, and cognitive orientation in Tzintzuntzan. *Ethos*, 1973, **1**, 106–121.

Foulkes, D. Theories of dream formation and recent studies of sleep consciousness. *Psychological Bulletin*, 1964, **62**, 236–247.

————. Children's dreams: Age changes and sex differences. *Waking and Sleeping*, 1977, **1**, 171–174.

————; Larson, J.D.; Swanson, E.M.; and Rardin, M. Two studies of childhood dreaming. *American Journal of Orthopsychiatry*, 1969, **39**, 627–643.

————; Pivik, T.; Ahrens, J.B.; and Swanson, E.M. Effects of "dream deprivation" on dream content: An attempted cross-night replication. *Journal of Abnormal Psychology*, 1968, **73**, 403–415.

————; ————; Steadman, H.S.; Spear, P.S.; and Symonds, J.D. Dreams of the male child: An EEG study. *Journal of Abnormal Psychology*, 1967, **72**, 457–467.

Freud, S. *The Interpretation of Dreams*. New York: Basic Books, 1955.

Gardner, R., Jr.; Grossman, W.I.; Roffwarg, H.P.; and Weiner, H. The relationship of small limb movements during REM sleep to dreamed limb action. *Psychosomatic Medicine*, 1975, **37**, 147–159.

Garfield, P.L. *Creative Dreaming*. New York: Simon & Schuster, 1974.

Gentil, L.F., and Lader, M. Dream content and daytime activities in anxious and calm women. *Psychological Medicine*, 1978, **8**, 297–304.

Gerber, G.L. Coping effectiveness and dreams as a function of personality and dream recall. *Journal of Clinical Psychology*, 1978, **34**, 526–532.

Goodenough, D.R.; Witkin, H.A.; Koulack, D.; and Cohen, H. The effects of stress films on dream effect and on respiration and eye-movement activity during rapid-eye-movement sleep. *Psychophysiology*, 1975, **12**, 313–320.

164   Bibliography

_____; _____; Lewis, H.B.; _____; and _____. Repression, interference
and field dependence as factors in dream forgetting. *Journal of Abnormal Psychology*, 1974, **83**, 32–44.
Greenson, R.R. The exceptional position of the dream in psychoanalytic practice. *The Psychoanalytic Quarterly*, 1970, **39**, 519–549.
Grene, D., and Lattimore, R. (eds.). *The Complete Greek Tragedies*. Chicago: The University of Chicago Press, 1953.
Grey, A., and Kalsched, D. Oedipus east and west: An exploration via manifest dream content. *Journal of Cross-Cultural Psychology*, 1971, **2**, 337–352.
Griffin, M.L., and Foulkes, D. Deliberate presleep control of dream content: An experimental study. *Perceptual and Motor Skills*, 1977, **45**, 660–662.
Griffith, R.M.; Miyagi, O.; and Tago, A. The universality of typical dreams: Japanese vs. Americans. *American Anthropologist*, 1958, **60**, 1173–1179.
Gutheil, E.A. *The Handbook of Dream Analysis*. New York: Liveright, 1951.
Hall, C.S. *The Meaning of Dreams*. New York: Harper & Brothers, 1953.
_____. "A ubiquitous sex difference in dreams" revisited. *Journal of Personality and Social Psychology*, 1984, **46**, 1109–1117.
_____, and Domhoff, B. A ubiquitous sex difference in dreams. *Journal of Abnormal and Social Psychology*, 1963, **66**, 278–280.
_____, and Van de Castle, R.L. *The Content Analysis of Dreams*. New York: Appleton-Century-Crofts, 1966.
Hartmann, E. The day residue: Time distribution of waking events. *Psychophysiology*, 1968, **5**, 222.
_____; Russ, D.; Oldfield, M.; Sivan, I.; and Cooper, S. Who has nightmares: The personality of the lifelong nightmare sufferer. *Archives of General Psychiatry*, 1987, **44**, 49–56.
_____. A note on the nightmare. *International Psychiatry Clinics*, 1970, **7**, 192–197.
Hauri, P. Effects of evening activity on subsequent sleep and dreams. Doctoral dissertation, University of Chicago, 1967.
_____. Dreams in patients remitted from reactive depression. *Journal of Abnormal Psychology*, 1976, **85**, 1–10.
_____; Sawyer, J.; and Rechtschaffen, A. Dimensions of dreaming: A factored scale for rating dream reports. *Journal of Abnormal Psychology*, 1967, **72**, 16–22.
Herman, J.; Roffwarg, H.; and Tauber, E.S. Color and other perceptual qualities of REM and NREM sleep. *Psychophysiology*, 1968, **5**, 223.
Herodotus. *The Persian Wars*. New York: Random House, 1942.
Hess, E. Attitude and pupil size. *Scientific American*, April 1965, **212**, 46–54.
Holy Bible. Revised Standard Version. New York: Thomas Nelson & Sons, 1952.
Homer. *The Iliad of Homer*. Translated by E. Rees. New York: Modern Library, Random House, 1963.
_____. *The Odyssey of Homer*. Translated by S.H. Butcher and A. Lang. New York: Macmillan, 1930.
Jersild, A.T.; Markey, F.V.; and Jersild, C.L. Children's fears, dreams, wishes, daydreams, likes, dislikes, pleasant and unpleasant memories. *Child Development Monographs*. No. 12. New York: Teachers College, Columbia University, 1933.
Jones, E. *The Life and Work of Sigmund Freud*. Vol. 1. New York: Basic Books, 1953.
_____. *On the Nightmare*. New York: Grove, 1959.
Jung, C.G. *The Development of Personality*. Vol. 17 of the *Collected Works*. Translated by R.F.C. Hull, Bollingen Series XX. Princeton, N.J.: Princeton University Press, 1954 (copyright renewed 1982).
_____. *Man and His Symbols*. New York: Doubleday, 1964.

Kahn, E.; Dement, W.; Fisher, C.; and Barmack, J.E. Incidence of color in immediately recalled dreams. *Science*, 1962, **137**, 1054–1055.

_____, and Fisher, C. Dream recall in the aged. *Psychophysiology*, 1968, **5**, 222.

Karacan, I.; Goodenough, D.R.; Shapiro, A.; and Starker, S. Erection cycle during sleep in relation to dream anxiety. *Archives of General Psychiatry*, 1966, **15**, 183–189.

Kirtley, D., and Cannistraci, K. Dreams of the visually handicapped: Toward a normative approach. *American Foundation for the Blind, Research Bulletin*, 1974, **27**, 111–133.

Kramer, M., and Roth, T. A comparison of dream content in laboratory dream reports of schizophrenic and depressive patient groups. *Comprehensive Psychiatry*, 1973, **14**, 325–329.

_____, and _____. Dreams and dementia: A laboratory exploration of dream recall and dream content in chronic brain syndrome patients. *International Journal of Aging and Human Development*, 1975, **6**, 169–178.

Krippner, S., and Hughs, W. Genius at work. *Psychology Today*, 1970, **4**, 40–43.

Kurland, M.L. Oneiromancy: An historical review of dream interpretation. *American Journal of Psychotherapy*, 1972, **26**, 408–416.

Lacoursiere, R.B.; Godfrey, K.E.; and Ruby, L.M. Traumatic neurosis in the etiology of alcoholism: Viet Nam combat and other trauma. *American Journal of Psychiatry*, 1980, **137**, 966–968.

Langs, R.J. Manifest dreams from three clinical groups. *Archives of General Psychiatry*, 1966, **14**, 634–643.

Laurendeau, M., and Pinard, A. *Causal Thinking in the Child*. New York: International Universities Press, 1962.

Lee, S.G. Social influences in Zulu dreaming. *Journal of Social Psychology*, 1958, **47**, 265–283.

Lessler, K. Sexual symbols, structured and unstructured. *Journal of Consulting Psychology*, 1962, **26**, 44–49.

Lester, D. The fear of death of those who have nightmares. *Journal of Psychology*, 1968, **69**, 245–247.

Lewis, N.D.C. The practical value of graphic art in personality studies. (I. An introduction and presentation of the possibilities.) *Psychoanalytic Review*, 1925, **12**, 316–322.

McGuigan, F.J., and Tanner, R.G. Covert oral behavior during conversational and visual dreams. *Psychosonomic Science*, 1971, **23**, 263–264.

Mack, J.E. Nightmares, conflict, and ego development in childhood. *International Journal of Psycho-Analysis*, 1965, **46**, 403–428.

Marshall, J.R. The treatment of night terrors associated with the posttraumatic syndrome. *American Journal of Psychiatry*, 1975, **132**, 293–295.

Martinetti, R.F. Cognitive antecedents of dream recall. *Perceptual and Motor Skills*, 1985, **60**, 395–401.

Meier, C.A.; Ruef, H.; Zeigler, A.; and Hall, C.S. Forgetting of dreams in the laboratory. *Perceptual & Motor Skills*, 1968, **26**, 551–557.

Meissner, W.W. Affective response to psychoanalytic death symbols. *Journal of Abnormal and Social Psychology*, 1958, **56**, 295–299.

Mendleson, J.H.; Siger, L.; and Solomon, P. Psychiatric observations on congenital and acquired deafness: Symbolic and perceptual processes in dreams. *American Journal of Psychiatry*, 1960, **116**, 883–888.

Merton, R.K. *Social Theory and Social Structure*. New York: Free Press, 1957.

Miller, J.B. Dreams during varying stages of depression. *Archives of General Psychiatry*, 1969, **20**, 560–565.

Miller, W., and DiPilato, M. Treatment of nightmares via relaxation and desensitization: A controlled evaluation. *Journal of Consulting and Clinical Psychology*, 1983, **51**, 870–877.

Money, J. Phantom orgasm in the dreams of paraplegic men and women. *Archives of General Psychiatry*, 1960, **3**, 373–382.

Morishige, H., and Reyher, J. Alpha rhythm during three conditions of visual imagery and emergent uncovering psychotherapy: The critical role of anxiety. *Journal of Abnormal Psychology*, 1975, **84**, 531–538.

Murray, H.A., and Wheeler, D.R. A note on the possible clairvoyance of dreams. *Journal of Psychology*, 1937, **3**, 309–313.

Ogilvie, R.; Belicki, K.; and Nagy, A. Voluntary control of dream affect? *Waking and Sleeping*, 1978, **2**, 189–194.

_____; Busby, K.; Costello, L.; and Broughton, R. The effects of pre-sleep suggestion upon REM sleep. *Canadian Journal of Behavioral Science*, 1975, **7**, 139–150.

Oppenheim, A.L. Mantic dreams in the ancient near east. In G.E. Von Grunebaum and R. Caillois (eds.). *The Dream and Human Societies*. Berkeley: University of California Press, 1966.

Papageorgiou, M.G. Incubation as a form of psychotherapy in the care of patients in ancient and modern Greece. *Psychotherapy and Psychosomatics*, 1975, **26**, 35–38.

Perls, F.S. *Gestalt Therapy Verbatim*. Moab, Utah: Real People Press, 1969.

Piaget, J. *The Child's Conception of the World*. New York: Harcourt, Brace, 1929.

Rados, R., and Cartwright, R.D. Where do dreams come from? A comparison of presleep and REM sleep thematic content. *Journal of Abnormal Psychology*, 1982, **91**, 433–436.

Redfering, D.L., and Keller, J.N. Influence of differential instructions on the frequency of dream recall. *Journal of Clinical Psychology*, 1974, **30**, 268–271.

Reed, H. Learning to remember dreams. *Journal of Humanistic Psychology*, 1973, **13**, 33–48.

Reyher, J. Free imagery: An uncovering procedure. *Journal of Clinical Psychology*, 1963, **19**, 454–459.

_____, and Morishige, H. Electroencephalogram and rapid eye movements during free imagery and dream recall. *Journal of Abnormal Psychology*, 1969, **74**, 576–582.

Rhine, J.B. *New World of the Mind*. New York: Morrow, 1953.

Rhine, L.E. Psychological processes in ESP experiences. (Part II. Dreams.) *Journal of Parapsychology*, 1962, **26**, 172–199.

Richardson, R.A. The cross-cultural validity of Freudian sexual symbolism. *International Journal of Symbology*, 1971, **2**, 1–7.

Robbins, P.R. An approach to measuring psychological tensions by means of dream associations. *Psychological Reports*, 1966, **18**, 959–971.

_____, and Houshi, F. Some observations on recurrent dreams. *Bulletin of the Menninger Clinic*, 1983, **47**, 262–265.

_____, and Tanck, R.H. Community violence and aggression in dreams: An observation. *Perceptual and Motor Skills*, 1969, **29**, 41–42.

_____, and _____. The Repression-Sensitization scale, dreams, and dream associations. *Journal of Clinical Psychology*, 1970, **26**, 219–221.

_____, and _____. The Dream Incident Technique as a measure of unresolved problems. *Journal of Personality Assessment*, 1978, **42**, 583–591.

_____, and _____. Sexual gratification and sexual symbolism in dreams: Some support for Freud's theory. *Bulletin of the Menninger Clinic*, 1980, **44**, 49–58.

_____; _____; and Houshi, F. Anxiety and dream symbolism. *Journal of Personality*, 1985, **53**, 17–22.

_____; _____; and Meyersburg, H.A. Psychological factors in smoking, drinking, and drug experimentation. *Journal of Clinical Psychology*, 1971, **27**, 450–452.

————; ————; and ————. A study of three psychosomatic hypotheses. *Journal of Psychosomatic Research*, 1972, **16**, 93–97.

Rofé, Y., and Lewin, I. The effect of war environment on dreams and sleep habits. *Series in Clinical & Community Psychology: Stress & Anxiety*, 1982, **8**, 67–79.

Roheim, G. The song of the sirens. *Psychiatric Quarterly*, 1948, **22**, 18–44.

Rosenblatt, G.; Hartmann, E.; and Zwilling, G.R. Cardiac irritability during sleep and dreaming. *Journal of Psychosomatic Research*, 1973, **17**, 129–134.

Ryan, J.H. Dreams of paraplegics. *Archives of General Psychiatry*, 1961, **5**, 286–291.

Schechter, N.; Schmeidler, G.R.; and Staal, M. Dream reports and creative tendencies in students of the arts, sciences, and engineering. *Journal of Consulting Psychology*, 1965, **29**, 415–421.

Schonbar, R.A., and Davitz, J.R. The connotative meaning of sexual symbols. *Journal of Consulting Psychology*, 1960, **24**, 483–487.

Schroetter, K. Experimental dreams. In D. Rapaport (ed.). *Organization and Pathology of Thought*. New York: Columbia University Press, 1951.

Shapiro, A.; Goodenough, D.R.; Binderman, I.; and Sleser, I. Dream recall and the physiology of sleep. *Journal of Applied Psychology*, 1964, **19**, 778–783.

Sheppard, E., and Karon, B. Systematic studies of dreams: Relationship between the manifest dream and associations to the dream elements. *Comprehensive Psychiatry*, 1964, **5**, 335–343.

Shweder, R.A., and LeVine, R.A. Dream concepts of Hausa children: A critique of the "doctrine of invariant sequence" in cognitive development. *Ethos*, 1975, **3**, 209–230.

Singer, J.L., and Streiner, B.F. Imaginative content in the dreams and fantasy play of blind and sighted children. *Perceptual and Motor Skills*, 1966, **22**, 475–482.

Stern, M.M. Free painting as an auxiliary technique in psychoanalysis. In Bychowski, G., and Despert, J.L. (eds.). *Specialized Techniques in Psychotherapy*. New York: Basic Books, 1952.

Stoyva, J.M. Posthypnotically suggested dreams and the sleep cycle. *Archives of General Psychiatry*, 1965, **12**, 287–294.

————. The effects of suggested dreams on the length of rapid eye movement periods. Doctoral dissertation, University of Chicago, 1961.

Strean, H.S. A paranormal dream. *Psychoanalytic Review*, 1969, **56**, 142–144.

Sylvia, W.H.; Clark, P.M.; and Monroe, L.J. Dream reports of subjects high and low in creative ability. *Journal of General Psychology*, 1978, **99**, 205–211.

Tanck, R.H., and Robbins, P.R. Pupillary reactions to sexual, aggressive, and other stimuli as a function of personality. *Journal of Projective Techniques and Personality Assessment*, 1970, **34**, 277–282.

Tart, C.T., and Dick, L. Conscious control of dreaming: The posthypnotic dream. *Journal of Abnormal Psychology*, 1970, **76**, 304–315.

Tauber, E.S.; Roffwarg, H.P.; and Herman, J. The effects of longstanding perceptual alterations on the hallucinatory content of dreams. *Psychophysiology*, 1968, **5**, 219.

Toboada, E.L. Night terrors in children: Causes and treatment. *Texas Medicine*, 1974, **70**, 70–72.

Tokar, J.T.; Brunse, A.J.; Castelnuovo-Tedesco, P.; and Stefflre, V.J. An objective method of dream analysis. *Psychoanalytic Quarterly*, 1973, **42**, 563–578.

Trosman, H.; Rechtschaffen, A.; Offenkrantz, W.; and Wolpert, E. Studies in psychophysiology of dreams. *Archives of General Psychiatry*, 1960, **3**, 602–607.

Ullman, M. Telepathy and dreams. *Experimental Medicine and Surgery*, 1969, **27**, 19–38.

————; Krippner, S.; and Vaughan, A. *Dream Telepathy*. New York: Macmillan, 1973.

Walker, P.C., and Johnson, R.F.Q. The influence of presleep suggestions on dream content: Evidence and methodological problems. *Psychological Bulletin*, 1974, **81**, 362–370.

Wallach, M.A. Two correlates of symbolic sexual arousal: Level of anxiety and liking for esthetic material. *Journal of Abnormal and Social Psychology*, 1960, **61**, 396–401.

Weiss, H.B. Oneirocritica Americana. *Bulletin of the New York Public Library*, 1944, **48**, 519–541.

Wilson, G.S. A prophetic dream reported by Abraham Lincoln. *American Imago*, 1940, **1**, 42–48.

Winget, C., and Kapp, F.T. The relationship of the manifest content of dreams to duration of childbirth in primipare. *Psychosomatic Medicine*, 1972, **34**, 313–320.

Wolpert, E.A. Studies in psychophysiology of dreams. (II. An electromyographic study of dreaming.) *Archives of General Psychiatry*, 1960, **2**, 231–241.

_____, and Trosman, H. Studies in psychophysiology of dreams. (I. Experimental evocation of sequential dream episodes.) *Archives of Neurology and Psychiatry*, 1958, **79**, 603–606.

Wood, P. Dreaming and social isolation. Doctoral dissertation, University of North Carolina, 1962.

Zepelin, H. Age differences in dreams. (II: Distortion and other variables.) *International Journal of Aging and Human Development*, 1981, **13**, 37–41.

Index

M

N

O

P

R